Praise for *Managing Retirement Wealth*

"I have found Julie Jason's *Managing Retirement Wealth* to be an excellent overview, a helpful and detailed guide in the investment process of my personal portfolio management."—Peter Hathaway, retired, former portfolio manager in charge of over $10 billion of assets for GE Asset Management's U.S. Equity Large Cap Value Strategy

"In your hand is a book that is chock full of information on everything from muni bonds to risk management. It is a great way for anyone trying to pick up the basics—or go beyond them—as they build a strategy for a new economic climate. And in an age with so many economic uncertainties, Julie Jason's *Managing Retirement Wealth* is as good a place as any to bone up on the bewildering but rewarding task of putting our futures in order."—Jonathan Dahl, editor in chief of *SmartMoney*, the personal finance magazine from the *Wall Street Journal*

"If you have not placed an emphasis on how you manage your portfolio, now is the time to do it. Julie will show you how."—Charles Rotblut, CFA, vice president, American Association of Individual Investors, author, *Better Good than Lucky*

"Julie Jason's *Managing Retirement Wealth* gets what most investment books miss—investing is a means to an end. If you achieve your goals and provide greater security and opportunity for your loved ones, that's what really matters. This fine text will prepare you to make smarter decisions about the choices that matter most, the ones that lead to your retirement success."—Don Phillips, managing director, Morningstar

"At some point in our lives, we will care deeply about preserving the money we've worked so hard to save. Julie Jason's newest book, *Managing Retirement Wealth,* will take you by the hand and show you how to create the only investment portfolio you will ever need in retirement."—Pam Krueger, executive producer and cohost of the award-winning PBS series *MoneyTrack* and EIFLE Financial Educator of the Year 2010

"Julie Jason's *Managing Retirement Wealth* is written with the reader in mind. The book provides clear explanations of complex financial market topics and guides the reader on how to design, manage, and evaluate a portfolio to meet retirement needs."—Tom Robinson, PhD, CFA, CAIA, CFP; managing director, Education Division, CFA Institute

"At last, a sensible guide to creating a sound retirement portfolio. It's all here—creating cash flow, understanding risk, and the actual mechanics of keeping your money working for you the rest of your life."—John F. Wasik, Reuters columnist and author of *The Cul-de-Sac Syndrome: Turning Around the Unsustainable American Dream*

"A sturdy, basic, thoughtful, and extremely useful primer to get the investor off the starting line and well down the track to a successful financial future."—Ben Stein

"Julie Jason gets it! Anyone who is interested in understanding personal portfolio management should read her book. She explains complex ideas simply and points out simple concepts that are easy to overlook. I thoroughly enjoyed, and learned a great deal from, her book, *Managing Retirement Wealth*."—Richard Berkowitz, Esq., senior partner, Berkowitz, Trager & Trager, LLC of Westport, CT

MANAGING RETIREMENT WEALTH

An Expert Guide to Personal Portfolio Management in Good Times and Bad

Julie Jason

Forewords by
Peter J. Hathaway, Jonathan Dahl, and Charles Rotblut

STERLING
New York

STERLING
New York

An Imprint of Sterling Publishing Co., Inc.
1166 Avenue of the Americas
New York, NY 10036

ISBN 978-1-4027-8272-5

Library of Congress Cataloging-in-Publication Data

Jason, Julie.
   Managing retirement wealth : an expert guide to personal portfolio management in good times and bad /
Julie Jason ; forewords by Peter J. Hathaway, Jonathan Dahl, and Charles Rotblut.
      p. cm.
   Includes bibliographical references and index.
   ISBN 978-1-4027-8272-5
   1. Retirement income--Planning. 2. Finance, Personal. 3. Portfolio management. I. Title.
HG179.J3274 2011
332.024'014--dc22

2011010300

Distributed in Canada by Sterling Publishing Co., Inc.
c/o Canadian Manda Group, 664 Annette Street
Toronto, Ontario, Canada M6S 2C8
Distributed in the United Kingdom by GMC Distribution Services
Castle Place, 166 High Street, Lewes, East Sussex, England BN7 1XU
Distributed in Australia by NewSouth Books
45 Beach Street, Coogee, NSW 2034, Australia

For information about custom editions, special sales, and premium and corporate purchases,
please contact Sterling Special Sales at 800-805-5489 or specialsales@sterlingpublishing.com.

Manufactured in the United States of America

4   6   8   10   9   7   5   3

www.sterlingpublishing.com

To Joanna, the newest member of our family

Contents

Foreword *by Peter J. Hathaway*

Speaking to you as an institutional portfolio manager working on domestic equity portfolios for the last thirty-five years, I can tell you that it is quite different developing and managing your own personal accounts using your own goals and objectives.

For me, it was a case of "the cobbler's son has no shoes," as I had neglected my own portfolio. What a great resource Julie's book, *Managing Retirement Wealth,* has been in helping me organize and access my individual needs and objectives based on my risk parameters.

Many of us have a "random assortment of assets," consisting of IRAs, CDs, savings accounts, 401(k)s, and other miscellaneous financial assets accumulated over a lifetime, that lacks an overall plan. This is not an easy task to solve, but Julie's book provides the framework for you to organize and manage your personal portfolio now and in the future.

You will benefit from Julie's knowledge and practical experience, which she has gained from helping others in the portfolio management process. It will help you choose wisely and avoid costly mistakes.

One of my favorite topics is her discussion of goals: "Investment objectives are goals. The big difference between having a collection of investments and having a portfolio is pursuing goals, actually making decisions that lead to the accomplishment of those goals, and keeping track of progress by monitoring your portfolio."

As you begin the process of managing your portfolio, you will find this not to be an easy task, but well worth the time and effort you put into it. Julie's book will prove to be an invaluable guide.

—Peter J. Hathaway (retired),
former portfolio manager for
GE Asset Management's U.S. Equity Large Cap Value Strategy,
responsible for portfolios with assets in excess of $10 billion

Foreword *by Jonathan Dahl*

In the world of personal finance, these are surely historic times of unprecedented change. A generation of Americans could once count on enjoying an easy retirement, thanks to the generosity of their employers and a combination of the robust housing and stock markets. That has all changed, of course: only a third of mid- and large-size American firms offer pensions these days, and the country's real estate bust has wiped out $3.3 trillion in market value in homes in five years.

Throw in the stock market crash of 2008, which battered people's 401(k) plans and sent many investors' carefully built portfolios essentially back to square one, and you have yourself a perfect storm for developments in personal finance.

But there is good news: help is on the way.

Investors today have more places to turn to for advice, including a growing number of books that deal with personal finance in a smarter way than before. The idea that a bookstore could fill a shelf with successful personal finance books would have been unthinkable a decade ago. Now, as Americans try to make sense of their future, these sorts of titles are coming out in great numbers, with advice and insights for all levels of investor.

In your hand is one such publication: Julie Jason's *Managing Retirement Wealth*.

It is a great way for anyone trying to pick up the basics—or go beyond them—as they build a strategy for a new economic climate. And in an age with so many economic uncertainties, Julie's book is as good a place as any to bone up on the bewildering but rewarding task of putting our futures in order.

—Jonathan Dahl, editor in chief of
SmartMoney,
the personal finance magazine from *The Wall Street Journal*

Foreword *by Charles Rotblut*

Your net worth is highly dependent on how well you manage your portfolio. Your ability to make the right decisions and follow the correct strategies will determine whether you have enough money to retire and enough to last you throughout your lifetime.

Yet, as important as this concept is, most people tend to be reactive, instead of proactive, with their investing. Decisions are often made based on what the market is doing rather than with the long-term goals in mind. If this describes you, do not feel bad.

Most people have not been given a comprehensive guide on how to effectively manage their portfolios. Rather, investing is commonly thought about in terms of what stock, bond, mutual fund, or ETF should be bought. Significantly less attention is given to what mix of securities and funds should be held in one's portfolio. As result, many investors find that their knowledge of how to manage a portfolio is acquired through trial and error.

Complicating matters is the volatility of the stock market. Two bear markets occurred over the past ten years, causing havoc with most investors' portfolios. The result was a lost decade with many people still not recouping the wealth they lost.

Yet, some investors weathered the storm and actually increased their net worth. What was their secret to success? These successful investors effectively managed their portfolios using the time-tested rules that Julie Jason explains in this book.

They stayed focused on their long-term goals and kept their investment risk at levels they were comfortable with. This gave them the luxury of not having to be reactive to the market's volatility, while ensuring they have enough wealth to last them a lifetime.

If you have not placed an emphasis on how you manage your portfolio, now is the time to do it. Julie will show you how.

—Charles Rotblut, CFA, vice president,
American Association of Individual Investors
and author of *Better Good than Lucky*

Preface

Each day, we all make decisions in every aspect of our lives that require an understanding of the risks, rewards, consequences, and options before us. Our continued security, our independence, and the comfort of our loved ones could very well hinge on how we choose to make important financial decisions as we live our lives and pursue our goals.

This book is designed to educate, motivate, and pass on what I have learned as an investment adviser, author, and financial columnist over many years—not only as a student of the markets but also as the guardian of each client —the unique person at the center of each portfolio that I structure and manage.

As you read this book, I hope that it will help you recognize that the first and most important analysis you must make is to try to understand "who you are and what you need" so that you can design and manage a portfolio to achieve *your* goals. Security comes from knowing yourself, where you are going, and how to get there—and making sure you don't get lost along the way.

Introduction

Teachers, social workers, business owners, lawyers, dentists, accountants, and corporate employees may not think of themselves as wealthy, yet millions of these everyday Americans have substantial assets that they have acquired through business ventures, personal savings, inheritances, and through their 401(k)s and other retirement plans at work.

Whether they are interested in the financial markets or not, at some point in their lives—possibly at or near retirement—these individuals come to question how they will provide for themselves after they stop working. They need to assure themselves that their investments can sufficiently supplement their Social Security retirement benefits and pensions for as long as they live, and possibly leave a legacy for their heirs. That's quite a challenge, considering the uncertainties all investors face.

Because of the way people invest *before* they reach this point in their lives—buying mutual funds, stocks, and bonds on their own, through a broker or through a retirement plan at work—they may not be aware of the discipline I call "Personal Portfolio Management."

Just what is a "portfolio"? Borrowing from Nobel Prize–winning economist and father of portfolio management Harry M. Markowitz, a portfolio is "more than a long list of good stocks and bonds . . . [it is a] balanced whole [that can provide you] with protections and opportunities with respect to a wide range of contingencies."

A "personal" portfolio is goal-oriented, meaning it focuses on your personal and unique situation and addresses the goals that you want to achieve.

What is "management?" It's the process of planning, executing, and, most important, watching progress toward your goals so that inevitable missteps can be observed and corrected, with the ultimate goals of achieving desired results.

The difference between buying a few stocks and bonds here and there and managing a portfolio is the difference between throwing up a tent at a campground on a trip with some friends and building a house for your family. Both might provide shelter. One satisfies a temporary need; the other offers a structure that your family will call "home" for many years to come.

How to Read This Book

I wrote this book in eight parts, with the intention of taking you through some facts and figures to lay a foundation while sharing some insights from years of actually constructing and managing personal portfolios.

Part 1: Building the Foundation for Managing Your Personal Portfolio

Part 2: Demystifying Risk and Uncertainty

Part 3: Creating Your Portfolio Objectives and Strategy

Part 4: Structuring Your Portfolio for Income and Your Retirement

Part 5: Investing for Three Different Goals

Part 6: Utilizing Independent Research: Choosing Stocks

Part 7: The Importance of Monitoring Your Portfolio

Part 8: Who Should Manage Your Portfolio?

You'll get the most out of this book by reading the parts in order. At the end of each chapter, I've summarized some key points and listed a few steps that you might want to take along the way.

You'll notice that there is quite a bit of market data in this book, including results of studies prepared for this book for illustration purposes, not as recommendations. If you wish to pursue a particular strategy or investment discussed in the book, be sure to verify the information yourself and review it with your adviser before taking any action.

In the back of the book, you'll find reference materials, including a comprehensive presentation on how to dig for information in financial statements, which is provided courtesy of AAII (the American Association of Individual Investors) (Appendices A through D).

AAII is a national nonprofit membership organization, with chapters in almost every state whose purpose is to educate the individual investor. AAII's website (*www.AAII.com*) provides educational and research materials that are both understandable and easily accessible. AAII kindly offered readers of this book a complimentary 12-month membership. To take advantage of this free offer, see the "Special Offers," section at the end of this book.

What This Book is Not

There are many investment books that offer get-rich-quick formulas and stock tips. If that is what you are seeking, you will not find it here. Instead, this book is for the thoughtful individual who wants to bring some discipline to his or her investment activity at an important transitional time of life. As such, it is a resource to both the novice who has substantial assets that need to be invested with care and the experienced investor who has a history of successfully investing for capital appreciation.

Most important, this book recognizes that investing retirement wealth calls for a very personal inward exploration, not only of goals, intentions, desires, strengths, concerns, and limitations, but also of the uncertainties that we all face in investing and in life.

It is my sincere wish that this book will give you some insights that you can apply in your decision making and as you plan for a secure financial life for yourself and your loved ones.

Do reach out to me if you have questions or comments. You can e-mail me at readers@juliejason.com. My best wishes to you and your family.

—Julie Jason

PART 1

Building the Foundation for Managing Your Personal Portfolio

As individuals acquire assets, there comes a time when they need to bring some oversight, planning, and management into their investment activities. This process of overseeing your investments I call "Personal Portfolio Management" (Chapter 1), and the person who takes on that task I call a "personal portfolio manager." Let's agree that you are that person, at least for now. (We'll explore alternatives in Part 8 of the book.)

Managing your portfolio is also about having the confidence and knowledge to make sound decisions over a lifetime. In Chapter 2 we'll discuss decision making in the context of long-term investment goals. I'll point out the pitfalls of striving for goals that may be unattainable, and I'll present six factors involved in making quality investment decisions.

Having a general understanding of the market helps put the risks and rewards of investing into context. In Chapters 3 and 4, I'll share my perspectives, debunk some popular misconceptions about the market, and give you some insights based on market and investor returns. We'll also examine market data from the first decade of 2000, a challenging period that academics and researchers will no doubt study for a long time to come. After reading these chapters, lessons might emerge to help you construct your own portfolio even in periods such as the "lost decade."

CHAPTER 1

Personal Portfolio Management

What's in It for You?

This chapter introduces the concept of Personal Portfolio Management and how you might benefit from applying some of these principles to your own situation. It explains why some investors need to be extra vigilant (those who need to live off their investments), and it starts you on the course to organizing your own investments.

Contents

Life Can Be Complicated

Some people have most of their assets in a single account, such as a 401(k). But, it is not uncommon for well-to-do individuals to have multiple accounts with a number of brokers, banks, and advisers. Take Michael and

Mary, a hypothetical couple based on a composite of people I might meet when they are searching for a professional money manager. Between them they have two 401(k) plans with former employers, a few IRA accounts held at brokerage firms a joint account with a popular online discount brokerage firm that Michael likes to use for "playing the market," and multiple savings and checking accounts. In addition, they have a number of "managed accounts" sold to them by two high-end "wealth managers" with well-known brokerage firms, who make available all the resources of their firms for any financial need imaginable, including help with financing the purchase of a yacht.

Michael is the financial decision maker in the family. He discusses stock ideas with his wealth managers. When he has time, he reads research reports they send him. Occasionally, he does some online research on his own. Michael reviews brokerage statements to see if his accounts are up or down from the previous month. He places trades in his online accounts, files his transaction confirmations, and gathers year-end tax data for his accountant. And that pretty much summarizes Michael's current routine, which has worked well for him until now.

The Big Picture

Even though Michael and Mary have wealth, they are uncertain about how to invest for the future, as is natural for people approaching retirement. After all, they have to address their changing circumstances and lay out an investment plan of action with a time horizon of thirty years or more.

Important questions arise. Will they be able to support the lifestyle they would like to have in retirement? How will their wealth be affected should there be a severe market decline after they retire? Ultimately, will assets and income be sufficient to last a lifetime?

What about their approach to investing? Do they need to change how they invest in any way or continue as usual? Do their accounts need to be consolidated? Do they need to change how they direct their financial service providers in order to accomplish a different set of goals? Do they need a different type of service altogether as they approach retirement?

Then, there are estate planning issues. Will they be able to leave a legacy for their heirs? How do their financial decisions impact their estate and charitable giving plans? Who can help them tee up and coordinate financial, tax, and legal decisions? And, importantly, what happens if Michael, as the family's financial decision maker, becomes ill, incapacitated, or predeceases Mary?

Survey data tell us that people with substantial assets can be confused about financial decisions, especially after living through a market decline (something we can expect to occur again during our lifetimes). At such times, their biggest fears are losing wealth, outliving assets, having to modify current lifestyles, having to replenish retirement savings, and having to postpone retirement. Research tells us that affluent Baby Boomers who are five to ten years away from retirement are panicked at such times, with a large number being forced to delay retirement.

This book is for all the pre-retirees and retirees who might face some of these issues. It addresses the fact that, at some point in life, people come to the realization that they are not satisfied without a big-picture plan on how to manage their assorted holdings, accounts, and advisers. What they need is a way to bring structure and organization to their investments through Personal Portfolio Management.

Personal Portfolio Management

I'm using the term "Personal Portfolio Management" to focus on (1) you and your family, the "personal" part of the equation, (2) your "portfolio," a collection of investments organized for a specific purpose, and (3) "management," the ongoing process of selecting, reviewing, and deselecting investments in order to achieve the portfolio's objectives.

This process, as we'll discuss together in the pages that follow, is applicable to all types of investors in all kinds of financial markets and economic cycles. The purpose of engaging in the process is to achieve what Harry M. Markowitz calls a "good portfolio." As he said in his classic book on portfolio management, *Portfolio Selection: Efficient Diversification of Investments*: "A good portfolio is more than a long list of good stocks and bonds. It is a balanced whole, providing the investor with protections and opportunities with respect to a wide range of contingencies." We will visit with Markowitz again in later chapters. The ultimate goal of *Personal Portfolio Management* is to improve returns and lessen risk.

Organization

Applying Personal Portfolio Management principles will bring some organization to your collection of investments, brokerage accounts, and financial advisers. It is not uncommon to have such a collection. Indeed, in addition to the usual investments, you may also own some variable annuities, limited partnerships, structured products, hedge funds, or private equity investments. Plus you may have an online trading account with a discount broker that you direct for fun. And, let's not forget your employee benefit plans, such as employee stock option plans, pensions, and even non-qualified employee plans.

Changing Needs

While everyone needs a plan, the need for one heightens at transitional points in life, such as getting married, starting a family, changing jobs, losing a spouse to death or divorce, facing an illness, or moving into retirement. Each such transition is a time of dislocation until a suitable path is discovered and followed. The search for the best way to proceed is necessarily a personal one, because one person's financial circumstances differ from just about every other's.

In retirement, for example, your personal cash flow will need to be addressed: how much money comes into the household (your income) compared to how much money goes out (your expenses). If the amount of your pension and Social Security combined cover your expenses, your portfolio needs will differ dramatically from someone who must rely on his investments to cover his expenses. (For help with cash-flow management, let me refer you to my book, *The AARP Retirement Survival Guide: How to Make Smart Financial Decisions in Good Times and Bad* [Sterling 2009], which you can find at your local library or bookstore or online at juliejason.com.)

That's why I put retirees into two camps: those who don't need to withdraw funds from their investment portfolios for living expenses and those who do. Those who do will need to be extra vigilant in how they manage their portfolios, since their livelihood depends on making a series of sound decisions for the rest of their lives, whether the markets are favorable or not. Ideally, they will create retirement income that will last a lifetime, offsetting inflation and potentially leaving a legacy for their heirs.

Do You Need Your Investments to Pay for Living Expenses?

Whether you are divorced, widowed, retired, or just starting a family, you may need your portfolio to support you—if not now, possibly later in life. If your cash-flow needs are not covered by income sources, such as pension and Social Security, your devotion to Personal Portfolio Management principles will help you formulate appropriate goals and a rational way to achieve them.

Investing for the Future

If you are investing to grow your assets for the future, adopting a Personal Portfolio Management approach to your investment activities will help you organize your efforts and potentially optimize your results.

Avoiding and Correcting Mistakes

Irrespective of your particular investment goals, understanding how to manage your holdings as a portfolio will help you avoid missteps, such as being drawn to financial instruments that promise guarantees during a bear market or to speculative investments during a market bubble. It will also help you identify investments that need to be replaced at the right time. And, it will guide you when you are tempted to take action based on what you see, read, or hear in the popular media—investing should not be reactionary.

Summary

As you might imagine, only the most organized individuals approaching an impending lifestyle change such as retirement have a big-picture overview of their holdings. Few have a master plan for managing investment decisions to achieve specific goals. And yet, that is precisely what individuals need if they want to grow their wealth or create cash flow for retirement.

Developing your own Personal Portfolio Management process will help you steer clear of trouble while enjoying the benefits of the financial results you set out to accomplish. Let's see if we can work together to achieve these objectives in the pages that follow. You can start the organizational process by following the "Steps to Take."

Key Points

1. Personal Portfolio Management is an organizational and review process focused on you and your needs.
2. Without a process, all you have is a collection of investments.
3. If you organize your efforts to achieve certain objectives, it is more likely that you will take a series of actions to achieve your goals. Without organization, goals are unstated and unachievable leaving successful retirement to chance.

Steps to Take

1. Gather all of your most recent account statements and put them into a binder. Include 401(k)s and other retirement plans, as well as insurance policies. Arrange them by owner of the account (you, your spouse, joint, etc.) and by type (taxable or tax-deferred, such as IRAs

and retirement plans). We'll refer to these statements again in Chapter 21.

2. Create a table of contents with four columns, listing each account, each financial adviser handling the account, the goal or objective of each account, and a column for notes. This list will help you start the organizational process. As you read ahead, you'll find it useful to record insights on how to handle these accounts. If you find that you don't have objectives at this point, come back to this list later, after reading Part 3 of the book.

3. Create a cover sheet. Make a note of two things:
   1. Portfolio manager: who is managing your overall portfolio today?
   2. Cash-flow needs: are you looking to your portfolio to support you today or in the future when you retire? If you are retired, make a note if your expenses are *not* fully covered by your pension and Social Security.

CHAPTER 2

Portfolio Management: A Series of Good Decisions

What's in It for You?

This chapter provides insights on decision making in the context of the long-term time frame of a retiree and introduces six decision-making elements that lead to effective outcomes. In later chapters, we'll discuss how to set objectives, organize, structure, and manage your own personal portfolio. We'll return to the six elements in Chapter 20.

Contents

A Series of Good Decisions

If you think about it, investing is all about decision making—and Personal Portfolio Management is all about making a series of good decisions based on planned objectives (Part 2 of the book) that are designed for, and executed over, the rest of your life. We're not talking about making a few winning trades here. We're focusing on the end game—making sure that we have enough resources to support ourselves and our families through retirement. That's a serious undertaking that calls for some thoughtful effort.

At the most basic level, you start with a decision to "buy" a stock, bond, mutual fund, or other investment. To take a profit, or to avoid a loss, you have to make a good "sell" decision. And, in between the buy and sell decisions, you choose to "hold," either in anticipation of selling at a higher price or to earn some money (dividends or interest).

You measure success based on positive outcomes. A purchase resulted in a profit (you sold for more than you paid). Or, you avoided a major loss (you sold for less than you paid to protect yourself from further declines). Or, a purchase produced some income (your bonds paid some interest; your stocks paid dividends).

Portfolio results go beyond buy, sell, and hold outcomes, of course. Success is meeting objectives within acceptable risk parameters, subjects we will discuss together in this book.

Wins Are Market-Dependent for Most People

If you were a market participant during the Internet bubble of the late 1990s, you will likely remember most of your trades as wins. Buys resulted in profits realized when you sold those stocks—positive outcomes indeed.

Those wins may have turned into losses during the subsequent market crash that started in January of 2000 and lasted through 2002. Some of the Internet stocks that lured normally cautious people into the market at the very top caused losses of as much as 90 or even 100 percent when companies with no revenues (but great appeal to a public hungry to make a killing in the market) went out of business.

If you need your investments to support you, focusing on a few home runs simply won't suffice. Taking the longer-term view, as you will need to do when managing your own portfolio, you need a series of positive outcomes in all types of markets, not just bull markets. There is a cost for failure that goes above and beyond a win or a loss on a particular trade: your livelihood may be at stake.

Time Horizon

With retirement portfolios, you still have to make good buy, sell, and hold decisions. But now, gains and losses need to be linked together. You need to make a series of continuing correct goal-oriented decisions while limiting (or reversing) incorrect decisions over the span of a lifetime that can last thirty or more years after you retire. Achieving long-term success is far more difficult than achieving short-term profits in a bull market, but it can be done by applying the type of process that we'll be discussing together. A series of good portfolio management decisions leads to successful portfolio outcomes, which are a function of your personal needs and objectives.

People Take Shortcuts When Confused

As students of decision making know, it's not an easy task to make good decisions when faced with the financial market ambiguity and uncertainty that every investor—professional and nonprofessional—encounters. (We'll discuss how to address the important subject of uncertainty in Chapters 5, 6, and 7.)

And indeed, in such situations, behavioral economists tell us that bad outcomes result from heuristics (behavioral shortcuts that people take when they are presented with a confusing array of choices), improper framing (inability to properly define the problem to be solved), and even overconfidence (not recognizing when we are making decisions based on oversimplification, wishful thinking, or even "blissful ignorance").

Six Factors for Making "Quality" Decisions

What makes investment decisions sound? Professor Ron Howard of Stanford University and Carl Spetzler, CEO of Strategic Decisions Group, articulate six elements that have equal weight in leading to "quality decisions"—those that are both effective and efficient. While quality decisions do not guarantee good outcomes, they increase their likelihood. I've adapted these elements to investment decision making:

1. "An appropriate frame"—What is the problem we're trying to solve? "Avoiding losses" can lead to buying a certificate of deposit, which can protect assets, but offers no growth potential. "Making the most money possible in the quickest amount of time" can lead to aggressive strategies such as concentrated portfolios and leverage (margin), increasing the possibility of losses if not managed properly.

2. "Creative, doable alternatives"—What investment or actions are we considering? Investment problems can be solved in more than one way. Alternatives may come to light that look appropriate but might not be optimal. For example, you may be offered an investment with upside potential, downside protection, and lifelong income. That may be a creative solution to a retirement income problem; or you may find that it is not a "doable alternative" to a well-balanced stock and bond portfolio because of limitations in the particular offering, such as lack of liquidity or high costs.

3. "Meaningful, reliable information"—Do we have current, relevant research at hand? Investment information is constantly in production. News travels fast in today's wired world. You will need to ignore some information and act on only data that are meaningful to you as an investor.

4. "Clear values and trade-offs"—Have we considered relevant opportunities and risks? Investing offers myriad choices that all have different risk-reward trade-offs—each such investment needs to be considered on its own merits and how it interacts with other investments you own,

so that the portfolio as a whole achieves the balance that you are seeking. For example, you may decide to hold a low-yielding Treasury bill or money market mutual fund for safety (discussed in Chapter 15), even though you can earn more interest elsewhere.

5. "Logically correct reasoning"—Are desired outcomes achievable considering all of the above? In investing, as in other fields, there might be a tendency to react positively to a powerful emotional message (a scarce investment that promises huge profits). It's better to rely on reason ("just how will the profits be delivered?") rather than emotion ("I'd love to make a big hit").

6. "Commitment to action"—At some point in the analytical process, it will be time to move forward with appropriate actions. Of course, there will be buy, sell, or hold decisions. But before anything is bought, sold, or held, we need to make a commitment to plan, implement, watch, and fix, as we will discuss in Parts 3 through 8 of the book.

Table 2-1 below summarizes these six decision-making elements.

Table 2-1. Six Decision-Making Elements

	Element	Consider
1	An appropriate frame	Problem being solved?
2	Creative, doable alternatives	Actions being considered?
3	Meaningful reliable information	Research supporting decision?
4	Clear values and trade-offs	Risk versus reward?
5	Logically correct reasoning	Desired outcomes achievable?
6	Commitment to action	Plan, implement, watch, and fix.

Even with this framework, we're left with the question of how quality decisions can lead to good outcomes when conditions are uncertain, as they necessarily are with long-term investment horizons. As Professor

Howard points out, important decisions are always made in the face of uncertainty.

The next question is whether one should refrain from acting if all the elements of a quality decision don't fall into place. That is, should you seek perfection—should you try to bat 1,000?

Should You Strive for Perfection?

In the practical world of investing, even the most effective professional portfolio managers cannot achieve perfection (all winning trades). Even the best of managers make mistakes—that's simply the nature of running portfolios.

Instead of seeking to achieve a perfect score, long-term investors are better off focusing on making more good decisions than bad ones both in magnitude (dollars committed) and quantity (number of decisions). After the trade is made, success comes from monitoring results and taking appropriate action when a position in the portfolio does not meet expectations. In the words of nineteenth-century philosopher Carveth Read, attributed to Warren Buffet, "It is better to be vaguely right than exactly wrong."

Summary

Making profits on trades is a function of good buy, sell, and hold decisions, which is difficult enough in the short term. When managing a personal portfolio, however, time horizon becomes an essential factor. Success is defined over the long term, in fact over a lifetime. Achieving that success is a much more difficult task when we consider how we make decisions and the shortcuts that we naturally take when choices are not clear.

Instead of trying for perfection, the Personal Portfolio Management process focuses on making more good decisions than bad ones, all in the context of a big-picture view of what needs to be achieved. The key to success is catching and correcting bad decisions, early before they can cause irreparable harm.

Key Points

1. Personal Portfolio Management sets you up to make a series of quality decisions over a lifetime, resulting in a series of positive outcomes even when conditions are uncertain.
2. Uncertainty can lead to confusion, which can lead to shortcuts, which can lead to negative outcomes.
3. Bad outcomes can be lessened by applying a structured approach to decision making, but they cannot be avoided altogether; perfection in investment decision making is neither desirable nor achievable.

Steps to Take

1. Review how you make your investment decisions. Do you strive for home runs? Do you take shortcuts when presented with a confusing array of investment choices? Do you strive for perfection—all buys resulting in profits?
2. Make a list of the six decision-making elements and consider how you might formulate actions based on where you are today.
3. Keep the list handy so that you can make notes of any insights you gain as you read ahead. Note that we will not be tackling the elements in order, since I want to lay a foundation first. Focus particularly on the problems you are trying to solve. This will help you set investment objectives, the subject of Part 3 of the book.

CHAPTER 3

Misconceptions About the Market

What's in It for You?

This chapter will be important to you in setting expectations. We'll draw some lessons from market returns, and we'll review data that shows how individual investors tend to act in different market periods. This information shows how some investors move in and out of the market at the wrong time and may help you avoid these mistakes yourself.

Contents

Lessons from a Difficult Market Period

There is no better time period to study in the financial markets than the 2000–2009 decade. In this relatively short period of time, we saw a heady boom (the Internet bubble) come abruptly to an end, a subsequent rise in the market, and a shift in market leadership to financial stocks. This was followed by a spectacular letdown with the fall of Lehman Brothers in September of 2008 and the entry of the federal government into the marketplace with bailouts and government ownership. We also saw the real estate boom come to an end and the gold market take off.

During this decade, the market as measured by the Dow Jones Industrial Average (the "DOW") peaked at 14,165 on October 9, 2007, and bottomed at 6,547 on March 9, 2009, posting a dramatic drop of about 54 percent.

During the height of the financial panic, from September 14, 2008, when Lehman Brothers filed for bankruptcy to November 20, 2008, the DOW lost over 30 percent. Down days followed down days. The market had absolutely no footing. No one was stepping up to buy—that would have been like trying to catch a falling sword.

Flash Crash

While the madness came to an end in March of 2009, we still saw aftershocks. From 2:42 pm through 2:47 pm on May 6, 2010, we experienced the "flash crash," a day in which the market fell by 5 percent in 5 minutes. A matter of minutes later, by 3:00 pm, most stocks had recovered. The flash crash added to the public's loss of confidence in the market.

From the bottom (March 9, 2009), the DOW quickly recovered 57 percent by the end of the year, a solid one-half of the way to full recovery (keep in mind that you need a 108 percent gain to offset a 54-percent loss). By March 31, 2011, the DOW had risen 88 percent from the March 9, 2009 low, still shy of, but pretty close to, its October 9, 2007, peak.

The Future

Because we as investors will see variations of these types of markets again in our lifetimes, let's talk about them now and the lessons that they teach us. Let's start with extremes (market bubbles, market crashes, and bears), followed by market timing, predicting the market, and what happens with winning trades. Then, let's put some historical context to our discussions by comparing market returns for different time periods. Finally, let's look at some data that give us insight into how individual investors perform compared to the market itself, focusing on longer periods of time that are more important to investors with retirement portfolios.

Bubbles

Looking back to the beginning of the 2000–2009 decade helps put future bubbles in perspective. In January 2000, John, a conservative 70-year-old gentleman with a balanced portfolio, asked me if he should sell everything to buy Internet stocks. At the time, returns for the highest flying stocks were dazzling everyone. The question I posed was, "What about risk?"

"This market is different," John replied. "Technology and Internet stocks will continue to go up. My friends are making money, and I don't want to be left behind."

This gentleman's outlook reflected the then-current wisdom: this was a "new economy" where new rules applied. When a normally conservative person buys into a current fad, it is a sign of the end of a speculative market. The incident made me think of Wall Street financier, Bernard Baruch, who, the story goes, sold all his stocks just before the great crash of 1929, after his shoeshine boy offered him a stock tip.

The technology bubble burst a few months after John's visit, and he was indeed happy that he had not thrown caution to the wind.

History teaches us that major technological advances fueled speculative fever in the past. In the 1920s, the automobile and the radio were the technological wonders of the time, both of which still play a major role in our lives. It took thirty-five years, however, for Radio Corporation of America (RCA) to recover its 1926 price peak.

The same was true of the late-1960s bull market. Dominated by the "Nifty Fifty," the S&P 500 Index was driven by consumer goods and technology stocks. However, higher inflation, monetary tightening, and cheaper imports from Japan led to two bear markets—first in 1969–1970 and again in 1973–1974. During the latter period, stock market averages dropped about 50 percent. Many of the Nifty Fifty dropped by as much as 80 to 90 percent, some reaching their ultimate lows in 1977 and 1978.

Boom markets create a careless attitude on the part of investors who, inspired by wishful thinking and the stories of fortunes being made by others, close their eyes to risk. Based on the belief that they are being left behind in a market that will not decline, they gleefully abandon their normal caution. Sadly, many who enter the fray at fever pitch do not recover their losses.

Bull markets have a hidden and dangerous underbelly—like sirens, they lure people into treacherous waters. When we see such markets again—which we will—be alert. Don't be tempted to take on excessive risk by the current fad of the day.

We Will See Bear Markets Again

Bear markets and crashes will visit us again. From time to time, the threat will be so severe that we'll believe that the market won't recover. The stock market will not go to zero. Bulls and bears are a natural function of a free market economy. As the economy expands or contracts, so do financial markets. The stock market will survive through the ups and downs that are sure to follow.

Where Is the Market Heading?

Although alchemy was a legitimate profession in the 1500s, attempting to predict the future movement of a stock or of the market is probably as fruitless as attempting to change base metals into gold. Purveyors of market-timing services take a different view. I'm not a believer. I have yet to see a predictive device that works—if one existed, we would all know about it and take advantage of it. But of course, once that happened, the system would fail given the need for a seller on the other side of every buy trade.

Predicting the Future

So the question becomes, should we even try to predict the future? "Yes" if you are a short-term trader—because if you want to make money, your decision to buy is based on your belief that prices are rising.

And, "no" if you are a long-term investor applying Personal Portfolio Management principles, since your results are not dependent on the short-term vicissitudes of the market. Your approach is to take the time to plan, manage, and monitor investments, pruning as needed to lessen mistakes.

Long-term investors who manage their positions will participate in the growth of the market over time, as long as they avoid major errors and repair minor ones as they discover them.

What's minor? Things you can correct. For example, buying a stock that fails to meet expectations.

What's major? Making a big commitment to an illiquid investment. Failing to monitor results. Failing to make repairs.

Winning Trades in an Up Market

Success in late 1999 and early 2000 gave many people the false notion that they were good investors. Individuals who were pulled along with the bull market didn't realize that their investment genius was trend-dependent. As Warren Buffett said in Berkshire Hathaway's 1996 annual report, referring to its 1995 performance, "This is a year in which any fool could make a bundle in the stock market. As we did. To paraphrase President Kennedy, a rising tide lifts all yachts."

Historical Market Returns Set Expectations

Historically, a diversified portfolio of large company stocks represented by the S&P 500 Index offered returns of just about 10 percent per year on average (1926 through 2015), according to Ibbotson Associates, a Morningstar® company and publisher of market data going back to 1926.

That 10 percent figure is "total return," which includes capital appreciation plus dividends. For example, in 2009, the total return was 26.5 percent (capital appreciation of 23.5 percent plus dividend yield of 3.0 percent). In 2010, the S&P 500 Index was up 15.1 percent (capital appreciation of 12.8 percent plus dividend yield of 2.3 percent). Annual swings from 1926 through 2015 ranged from a high of 54.0 percent in 1933 to a low of –43.3 percent in 1931, according to Ibbotson.

Investors lost confidence in the markets during the 2008 market, when the S&P 500 Index lost 37 percent. The 2000–2009 decade itself, however, returned nothing close to 10 percent. In fact, it went nowhere.

The 2000–2009 Decade Compared to Others

Historically, the broad stock market has averaged about 10 percent per year, but the 2000 decade lost just shy of 1 percent (average annual return)— the worst showing of all the decades from 1926 through 2015.

Compare other historical periods, and you'll see that the 2000–2009 decade is comparable to 1930–1939, the decade that contained the Great Depression. No other decades since the 1930s had negative returns. The range of positive decade returns varied between a low of 5.9 percent (1970s) to a high of 19.4 percent (1950s), as you can see from Table 3-1 and Graph 3-1. Note that the 1920 data in the table and graph is for a short period (1926 through 1929).

Table 3-1. Decades' Compared Average Annual Returns for Large Capitalization Stocks

(Source: Ibbotson)

1920	1930	1940	1950	1960	1970	1980	1990	2000
19.2%	−0.1%	9.2%	19.4%	7.8%	5.9%	17.6%	18.2%	−0.9%

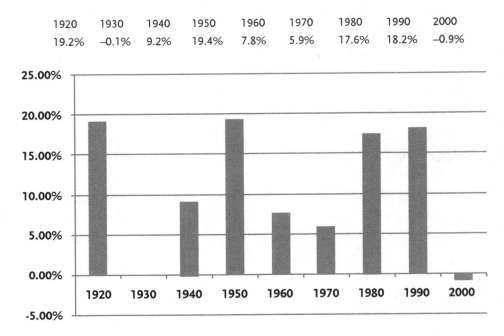

Graph 3-1. Large Capitalization Stocks (Average Annual Returns) Compared for Decades Shown (see Table 3-1). (Source: Ibbotson)

If you look at what came before the 2000–2009 decade's poor performance, you'll notice that the market had overshot itself in the late 1990s. It corrected much more severely and deeply in the early part of the decade, after the Internet bubble crashed (2000, 2001, and 2002). See Table 3-2 below for annual returns for the 2000–2009 decade.

Table 3-2. 2000–2009 Annual Returns for Large Capitalization Stocks

(Source: Ibbotson)

2000	2001	2002	2003	2004	2005	2006	2007	2008	2009
−9.1%	−11.9%	−22.1%	28.7%	10.9%	4.9%	15.8%	5.5%	−37.0%	26.5%

Compare Table 3-3 below, showing the 1930–1939 decade. You'll see that this ten year period contained six loss years and four up years. In comparison, there were four loss years in the 2000–2009 decade.

Table 3-3. 1930–1939 Annual Returns for Large Capitalization Stocks
(Source: Ibbotson)

1930	1931	1932	1933	1934	1935	1936	1937	1938	1939
–24.9%	–43.3%	–8.2%	54.0%	–1.4%	47.7%	33.9%	–35.0%	31.1%	–0.4%

Graph 3-2 (below) overlays the two decades. You can see from the graph that the 1930–1939 decade was much more volatile than the 2000–2009 decade, with lower lows and higher highs. The statistical measure for volatility is "standard deviation," a concept we'll return to in Chapter 7, when we'll discuss how to harness risk. The standard deviation for the 1930–1939 decade is significantly higher (0.346) than that of the 2000–2009 decade (0.211).

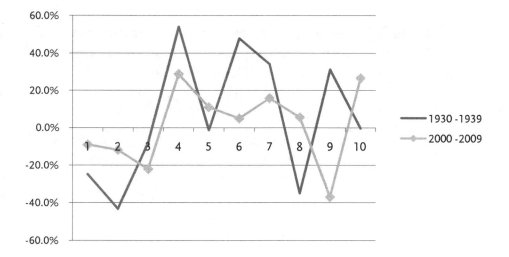

Graph 3-2. Annual Large Capitalization Stock Returns (annual): 1930–1939 compared to 2000–2009.

Our discussions up to now have focused on market returns, which reflect a diversified portfolio of large company stocks. You might well ask, where is the individual investor in all this?

How Do Investors Perform?

It's possible to measure how investors perform by studying the inflows and outflows of money into mutual funds. Morningstar's "investor return," is a dollar-weighted return, meaning it measures the impact of cash flows on returns when investors move out of a fund by redeeming shares or into a fund by buying shares. As such, investor return is probably a better reflection of the average investor's experience than the fund's total return.

What does the data tell us?

A search of all U.S. equity funds with ten-year performance using Morningstar® Principia®, a database published by Morningstar, Inc. of Chicago, (2010) revealed that overwhelmingly, the majority of times, investor performance lagged the fund's performance. Ten-year investor returns are more reliable than shorter period returns, according to Morningstar. Table 3-4 tells the story.

Table 3-4. Percent of Investors Underperforming and Outperforming All US Equity Funds with 10 Year Total Returns Through 2010

(Source: Morningstar Principia)

Period Ending 2010	Percent of Investors Underperforming the Fund	Percent of Investors Outperforming the Fund
10 years	73%	27%
5 years	77%	23%
3 years	77%	23%
1 year	82%	18%

The difference between a fund's return and investor returns can be quite significant, as you can see in Table 3-5, below. Look at the "Investor Is Behind by" column. For example, a small growth fund (Fund A in the table) lost 1.8 percent for the ten-year period ending 2010, which was a far superior return than investors achieved (loss of 17.5 percent). Investor returns were behind by 15.7 percent, due to buying and selling at the wrong time.

Table 3-5. Ranking of Investor Underperformance of All US Equity Funds with 10 Year Total Returns Through 2010
(Source: Morningstar Principia)

Ten years ending 2010 Annualized Total Returns. Source: Morningstar Principia Search of all U.S. Equity Funds Sorted by Highest Discrepancy between Fund's Return and Investor Return

Fund	Morningstar Category	Fund's Return (%)	Investor Return (%)	Investor is Behind by (%)
Fund A	Small Growth	−1.8	−17.5	15.7
Fund B	Financial	3.1	−10.7	13.7
Fund C	Small Growth	−3.0	−15.7	12.6
Fund D	Small Blend	10.2	−2.4	12.5
Fund E	Large Growth	5.3	−6.7	12.0
Fund F	Natural Res	15.3	3.4	11.8
Fund G	Small Value	8.3	−3.1	11.4
Fund H	Mid-Cap Blend	8.7	−2.5	11.1
Fund I	Mid-Cap Growth	1.9	−9.0	10.9
Fund J	Large Blend	1.0	−9.4	10.4
Fund K	Mid-Cap Value	8.2	−1.9	10.1

To arrive at the above list, I used Principia to search for the greatest disparity between total return and investor return for all domestic equity funds. The column headed "Investor Is Behind by" is the difference between "Total Return," which is the fund's return, and "Investor Return," which is the return investors achieve on a dollar-weighted basis.

According to Morningstar:

> The gap between investor return and total return indicates how well investors time their fund purchases and sales. When investor return is less than total return, it means that investors didn't participate equally in the funds' monthly returns—more investors participated in the downside returns and less in the upside returns. This sometimes happens when investors chase returns and assets flow into a fund at its peak of performance. This effect can be exacerbated when investors aim to break even and refuse to sell a losing fund.

On the other side of the coin are the funds in which investor return exceeded total returns, something that occurred only 27 percent of the time for the ten-year period ending 2010, as you can see from Table 3-4.

In Table 3-6 below, see the column labeled "Investor Is Ahead by," which shows the highest discrepancy between investor return and total return. For example, the investors in Fund L, a small blend fund, moved in and out of the fund in such a way as to handily outperform the fund by a wide margin. Investor return was 32.9 percent, compared to 8.6 percent for the fund, putting the investor ahead by 24.3 percentage points.

"When investor return is greater than total return," according to Morningstar, "it means that more investors participated in the fund's upswing and less in the downswing. This can happen when investors are committed to a diversification strategy and continue to invest new monies into a fund, even when its style of investing has gone out of favor."

Table 3-6. Ranking of Investor Outperformance of All US Equity Funds with 10-Year Total Returns Through 2010
(Source: Morningstar Principia)

Fund	Morningstar Category	Fund's Return (%)	Investor Return (%)	Investor is Ahead by
Fund L	Small Blend	8.6	32.9	24.3
Fund M	Mid-Cap Growth	−0.8	14.2	15.0
Fund N	Real Estate	10.0	24.6	14.6
Fund O	Large Growth	−13.4	−1.8	11.6
Fund P	Mid-Cap Growth	5.4	15.8	10.5
Fund Q	Mid-Cap Growth	3.2	11.6	8.4
Fund R	Small Growth	8.6	16.3	7.7
Fund S	Large Blend	2.1	9.3	7.1
Fund T	Large Blend	−7.2	−0.6	6.6
Fund U	Small Blend	2.5	9.0	6.6
Fund V	Real Estate	9.4	15.9	6.5

Some conclude that how well an investor does is actually more dependent on *investor behavior* than on fund performance.

This sort of movement in and out of a fund comes about when investors react to market swings. It's far better to be prepared for such moves and to anticipate how you will react.

A Review System Will Help You

Now that we've reviewed the averages—market averages and investor averages—we need to think about how you can do better by managing your individual portfolio. And indeed, in later chapters, we'll discuss how you can avoid inopportune buys and sells by having a system or rule-set that you apply when markets change, as they will inevitably do over time. In Chapter 21, we'll look at a ten step review system to help you effectively monitor your portfolio.

Now, let's dive into more market data, which can help you see market returns in a different light. Then, in Chapters 5, 6, and 7, we'll turn to what I feel is the most important element of investing significant sums of money—uncertainty and how to manage it.

Summary

This chapter establishes a foundation in historical returns for the broad market and sets the stage for closer scrutiny in the next chapter.

Approaching investing from the perspective of being your own portfolio manager will help you avoid the lagging results experienced by some investors.

Key Points

1. The future will be some reflection of the past. We will see bulls and bears again.
2. Studies conclude that individual investors' returns lag market returns because individual investors move in and out of their investments at the wrong time.
3. Deciding to buy based on feeling left out (in a bull market) or sell based on fear (in a bear market) is not a sound way to make investment decisions.

Steps to Take

1. Create a record of when and why you made buy and sell decisions over the last year. What factors influenced your decisions?
2. Consider how you might make buy and sell decisions in the next bear market.
3. Consider how you might make buy and sell decisions in the next bull market.

CHAPTER 4

The "Lost" Decade?

What's in It for You?

If you think of the first decade of 2000 as the "lost decade" because stock market returns, as measured by the S&P 500 Index, went nowhere, you might be left with the sense that it doesn't pay to invest in stocks. That impression is wrong. This chapter will show you why.

The chapter is rich with return data on stocks (and stock mutual funds) that outperformed (and underperformed) the averages. This is the type of data investors need to review to build a foundation upon which to make good investment decisions. As you read this chapter, you may find that you'll want to expand on the research you see here to develop your own stock selection criteria, a subject we'll discuss in Part 6 of the book. We'll touch on how your results can be affected by when you buy as much as what you buy.

Contents

The "Lost" Decade?

It has been said that the first decade of the 2000 millennium was the "lost decade" in terms of stock market returns. That is indeed the case for investors who bought and held an S&P 500 Index fund that replicated the S&P 500 Index. If you had invested $10,000 in January 2000, you would have had about $9,000 at the end of 2009 for an average annualized loss of 1 percent and cumulative loss of 9.8 percent for the period, according to Morningstar Principia.

Averages don't tell the whole story, however, as you will see in this chapter. We'll go beyond the averages to the individual stocks that trade in the marketplace. We'll review the top—and the bottom—of the pack. And, we'll also consider how formula investing (dollar cost averaging) might affect results.

You'll see that relying on other people's views about the markets can leave you with incorrect conclusions about your own investing. Averages shouldn't encourage or discourage individual investors who need to manage their portfolios.

Mining the Data: The Top Stocks of the S&P 500 Index for the Decade

If the market benchmark (S&P 500 Index) disappointed over the 2000–2009 decade, was the stock market a bad place to invest during that time? To answer that question, I used Morningstar Principia to search for top performing stocks for the ten-year period ending 2009.

First, I screened for the top 100 stocks represented in the S&P 500 Index. The "average annual return" for the top 100 performers of the S&P 500 Index for the decade was 19.2 percent, far surpassing the broad market average of minus one percent. The median was 16.6 percent, the lowest return for the period was 12.5 percent, and the highest return was 42.7 percent. Table 4-1 provides a quick summary.

Table 4-1. Average Annual Returns of the Top 100 Performing S&P 500 Index Stocks for the 2000–2009 Decade

(Source: Morningstar Principia)

Average annual return	19.1%
Median	16.6%
Minimum	12.5%
Maximum	50.3%

Then I searched the entire Morningstar Principia database of over 5,000 stocks with ten-year performance records as of December 31, 2009. This second screen of all stocks, which includes the more risky small capitalization stocks that trade over the counter, proved to have even better top-stock performance for the period.

As you can see from Table 4-2, below, the average annual return for these top 100 stocks of the decade was 39.8 percent, far surpassing the broad market average loss of 1 percent. The median was 34.7 percent, the lowest return for the period was 30.0 percent, and the highest return was 107.9 percent.

Table 4-2. Average Annual Returns of the Top 100 Performing Stocks for the 2000–2009 Decade
(Source: Morningstar Principia)

Average annual return	39.8%
Median	34.7%
Minimum	30.1%
Maximum	107.9%

The stocks represented in both Tables 4-1 and 4-2 not only withstood the tumult of the decade but far surpassed the averages in stock performance.

How Many Stocks Beat the S&P 500 Index?

Of the 5,295 stocks with ten-year performance records in the Morningstar Principia December 31, 2009, database, 2,941 stocks (more than 55 percent) beat the decade's S&P 500 Index return, the benchmark for the broad market (an average annual loss of 1 percent for the decade). One-fifth, or 1,148 stocks, returned more than 10 percent average annual returns for the decade. About 6 percent (325 stocks) averaged more than 20 percent per year for the decade.

Bottom-Performing Stocks

To balance out our discussion, we need to look at the bottom performers as well. Of the 5,295 stocks with ten-year returns in the Morningstar Principia December 31, 2009, database, 1,895 (nearly 36 percent) lost more than 10 percent (average annual returns for the ten-year period ending 2009). Of those, 1,318 lost more than 20 percent; 921 lost more than 30 percent; 632 lost more than 40 percent; and 405 lost more than 50 percent.

Let's focus more narrowly than sectors as we examine the bottom performers. Morningstar subdivides its twelve sectors into more than ninety industries, which indicate a "company's primary area of business." (Note that S&P organizes stocks into ten, not twelve, sectors.)

The worst performer during this period was the Internet Service Provider industry, with an average annual loss for the decade of 28.6 percent, as you can see from the Table 4-3. The Broadcasting—Radio industry recorded an annual loss of 27.3 percent for the decade.

Table 4-3. Bottom-Performing Industries for the 2000–2009 Decade

(Source: Morningstar Principia)

Morningstar Sector	Morningstar Industry	Average Annual Total Returns for the 10 Years Ending 2009 (%)
Telecommunications	Internet Service Providers	−28.6
Media	Broadcasting—Radio	−27.3
Telecommunications	Internet Software & Services	−22.5
Telecommunications	Communication Equipment	−13.8
Hardware	Computer Peripherals	−13.2
Hardware	Printed Circuit Boards	−11.6
Media	Entertainment—Diversified	−10.4
Financial Services	Mortgage Investment	−10.2
Hardware	Semiconductor Equipment & Materials	−10.2

As you can see, investors could have done much more poorly than market averages if they had invested in these industries or in the many stocks that had substantially greater underperformance than the market averages.

Now let's turn to the 500 stocks in the S&P 500 Index.

Best of the S&P 500 Index

The top 50 stocks of the S&P 500 Index returned an average of 23.9 percent per year—hardly a lost decade for those who invested in these stocks. The median was 23.9 percent. The highest performer was Southwestern Energy Company (SWN), with a 50.3 percent per year return for the decade. The bottom-ranked stock of the highest 50 returned an average annual return of 16.6 percent.

The full list of the top 50 S&P 500 Index stocks of the decade is provided in Table 4-4, below. As you peruse the list, you might find some stocks that you will want to research later. This is not a "buy" list.

Table 4-4. Top 50 Performers of the S&P 500 Index for the 2000–2009 Decade

(Source: Morningstar Principia)

Count	Company Name	Ticker	Morningstar Sector	Average Annual Return for the 10-Year Period Ending 2009 (%)
1	Southwestern Energy Company	SWN	Energy	50.3
2	XTO Energy, Inc.	XTO	Energy	42.7
3	Range Resources Corporation	RRC	Energy	37.3
4	Precision Castparts Corp.	PCP	Industrial Materials	32.7
5	FLIR Systems, Inc.	FLIR	Industrial Materials	32.0
6	Denbury Resources, Inc.	DNR	Energy	30.1
7	Ventas, Inc.	VTR	Financial Services	30.0
8	Davita, Inc.	DVA	Healthcare	29.4
9	Gilead Sciences, Inc.	GILD	Healthcare	29.0
10	Stericycle, Inc.	SRCL	Industrial Materials	27.9
11	Chesapeake Energy Corp.	CHK	Energy	27.8
12	Titanium Metals Corporation	TIE	Industrial Materials	27.6
13	EOG Resources	EOG	Energy	27.5

Count	Company Name	Ticker	Morningstar Sector	Average Annual Return for the 10-Year Period Ending 2009 (%)
14	Express Scripts	ESRX	Healthcare	26.9
15	Consol Energy, Inc.	CNX	Energy	26.8
16	Western Digital Corporation	WDC	Hardware	26.6
17	Cognizant Technology Solutions Corporation	CTSH	Software	25.8
18	Celgene Corporation	CELG	Healthcare	25.3
19	Reynolds American, Inc.	RAI	Consumer Goods	24.2
20	Cabot Oil & Gas Corporation	COG	Energy	23.6
21	Occidental Petroleum Corporation	OXY	Energy	23.4
22	Quest Diagnostics, Inc.	DGX	Healthcare	23.4
23	Apple, Inc.	AAPL	Hardware	23.4
24	Laboratory Corporation of America Holdings	LH	Healthcare	23.3
25	Coventry Health Care, Inc.	CVH	Healthcare	23.3
26	Hudson City Bancorp, Inc.	HCBK	Financial Services	22.9
27	AmerisourceBergen Corporation	ABC	Consumer Services	21.9
28	Noble Energy, Inc.	NBL	Energy	21.3
29	Apollo Group, Inc.	APOL	Business Services	21.1
30	Apache Corporation	APA	Energy	20.9
31	CH Robinson Worldwide, Inc.	CHRW	Business Services	20.3
32	Varian Medical Systems, Inc.	VAR	Healthcare	20.2
33	Questar Corporation	STR	Energy	19.8
34	EQT Corp.	EQT	Utilities	19.7
35	Flowserve Corporation	FLS	Industrial Materials	19.1
36	National Oilwell Varco, Inc.	NOV	Energy	18.8
37	Amphenol Corporation	APH	Hardware	18.8
38	Ball Corporation	BLL	Consumer Goods	18.7

Count	Company Name	Ticker	Morningstar Sector	Average Annual Return for the 10-Year Period Ending 2009 (%)
39	Pioneer Natural Resources Company	PXD	Energy	18.7
40	Humana	HUM	Healthcare	18.3
41	Airgas, Inc.	ARG	Consumer Services	18.1
42	PACCAR, Inc	PCAR	Consumer Goods	17.9
43	Altria Group Inc.	MO	Consumer Goods	17.8
44	AutoZone, Inc.	AZO	Consumer Services	17.2
45	Pepsi Bottling Group, Inc.	PBG	Consumer Goods	17.2
46	Polo Ralph Lauren Corporation	RL	Consumer Goods	17.1
47	St. Jude Medical, Inc.	STJ	Healthcare	17.0
48	NVIDIA Corporation	NVDA	Hardware	16.9
49	Devon Energy Corporation	DVN	Energy	16.7
50	People's United Financial, Inc.	PBCT	Financial Services	16.6
			Average	23.9
			Median	23.1
			Maximum	50.3
			Minimum	16.6

What sectors did these stocks represent?

As you'll see from the next table (Table 4-5), while the sector with the highest total return was Software at 25.8 percent, most of the stocks in this top fifty list were represented by Energy stocks (seventeen stocks or 34 percent of the fifty), followed by Industrial Materials (eight stocks or 16 percent), Healthcare (five stocks or 10 percent), and Consumer Services (five stocks or 10 percent). You'll want to be aware of the sector representation of your own portfolio.

Table 4-5. Sector Representation for Top Fifty Performers of the S&P 500 Index for the 2000–2009 Decade Sorted by Number of Stocks

(Source: Morningstar Principia)

Morningstar Sector	Average Annual Total	Number of Stocks	Percentage of Total Returns for the 10 Years Ending 2009 (%)
Energy	24.8	17	34
Industrial Materials	21.6	8	16
Healthcare	23.9	5	10
Consumer Services	17.3	5	10
Consumer Goods	17.7	4	8
Hardware	22.9	3	6
Financial Services	23.2	2	4
Business Services	18.2	2	4
Utilities	17.1	2	4
Software	25.8	1	2
Telecommunications	14.9	1	2
Total		50	100%

Other Ten-Year Periods

Having examined the decade ending 2009, I wanted to compare each of the other ten-year holding periods during the decade (the ten years ending 2008, the ten years ending 2007, and so forth). I wanted to see how many S&P 500 Index stocks delivered an average of more than 10 percent per year for each ten-year period. As you can see from Table 4-6, a substantial number of companies passed the test.

Table 4-6. Number of S&P 500 Index Stocks Returning More Than 10 Percent for the Ten-Year Periods Shown
(Source: Morningstar Principia)

Ten Years Ending	Number of Stocks	Average Annual Total Returns for the 10-Year Periods Shown in Column 1 (%)
1999	160	26
2000	174	24
2001	96	20
2002	62	17
2003	150	18
2004	202	18
2005	156	17
2006	176	17
2007	118	18
2008	11	24
2009	84	18

As you might expect, the lowest representation of S&P 500 Index stocks that returned more than 10 percent per year was in the ten-year period ending 2008, the year that the S&P 500 Index lost 37 percent; only eleven stocks returned a ten-year average return greater than 10 percent. The second lowest number of stocks was the ten-year period ending 2002 (sixty-two), the year in which the S&P 500 Index fell by 22 percent, after falling by 12 percent the previous year.

The three ten-year periods representing the highest number of S&P 500 Index stocks that delivered more than 10 percent per year were the ten years ending 2004 (202), when the S&P 500 Index was up 10.9 percent for the year, followed by 2006 (176), when the S&P Index gained 15.8 percent, and 2000 (174), when the S&P 500 Index lost 9.1 percent.

Further research might take you to exploring these outperforming stocks in greater detail.

Mutual Fund Returns for the Decade

What about mutual funds? Again, using the Morningstar Principia database, I reviewed the top fifty performers for the decade ending 2009. The average annual return was 17.3 percent for the decade. The median was 17.0 percent, the highest performer returned 24.4 percent, and the lowest performer in the top fifty was 13.9 percent, as shown in Table 4-7.

Table 4-7. Average Annual Returns for the 2000–2009 Decade for the Fifty Top-Performing Mutual Funds
(Source: Morningstar Principia)

Average annual returns	17.3%
Median	17.0%
Maximum	24.4%
Minimum	13.9%

The entire top-fifty list for the decade is provided in Table 4-8, which also includes the Morningstar category. Don't view this list as a list of funds to buy. There is a lot more to mutual fund selection than past performance, as we will discuss in Chapter 19.

Table 4-8. Fifty Top-Performing Mutual Funds for the 2000–2009 Decade
(Source: Morningstar Principia)

Count	Fund Name	Ticker	Morningstar Category	Average Annual Total Returns for the 10 Years Ending 2009 (%)
1	USAA Precious Metals and Minerals	USAGX	Equity Precious Metals	24.4
2	ING Russia A	LETRX	Europe Stock	23.8
3	BlackRock Energy & Resources Inv A	SSGRX	Equity Energy	23.1

Count	Fund Name	Ticker	Morningstar Category	Average Annual Total Returns for the 10 Years Ending 2009 (%)
4	Evergreen Precious Metals B	EKWBX	Equity Precious Metals	21.8
5	Tocqueville Gold	TGLDX	Equity Precious Metals	21.7
6	First Eagle Gold A	SGGDX	Equity Precious Metals	21.4
7	Van Eck Intl Investors Gold A	INIVX	Equity Precious Metals	21.4
8	GAMCO Gold AAA	GOLDX	Equity Precious Metals	20.3
9	OCM Gold	OCMGX	Equity Precious Metals	19.7
10	Oppenheimer Gold & Special Minerals A	OPGSX	Equity Precious Metals	19.6
11	DWS Gold & Precious Metals S	SCGDX	Equity Precious Metals	19.3
12	CGM Realty	CGMRX	Real Estate	19.0
13	Bruce	BRUFX	Moderate Allocation	18.9
14	Franklin Gold and Precious Metals A	FKRCX	Equity Precious Metals	18.6
15	T. Rowe Price Latin America	PRLAX	Latin America Stock	18.4
16	U.S. Global Investors Gold and Prec Mtls	USERX	Equity Precious Metals	18.3
17	BlackRock Latin America A	MDLTX	Latin America Stock	18.3
18	AIM Gold & Precious Metals Inv	FGLDX	Equity Precious Metals	18.1
19	ICON Energy	ICENX	Equity Energy	18.0
20	U.S. Global Investors Wld Prec Minerals	UNWPX	Equity Precious Metals	17.9

Count	Fund Name	Ticker	Morningstar Category	Average Annual Total Returns for the 10 Years Ending 2009 (%)
21	CGM Focus	CGMFX	Large Growth	17.9
22	Vanguard Precious Metals and Mining	VGPMX	Natural Res	17.8
23	Jennison Natural Resources B	PRGNX	Natural Res	17.5
24	Matthews China	MCHFX	Pacific/Asia ex-Japan Stk	17.2
25	Fidelity Select Gold	FSAGX	Equity Precious Metals	17.1
26	U.S. Global Investors Global Res	PSPFX	Natural Res	16.9
27	American Century Global Gold Inv	BGEIX	Equity Precious Metals	16.7
28	RS Global Natural Resources A	RSNRX	Natural Res	16.4
29	RiverSource Precious Metals & Mining A	INPMX	Equity Precious Metals	16.4
30	Vanguard Energy	VGENX	Equity Energy	16.3
31	Oppenheimer Developing Markets A	ODMAX	Diversified Emerging Mkts	15.8
32	U.S. Global Investors Eastern European	EUROX	Europe Stock	15.5
33	Templeton China World A	TCWAX	Pacific/Asia ex-Japan Stk	15.5
34	AIM Energy Inv	FSTEX	Equity Energy	15.4
35	Van Eck Global Hard Assets A	GHAAX	Natural Res	15.1
36	Fidelity Latin America	FLATX	Latin America Stock	14.9
37	Dreyfus Greater China A	DPCAX	Pacific/Asia ex-Japan Stk	14.9

Count	Fund Name	Ticker	Morningstar Category	Average Annual Total Returns for the 10 Years Ending 2009 (%)
38	GMO Emerging Country Debt III	GMCDX	Emerging Markets Bond	14.9
39	Robeco Long/Short Eq I	BPLSX	Long-Short	14.8
40	Ivy Global Natural Resources A	IGNAX	Natural Res	14.6
41	Lord Abbett Micro Cap Value I	LMVYX	Small Blend	14.5
42	DWS Latin America Equity S	SLAFX	Latin America Stock	14.3
43	Burnham Financial Services A	BURKX	Financial	14.2
44	Delaware Pooled Emerging Markets	DPEMX	Diversified Emerging Mkts	14.2
45	BlackRock Natural Resources B	MBGRX	Natural Res	14.1
46	Third Millennium Russia A	TMRFX	Europe Stock	14.1
47	ING Global Natural Resources A	LEXMX	Natural Res	14.1
48	BlackRock Health Sciences Ops Inv A	SHSAX	Health	14.0
49	Fidelity Advisor Latin America A	FLTAX	Latin America Stock	13.9
50	DFA Emerging Markets Value I	DFEVX	Diversified Emerging Mkts	13.9
			Average	17.3
			Median	17.0
			Maximum	24.4
			Minimum	13.9

You'll notice that many of these top-performing funds were precious metals funds, which is reflective of the gold and precious metals boom during the decade.

Bottom-Performing Mutual Funds for the Decade

When it comes to mutual funds, the bottom performers suffered less than stocks, as you might expect, since most funds are diversified across different sectors and industries. In addition, you have to consider the effect of "survivorship bias"—funds can be closed or gobbled up by other funds when performance drags, so the returns reflect the results of the funds that made it to the end of the measuring period.

There were no mutual funds in the Morningstar Principia database of more than 25,000 mutual funds that lost more than 30 percent per year over the last decade. Only five lost more than 20 percent per year for the decade, and only fifteen lost more than 10 percent. However, 602 made no money for investors for the ten-year period.

If you compare the best of the mutual funds to the best of the stocks in this chapter, you'll see that the stocks achieved higher highs and lower lows than the mutual funds for the period. Generally, you will find that to be the case: most often funds that invest in a diversified list of stocks tend to have lower highs and higher lows than individual stocks. However, that is not the case for leveraged funds, which you should expect to exhibit greater volatility.

Other Indices

You may also be interested in knowing that the S&P SmallCap 600 Index returned a 6.3-percent average annual return for the decade ending 2009. The S&P MidCap 400 Composite Index returned 6.1 percent. Bonds returned 6.3 percent for the decade, as measured by the Barclays Aggregate Bond Index.

Dollar Cost Averaging

All of the data in this chapter measures returns as if a single investment were made at the beginning of the period and held to the end. An investment in a representative S&P 500 Index fund at the beginning of 2000 and held until the end of 2009 would have resulted in a loss. As we discussed earlier, an investment of $10,000 in January 2000 would have lost about $1,000 by the end of 2009 for an average annualized return of –1 percent and a cumulative return of –9.8 percent for the period, according to Morningstar Principia.

Using the very same investment vehicle, you could have substantially improved your results had you made your purchases over time, a technique called "formula investing" or "dollar cost averaging." If you had invested each month of the decade, instead of just at the beginning of the decade, your annual return would have been 1.2 percent for a cumulative return of 13.2 percent for the ten-year period. Generally, dollar cost averaging improves returns in volatile markets such as the lost decade, but not in a rapidly rising market.

Summary

The decade ending 2009 was not "lost" to individuals who were selective in their stock and stock mutual fund choices or circumspect about how they purchased those investments (dollar cost averaging). It was not lost to people whose portfolios were structured to include bonds (Chapter 14). This was not, however, a good decade for the passive S&P 500 Index fund investor who invested in the beginning of the period and held on to the end.

Just about every portfolio will need to have a stock or (stock mutual fund) component as we will discuss in later chapters. You will not, of course, want to choose the top performers we reviewed in this chapter solely because they outperformed the market. However, some of the data we reviewed together may spur you to do further research. In the Resources section at the back of the book, you'll find a list of recommended research tools.

Key Points

1. Decades are not "lost" to investors. There are always ways to make money.
2. Market averages are just that—averages.
3. Doing some very basic research helps investors build a foundation upon which good investment decisions can eventually be made.

Steps to Take

1. Consider how the return data we've reviewed together in this chapter might affect your investment decisions.
2. Consider whether dollar cost averaging is a desirable method of buying stocks or stock mutual funds, especially if you participate in a 401(k) or retirement plan at work in which you make investments every pay period.
3. Construct questions you would like to answer with further research. For example, you might want to research the characteristics of the stocks that outperformed the market during the "lost decade."

Demystifying Risk and Uncertainty

Risk is an inherent feature of investing. And one of the biggest challenges investors face is learning how to assess and manage risk. Gaining the skills to harness risk, rather than fearing or ignoring it, can be crucial to realizing your financial goals. Part 2 covers techniques and strategies to help you accomplish this.

In Chapter 5, we'll discuss uncertainty in the markets and how that can impact your portfolio decisions. We'll also examine the "investor's dilemma" of wanting high returns with no risk—an unlikely prospect. And we'll look to Harry Markowitz's *Portfolio Selection* for further insights.

Then in Chapter 6, I'll demonstrate a strategy to help you evaluate a security so you can decide if it's too risky for you. Whether or not you're a math whiz, you'll be able to apply these principles either by doing the calculations or by looking at the underlying concepts. I'll also provide data on stocks with different "betas," a measurement of risk described in the chapter.

In Chapter 7, we'll review how to lower risk by managing portfolio volatility. You'll see how to use measures like standard deviation to compare the volatility of stocks or mutual funds to help you determine which best fit your risk profile. You'll also learn about "downside exposure" and methods to lessen uncertainty when you manage your portfolio.

CHAPTER 5

Dealing with the Investor's Dilemma: Uncertainty

What's in It for You?

Uncertainty is part of every investor's life. In this chapter, we'll discuss what to make of uncertainty in the context of portfolio decision making.

Contents

Uncertainty

Irrespective of market gyrations, economic cycles, the rise and fall of the dollar, the expansion or contraction of government, inflationary or deflationary pressures, consumer spending and saving trends, globalization, wars, political upheavals, taxes, or changes in leadership in Washington, investment decisions need to be made and portfolios need to be managed.

In every type of situation you can imagine, challenges and opportunities will present themselves. Experts will opine. Thought-leaders will influence. Events will provoke reactions. And you, as an investor, will be called upon to make choices.

Bear Market

As we touched on in the last chapter, during a bear market, you might run for cover by selling at the wrong time, such as a market bottom, fearing that the market will never right itself. Or, you might search for "guaranteed" products or "down-market strategies" such as short selling or alternative, noncorrelated investment opportunities.

Bubble

During a bubble, you might be drawn to speculative investments with the false belief that a new era has arrived, with new opportunities governed by a new set of rules. We saw that happen during the Internet bubble leading up to the 2000–2009 decade, when people operated under the popular delusion that stock market rules had changed—stocks only went up, and never went down.

In either type of market, investors make the wrong decisions, moving in and out of investments at market turns, buying high and selling low. As we saw in the last chapter, investor returns suffer as a result of these inopportune moves. Managing a portfolio based on your own personal strategy will help prevent such errors.

Insights About Risk from Academia

A great body of academic work focuses on risk in the financial markets. Nobel Prize–winning economist Harry Markowitz posited the investor's dilemma (wanting a risk-free high rate of return) in his book *Portfolio Selection: Efficient Diversification of Investments.*

Originally published as his doctoral thesis, the work helps quantify risk and return expectations, forming the foundation for modern portfolio theory. This theory still guides the hands of many institutional portfolio managers who manage large pensions and mutual funds, as well as stock analysts who produce stock research reports. Many are Chartered Financial Analyst designees, also called CFA Charterholders or simply CFAs.

According to Markowitz:

> Uncertainty is a salient feature of security investment. Economic forces are not understood well enough for predictions to be beyond doubt or error. Even if the consequences of economic conditions were understood perfectly, noneconomic influences can change the course of general prosperity, the level of the market, or the success of a particular security. The health of the President, changes in international tensions, increases or decreases in military spending, an extremely dry summer, the success of an invention, the miscalculation of a business management—all can affect the capital gains or dividends of one or many securities.

> We are expecting too much if we require the security analyst to predict with certainty whether a typical security will increase or decrease in value. . . . Only the clairvoyant could hope to predict with certainty.

> Uncertainty is an essential ingredient of an investment.

The Investor's Conflict: Wanting Reward without Risk

As Markowitz says, two objectives are common to all investors. In his words, investors want their return to be "high" (however people define return, "they prefer more of it to less of it"). And, "They want this return to be dependable, stable, not subject to uncertainty."

And, therein lies the conflict of the investor: how to achieve high return and low risk at the same time. How does the investor solve this dilemma?

Solving the Dilemma

First, let me give you my view based on many years of managing portfolios for individual investors and interviewing them for my columns, books, and classes. Then, we'll return to the academic view.

In my experience, the most satisfied investors are those who embrace the investor's conflict, understanding that risk and reward are the opposite sides of a single coin. They accept that they cannot control the ups and downs of the market, cannot predict when the market will take a dive or spring toward the heavens, and cannot outmaneuver large institutions that may have much more data and power to be faster and smarter about finding bargains.

These investors realize that the goal is not to try to achieve the impossible (high returns with no risk). They focus on managing their portfolios to achieve their own personal objectives, which they set based on their personal preferences, while managing risk and tempering expectations to what the markets can reasonably provide. We'll discuss their techniques throughout the book.

Efficient Portfolios: Correlation and Diversification

First, we need a foundation. What do the experts say about structuring portfolios that could be useful? How would you attempt to structure a personal portfolio that has a good risk/return profile?

Markowitz suggested: consider different portfolios and choose the one that offers the highest return with the least uncertainty or risk. Anything else is inefficient and undesirable.

In Markowitz's words:

> The portfolio with the highest "likely return" is not necessarily the one with the least "uncertainty of return." The most reliable portfolio with an extremely high likely return may be subject to an unacceptably high degree of uncertainty. The portfolio with the least uncertainty may have an undesirably small "likely return." Between these extremes would lie portfolios with varying degrees of likely return and uncertainty.

> If portfolio A has both a highly likely return and a lower uncertainty of return than portfolio B and meets the other requirements of the investor, it is clearly better than portfolio B. Portfolio B may be eliminated from consideration, since it yields less return with greater uncertainty than does another available portfolio. We refer to portfolio B as "inefficient."

How does one create a portfolio like portfolio A, with a highly likely return and a lower uncertainty of return?

How to Lessen Uncertainty and Risk

Again, lessons from academics and logic teach us that you would want the portfolio to contain assets that are not all going to act the same way at the same time. Part of the exercise is to review each holding's risk and reward parameters to see how all the holdings interrelate with each other, which is the concept of *correlation*. "A . . . salient feature of security investment is the correlation among security returns," says Markowitz.

If a portfolio holds assets that are noncorrelated, the portfolio is said to be "diversified." According to Markowitz,

The correlation among returns is not the same for all securities. We generally expect the returns on a security to be more correlated with those in the same industry than those of unrelated industries. . . . To reduce risk it is necessary to avoid a portfolio whose securities are all highly correlated with each other. One hundred securities whose returns rise and fall in near unison afford little more protection than the uncertain return of a single security.

Diversified Portfolios: Risk Free?

Based on this theory, the goal for the investor would be to construct a portfolio that is diversified, meaning that it contains holdings that have different risk-reward characteristics. This type of portfolio would be less volatile and less "uncertain."

In contrast, a concentrated portfolio—say a portfolio that invested in financial institutions—would suffer greatly if that single sector dropped dramatically in price. A portfolio representing multiple sectors of the economy with different risk and reward parameters would suffer less.

Diversification Is Not a Guarantee against Losses

Markowitz cautions, however, that "[t]he fact that security returns are highly correlated, but not perfectly correlated, implies that diversification can reduce risk but not eliminate it." This statement is noteworthy. The principles of diversification do not guarantee someone against losses, as we saw in 2008. Even a well-diversified portfolio will suffer when the entire financial system is threatened with collapse.

Are Markets Efficient?

The efficient market theory essentially assumes that market prices reflect the presence, size, and scope of professional traders and arbitrageurs in the marketplace, as expressed by Eugene Fama, professor at the University of Chicago Booth School of Business.

Given the ability of professionals to act more quickly on previous prices and publicly available information than the public, pricing inefficiencies are short-lived, leaving little opportunity for the individual investor to locate or exploit them.

After the market dislocation of 2007 and 2008, and earlier during the Internet bubble, many challenged the efficient market theory—weren't we seeing pricing inefficiencies?

Few can disagree that, in Professor William F. Sharpe's words, for the average investor it is "impossible to make abnormal profit (other than by chance)." Sharpe introduced the Sharpe Ratio, a measure of an investment's reward relative to its risk.

Can You Outsmart the Market?

Whether or not you are a believer in the efficient market theory, we know from experience that a novice investor is at a disadvantage in the financial marketplace if his expectations are unrealistic based on inexperience.

For example, I recall meeting a widow who received a $1 million insurance check shortly after her husband died. She purchased a CMO (collateralized mortgage obligation) because the salesman offered her "9-percent interest on a safe, government-guaranteed bond," when other like bonds were yielding only 3 percent.

Thinking that was she extraordinarily lucky to have found this hidden gem, she went ahead with the purchase, only to find out later that she paid a premium to buy the bond to reflect the current 3-percent market. (Interest rates had declined significantly after the bond issued.)

Had she understood that such gems—if they did exist—would be gobbled up by institutions, she would have been a little more skeptical before the purchase. As it turned out, she also didn't understand that CMO distributions included repayment of principal, which she spent, not realizing that she was eating up her $1 million principal.

Skepticism

Everyone needs to approach investing with a healthy dose of skepticism. As Nassim Nicholas Taleb states in his book *The Black Swan,* "A vexing problem in the history of human thought is finding one's position on the boundary between skepticism and gullibility, or how to believe and how to not believe. And how to make decisions based on these beliefs, since believers without decisions are just sterile . . . Clearly, you cannot doubt everything and function, you cannot believe everything and survive."

Diversification Is Not for Everybody

Good deals do exist in the market, but it takes a bit of work to find them, and some money management skills to properly put them to work. For example, some investors successfully choose the more risky approach of concentrating in a few sectors of the market or on a few stocks. An example of such an investor might be someone like Warren Buffett, who buys and holds stocks of strong companies that he views as underappreciated by the market at the time of purchase.

Buffett prefers to concentrate his investments in a select number of strong companies that are priced well. In fact, he is reported to have said that "diversification is a protection against ignorance. It makes very little sense for those who know what they're doing." And, "I prefer to keep all my eggs in one basket and watch that basket closely." Concentration is a fine strategy for someone who wants to outperform the market and is confident in his stock selection skills. However, it is a risky strategy for anyone else.

Summary

Every individual needs to face the investor's conflict: wanting reward without risk. The successful investor will embrace this conflict by focusing on how to lessen risk in order to improve results, a natural outcome of Personal Portfolio Management.

Key Points

1. Uncertainty (and risk) is unavoidable. There is no potential for gain without risk.
2. Different theories of portfolio construction focus on balancing risk and reward.
3. Diversification reduces risk, but does not eliminate it.

Steps to Take

1. Consider how you make investment decisions. How does your attitude about uncertainty and risk affect your investment decisions?
2. Construct a set of rules to use in managing the risk you want to assume in your portfolio.
3. Review your current portfolio in light of the risk and reward principles we discussed in this chapter.

Enhancing Portfolio Returns

What's in It for You?

Risk might intimidate some investors. Rather than avoid or ignore risk, this chapter gives you a strategy to help assess the potential risk of an investment and then determine whether it makes sense for you to add it to your portfolio.

Contents

Should You Add a Risky Investment to Your Portfolio?

As we discussed in the last chapter, investors are faced with uncertainty and conflict: wanting high returns with no risk. We explored how to lower risk and increase returns through diversification and touched on the challenges to the efficient market theory upon which an efficient (properly diversified) portfolio rests.

CHAPTER 6

In this chapter, let's explore another foundational concept: how to determine whether adding a particular stock to your portfolio is worth the risk. An intriguing way to judge risk and reward is based on the capital asset pricing model (CAPM) developed by Nobel Prize–winner William F. Sharpe, professor emeritus of finance at Stanford University's Graduate School of Business.

Making Comparisons

The underlying concept is this: individuals should buy risky stocks only if they are rewarded for that risk—who can argue with that? You can see that this assessment can be very helpful in making buy, sell, and hold decisions, since it gives you a basis for assessing whether or not you want to take on more risk (and presumably potential reward) than market risk—something you can achieve by purchasing a stock index mutual fund.

I'll show you the calculation to illustrate the theory. If you don't care to do the math on your own investments, instead, look at the underlying concepts, which, again, can be quite valuable.

First, let me set the stage. CAPM asks you to predict the future return of the market and to project the future price of the security you have in mind to purchase, which is something that analysts do based on discounted cash-flow models and other forecasting metrics.

You can look at research reports from independent research houses such as Morningstar, Value Line, and Standard & Poor's for their *target* prices on the stock in question. Bear in mind that they won't necessarily concur. You'll have to compare and contrast their methodology to determine the target of your choice, or create your own. If you want to develop your own target price, you'll find many online tools to help you. You'll see shortly how your target price comes into the picture.

Risk: Reward

CAPM focuses on the risk-reward relationship of a security. This is based on three elements: (1) risk-free return (which represents the time value of money), (2) risk, and (3) the expected return of the market. Risk is expressed as "beta," which is a measure of volatility. A security with a beta of 1 is as volatile as the market as a whole; a beta above 1 is more volatile and more risky than the market; a stock with a beta below 1 is less volatile and less risky. (You can look up a stock's beta on Morningstar.com or Bigcharts.com.)

Under this theory, you would want to invest in stocks that are riskier than the market *only* if justified by the belief that they are expected to outperform the market—a logical and useful premise when structuring a portfolio.

Example

Let's go through an example. CAPM compares market risk (beta of 1) with the beta of the stock in question (assume yours is twice as volatile as the market, thus sporting a beta of 2). Factor in a risk-free return to measure safety (assume a twelve-month U.S. Treasury bill, which has no volatility or risk, is yielding 3 percent). Assume that you will be holding the stock for twelve months.

Further, assume a reasonable market rate of return is 8 percent per year, based on historical market data from Ibbotson Associates.

What would your security (with a beta of 2—which is double the risk of the market) need to produce to make it more desirable than the market? That's your "required rate of return."

Again, the concept is that you would not invest in that security unless you believed that you could earn at least your required rate of return, because otherwise, you could invest in an S&P 500 Index fund and achieve that 8-percent market return at one-half the risk (the S&P 500 Index fund has a beta of 1, whereas the security in our example has a beta of 2).

How to Arrive at Required Rate of Return

Here is the formula for required rate of return using the above example:

To arrive at the required rate of return:

A. Find the market's excess return over the risk-free return.

Subtract:

expected market return − risk-free T-bill yield = excess market return

8%   −   3%   =   5%

B. Multiply the excess market return (5 percent) by the stock's beta (2): 5 × 2 = 10.

C. Add the risk-free return of the T-bill (3 percent) to the result (10 percent): 13 percent is your required rate of return.

In this example, your required rate of return is 13 percent. What that means is that you would not buy the stock unless you feel it would go up by 13 percent or more over the next 12 months. That is, if the current price of the stock, when compared to the "target price" is not at least 13 percent lower than the target price, you don't buy the stock. The projected return is insufficient to justify the assumed risk.

If your expected return on the market is 10 percent, the required return is even higher [17 percent figured as follows: 2 × 7 (10 percent minus 3 percent) = 14 + 3 (the risk-free return)]; you would not buy the stock unless you think the stock will go up 17 percent within the next twelve months.

Comparing Three Stocks

Table 6-1, below, shows you the required rate of return for three stocks with different betas. Notice that higher-beta stocks call for higher required rates of return while the opposite is true for lower-beta stocks. Again, this is a logical conclusion, since you would not want to risk more unless the potential reward were great enough to compensate for the added risk.

Table 6-1. Calculation of Required Rate of Return

	Stock 1	Stock 2	Stock 3
Beta	2	1.2	0.8
Expected market return	8.0%	8.0%	8.0%
Risk-free return	3.0%	3.0%	3.0%
Required rate of return	13.0%	9.0%	7.0%

Different Betas

Comparing the stocks in Table 6-1, Stock 1, which is the most risky (beta of 2), would be worthwhile purchasing if the target return were 13 percent or greater.

On the other hand, Stock 2 with a beta of 1.2 only needs a target return of 9 percent and Stock 3 with a beta of 0.8 needs a target return of 7 percent.

Target Price

Suppose you are using Value Line, a publisher of independent stock analyses, as your research tool. You notice the stock you want to purchase has a beta of 1.2 and a target price of $55. The stock is currently trading at $50. If it reaches its target, your return is 10 percent. Let's call this your target "ROR" or target rate of return. To make things simple, assume that 10 percent is also your profit expectation on the market. Using the logic underlying CAPM, you would not make this purchase, since you can achieve the same return with lower risk by buying an S&P 500 Index fund. No calculation need be made.

Say the stock became available at a lower price. When would it be a potential "buy"? Now you need your required rate of return.

If you look at Table 6-2, you'll see a comparison of the required rate of return (ROR) to the target rate of return on the stock in question. If the value in the bottom row is a negative number, you would *not* want to buy, since that means you won't be able to achieve the required rate of return. If the number is positive, the current price of the stock is low enough to justify a purchase. (The bottom row of Table 6-2, "Possible purchase if value is positive [required ROR compared to target ROR]," subtracts the required rate of return from the target rate of return.)

Table 6-2. Assume a Single Stock Fluctuates in Price: The Effect of Lower Prices on the Decision to Buy

Current price	50	49	48	47	46	45
Beta	1.2	1.2	1.2	1.2	1.2	1.2
Expected market return	10.0%	10.0%	10.0%	10.0%	10.0%	10.0%
Risk-free return	3.0%	3.0%	3.0%	3.0%	3.0%	3.0%
Required rate of return	11.4%	11.4%	11.4%	11.4%	11.4%	11.4%
Current price	50	49	48	47	46	45
Target price	55	55	55	55	55	55
Target rate of return	10.1%	12.1%	14.6%	17.0%	19.6%	22.2%
Possible purchase if value is positive (required ROR compared to target ROR)	−1.4%	0.8%	3.2%	5.6%	8.2%	10.8%

Notice the negative number in the bottom row for the stock at a price of $50. Since the number is negative, $50 is too high a price to pay considering you want to achieve the required rate of return of 11.4 percent. Therefore, you would not buy the stock.

Notice the last column, where the stock is priced at $45. At that price, the stock is a buy. The lower the current price of the stock, the more likely the purchase is justified under CAPM.

Because all projections are imprecise, there is no standard guideline for how much into positive territory the required rate of return comparison should be in order to justify the increased risk. There are many other factors to stock selection, however, and this is only one measure of attractiveness. We will discuss stock selection again in Chapters 16 through 18.

Why Not Buy an S&P 500 Index Fund?

These concepts might be helpful to you in assessing whether a risky stock is worth purchasing, given the alternative of buying a stock index fund that replicates the market. Sometimes, it will make more sense to choose an S&P 500 Index Fund over the stock in question, the rationale being that you don't want to assume more risk than is justified by the profit you hope to make.

Summary

As you can see, calculating required rate of return can help an investor assess the potential risk of an investment before taking it on. It is a method of harnessing risk, instead of avoiding it, or, worse, ignoring it. It also sets the stage for putting together a portfolio based on your risk appetite. Keep in mind that the risk of a portfolio can be lowered by adding lower beta securities to the mix. Another less mathematical approach to managing risk, relative value, is discussed in Chapter 7. We'll also talk about another way to manage risk by studying volatility by assessing standard deviation.

Key Points

1. Risk is always an integral part of investing, and it is important to understand and manage it rather than avoid or ignore it.
2. The capital asset pricing model (CAPM) establishes the foundation for measuring risk based on beta and expected rate of return.
3. You can use a simplified version of CAPM to help you decide whether the risk of a potential investment will suit your investment goals.

Steps to Take

1. Calculate your required rate of return for a security you are considering purchasing using the formula on page 60 under "How to Arrive at Required Rate of Return."
2. Using a research tool such as Value Line, determine the beta and price target for a stock of interest to you.
3. If you are researching stocks, create a Table 6-2 for yourself to help you see at what price that stock might become a "buy" for your portfolio.

Harnessing Risk by Understanding Volatility

CHAPTER 7

What's in It for You?

This chapter gives you another tool for assessing risk: measuring a stock's volatility through standard deviation. Standard deviation can help you find lower-risk, higher-reward investments that can help lessen the downside exposure of your portfolio. We'll also talk about other risks and touch on hedging.

Contents

Achieving Good Outcomes

In the last two chapters, we talked about how to lower risk and enhance returns through diversification and by understanding beta, which measures the risk of a stock in comparison to the market. In this chapter, let's discuss how to lower risk and improve portfolio returns through volatility management using standard deviation, which measures prior price movement without comparison to a benchmark. We'll also talk about removing risk altogether through hedging, a technique that can be used to counteract risk.

Managing Risk

Given that risk is an essential element of each and every investment, your first job is to estimate that risk. As we discussed in Chapter 2, no measure is perfect, since events can intervene, such as the financial market meltdown of September 2008, when the global financial system was on the brink of collapse after the bankruptcy of Lehman Brothers, the failure of Bear Stearns, and the eleventh-hour government intervention that saved Merrill Lynch and AIG from a similar fate.

Volatility Management: Standard Deviation as a Measure of Risk

Let's start with the obvious: the price of a stock (or another investment) fluctuates in response to the activity of buyers and sellers. When there are more buyers, the price of a stock goes up. When there are more sellers, the price drops. Price is a function of supply and demand.

This change in price occurs throughout the trading day and beyond if a stock sells in the after-hours marketplace. As long as there are sellers and buyers, the stock price will move up and down.

This price action is something that can be measured over different periods of time, and these measures can be useful to investors who want to manage their portfolios.

Illustration

Let's compare three investments that returned an average of 9 percent per year over six years, each arriving at the average in different ways, due to price action.

In the first year, Stock A lost 10 percent. In the following year, the stock rose 10 percent. In year 3, it suffered a minor loss (–1 percent), and then had three great years in a row (18 percent, 13 percent, then 24 percent). Stock B lost 20 percent in the first year, then gained 30 percent in the second year. In the third year, it lost 10 percent, then went through major fluctuations the next three years. Stock C steadily gained 9 percent each year.

Which of the three would you rather own in your portfolio? If you are concerned about risk, as every investor should be, you would want to compare the price action of all three stocks.

While the statistical measure for doing that is "standard deviation," you'll be able to see my point by looking at the return comparisons in Table 7-1. Focus on the Return (%) column, which shows the yearly return for each stock. The bottom row shows the standard deviation (SD) calculation for each stock.

Table 7-1. Comparing Standard Deviation of Three Stocks

Stock A		Stock B		Stock C	
Year	Return (%)	Year	Return (%)	Year	Return (%)
1	–10	1	–20	1	9
2	10	2	30	2	9
3	–1	3	–10	3	9
4	18	4	40	4	9
5	13	5	–30	5	9
6	24	6	44	6	9
Average	9	Average	9	Average	9
SD	13	SD	33	SD	0

Now look at Table 7-2. If you compare the highs to the lows in Table 7-2 for each stock, you can see that the stocks with the widest swings in prices also had the highest standard deviations (bottom row). Statistically, a stock with a standard deviation of 13, like Stock A, will return between 22 percent and −4 percent two-thirds of the time. Whereas a stock with a standard deviation of 33, like Stock B, will return between 42 percent and −25 percent two-thirds of the time.

Where do those figures come from? For Stock A, take the average of 9 percent and add 13 for the upper limit (22 percent) and subtract the 13 for the lower limit (−4 percent). For Stock B, take the average of 9 percent and add 33 for the upper limit (42 percent) and subtract the 33 for the lower limit (−25 percent). (See Table 7-2.)

Table 7-2. Comparison of Returns and Standard Deviations of Three Stocks

	Stock A Return (%)	Stock B Return (%)	Stock C Return (%)
Average	9	9	9
SD	13	33	0
1SD high	22	42	9
1SD low	−4	−24	9

And indeed, this is a rule you can apply: the higher the standard deviation, the wider the price swings; and the wider the swings, the more likely an investor might get caught losing money on a downswing. The opposite is also true: the higher the standard deviation, the more an investor can profit on an upswing. So, it naturally follows that a high standard deviation indicates higher risk and lower standard deviation indicates lower risk.

Volatility of a Portfolio

This illustration compares three investments. If you wanted to judge the volatility of your portfolio, you would need software (or an Excel spreadsheet) to help you do the calculations (to account for the weightings and correlations of your holdings, see Chapter 5). For example, if the portfolio has only two holdings of equal weight (50 percent each), and they are perfectly negatively correlated, they essentially cancel each other out—there is no variability in the portfolio (standard deviation is zero), and the expected return of the portfolio is zero.

You cannot compute an average weighted standard deviation of a portfolio unless each holding is positively correlated, however. When CFA Charterholders compute estimated expected returns, standard deviations, and correlation coefficients for each holding, they might plot an "efficient frontier" representing an array of portfolios with different risk and reward characteristics. (See Graph 7-1.)

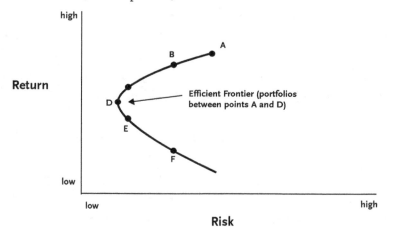

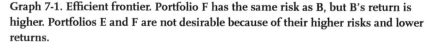

Graph 7-1. Efficient frontier. Portfolio F has the same risk as B, but B's return is higher. Portfolios E and F are not desirable because of their higher risks and lower returns.

Seeing alternatives this way, you can choose among high risk–high reward portfolios, medium risk–medium reward portfolios, or low risk–low reward portfolios. For obvious reasons, you would not want to choose high risk–low reward alternatives.

In my money management practice, we use software to calculate the standard deviations (and betas) of client portfolios to measure risk. We use these assessments in our monitoring process (more on monitoring in Chapters 20 and 21) and make judgments about returns based on how much risk we are assuming. These assessments give us information upon which to base risk decisions—we can raise and lower the risk (and potential reward) of a portfolio through investment selection and investment weightings.

Standard Deviation: Why It's Important

You can put volatility management to work in your portfolio to raise or lower the risk along with the potential reward of your portfolio.

A more conservative investor would want to choose the portfolio with lower risk and more modest return expectations than a more aggressive investor who could accept more risk for higher potential returns.

An Adaptation: Downside Exposure

While this is an inexact measure, you can use standard deviation to compute what I call "downside exposure" of a portfolio. Downside exposure gives you a rough idea of how far you should expect your investment to drop in normal markets. To explain the concept, let's go back to our illustration of Stocks A, B, and C.

Assume that your portfolio consists of $300,000 represented by $100,000 of each of the three stocks with the standard deviations that we've discussed. Now, let's take it a step further and determine expectations based on 1 standard deviation, which measures what can be expected to occur two out of three times. If return is 9 percent and standard deviation is 13 as with Stock A, then the upper limit of 1 standard deviation is 22 (9 + 13) (see 1SD high in Table 7-3) and the lower limit is –4 (9 – 13) (see 1SD low in Table 7-3).

Table 7-3. Comparison of Three Stocks

	Stock A Return (%)	Stock B Return (%)	Stock C Return (%)
Average	9	9	9
SD	13	33	0
1SD high	22	42	9
1SD low	–4	–24	9

Focusing on the lower band (1SD low) for each of the stocks, we can add them together to come up with a return expectation based on 1 standard deviation. Then, you can translate that figure into a dollar amount, which will give you a rough idea of how much a portfolio might be expected to decline based on normal market fluctuations (two-thirds of the time).

As seen from Table 7-4, the downside exposure for this three-stock portfolio is 6.3 percent, or a potential loss of just under $19,000 on a $300,000 portfolio consisting of $100,000 of each stock.

Table 7-4. Showing Portfolio Downside Exposure Based on 1 Standard Deviation

Stock A	−4.0%
Stock B	−24.0%
Stock C	−9.0%
Average	−6.3%
$300,000	$(19,000)

To figure the upside potential, you do the same calculation, as shown in Table 7-5. The upside potential is 24.3 percent for a potential gain of nearly $73,000 on a $300,000 portfolio consisting of $100,000 of each of these three stocks, again based on 1 standard deviation. Note that in this table (7-5) and the next (7-6), in order to be conservative (assuming higher volatility), we are taking the simple average of the standard deviations; if the assets are not fully correlated the portfolio standard deviation would be lower.

Table 7-5. Showing Portfolio Upside Potential Based on 1 Standard Deviation

Stock A	22.0%
Stock B	42.0%
Stock C	9.0%
Average	24.3%
$300,000	$73,000

Downside exposure is not an absolute loss point; it's useful because it sets an expectation. The number, while inexact, represents a monetary figure reflecting potential declines—what we expect to happen two out of three times, based on 1 standard deviation.

It can be useful quantifying how much risk someone is assuming at any point in time, with the caveat that actual losses can be far greater in normal markets (3 standard deviations take in 99 percent of the statistical possibilities)—or more in a Black Swan event, such as we experienced in the Fall of 2008. (The book *The Black Swan,* by Nassim Nicholas Taleb, 2007, describes unpredictable events such as the 9/11 attacks as "black swan events.")

Illustration of Downside Exposure

You can use downside exposure to lower the risk of a portfolio. For example, you can construct a portfolio with downside exposure of 25 percent. If you have a $1 million portfolio, your expectation is that it will likely decline to $750,000 in two out of three times (1 standard deviation), just as it will likely rise by that amount.

If this is too much risk to bear, you can add lower-risk investments, thus lowering the downside exposure of the portfolio. For example, we can add three-month U.S. Treasury bills, in such an amount that would decrease the potential decline to $800,000 instead of $750,000.

How to Lessen Uncertainty

For someone who wants minimal downside exposure, we can structure a portfolio entirely of short-term three-month U.S. Treasuries, which will preserve capital, but provide no growth. Assuming no Treasury bills had to be sold before maturity, that portfolio would be "risk-free."

In Markowitz's terms, since safety is of extreme importance in such a case, we sacrifice return to decrease uncertainty. You give up growth; you get preservation of capital. Of course, that does not eliminate the risk of inflation or taxes, both of which affect real return.

Now, let's turn to other risks that need to be understood when managing a portfolio.

Amount at Risk and Leverage

Since a company can go out of business, an investment in a stock or bond can go to zero. With some investments, you can lose more than you invest. For example, if you buy a stock on margin, write options, sell a stock short, or buy or sell futures contracts, you are borrowing money from the brokerage firm to execute the transaction. You can owe money to the brokerage firm that extended the loan to you if the value of your investment sinks below the value of your collateral. Each of these transactions is leveraged, meaning you are borrowing money to do the trade.

Before entering into any leveraged transactions, always assess how much you can possibly lose, remembering that you will be signing an agreement with the brokerage firm to allow them to go after collateral, such as your home and other assets, if your trade turns against you. (Always be sure to read the fine print of your margin, options, futures, and trading agreements. You don't want to be surprised when the lender forecloses on a debt you owe that is above and beyond the value of your brokerage account.)

Liquidity Barriers

Another risk to assess is the risk of not being able to get to your money. Some financial products have liquidity barriers such as surrender charges that function like early withdrawal penalties. Or, withdrawals may be limited to a certain percentage (say, 10 percent) during the first year or two, for example. Or they may be limited to a particular date, such as the end of a calendar quarter, and require that you make a written request for withdrawal a certain number of days in advance. Liquidity is of particular concern to people who are depending on their investments as a source of income.

Speculation

The short-term online trader often tries to make the most money in the shortest amount of time, embracing uncertainty of return. This is a valid objective for a speculative risk-oriented trader. It moves him to look for opportunities for big stock price swings in high volume. If skilled, the trader will sell quickly out of losing positions and let the winners ride. There may be a lot of trading for quick profits. And, there is the significant risk of a crash-and-burn outcome, many times because the trader ignores downside exposure.

The Internet bubble at the beginning of the 2000–2009 decade gives us the best illustrations of what a trader could experience. An Internet software company opened the year 2000 at $85 a share and dropped 40 percent by February 28. From there, it shot up 64 percent to its high of the year. By May 15, the stock was at $13, a drop of 84 percent from the former high it set on March 10, 2000.

In comparison, an investment of $100 in an S&P 500 Index fund would have seen a drop to $91 by the end of February, a jump to $105 by March 23, back down to $93 in April, ending at $96 by May 15, 2000.

Removing Risk

Before we leave the subject of risk, we need to talk about lessening risk through hedging, the goal of which is to neutralize the risk of an investment.

Farmers hedge to bring certainty to their earnings. For example, a farmer who plants his corn crop in the spring calculates his costs for bringing in the crop and the markup he needs to turn a profit so that he can feed his family. If the price of corn drops when it's time to go to market, he stands to lose, not make, money.

While the farmer can't prevent market declines, he can offset his potential loss by selling September corn futures contracts. Futures contracts are traded on exchanges, such as the New York Mercantile Exchange or the Chicago Board of Trade; futures are regulated by the Commodity Futures Trading Commission, a federal agency.

If the futures contracts decline in price between now and the expiration date, the farmer can close out the contracts at a profit to offset his losses in the cash market when he goes to sell his corn. If the contracts increase in price, he does not profit. Instead, he will likely deliver the corn at the expiration of the futures contract.

The hedge takes the uncertainty out of the transaction—and with it, the potential for profit or loss. As an investor, you would not want to take the risk out of the investment (there are exceptions of course, such as wanting to hedge a large employer stock position). By doing so, you would also take out the potential for gain. Without uncertainty, there is no risk. Without risk, there is no investment, and no opportunity for profit.

However, you might want to lower risk using hedging techniques. While we've been talking about futures contracts, you can hedge stock portfolios with options and other strategies. Inverse ETFs (a certain type of exchange-traded fund) can be used for this purpose, but only by the most experienced of investors. I'll point out some of the risks in inverse ETFs in Chapter 19.

Summary

Risk is a difficult issue to tackle. It is inevitable, and in fact, it is desirable. Without risk, you cannot expect to make a profit. In your own personal situation, your job is to understand the risk you are assuming in each investment you make, as well as the risk of your overall portfolio. We will talk about risk some more in the chapters dealing with stocks, bonds, and money market instruments. Risk also includes the loss of purchasing power due to inflation, taxes, and other factors, such as costs, that influence your real return.

Key Points

1. Using standard deviation as a measure of the risk of a portfolio can provide opportunities to lower risk and enhance returns.
2. Standard deviation can also be used to calculate the downside exposure of your portfolio, thus giving you

a rough estimate of how much the portfolio would be expected to decline.

3. Risk can be measured and managed.

Steps to Take

1. Calculate the standard deviation for three stocks from your own portfolio using Table 7-1 as an example.

2. Using those three stocks, follow the steps in "An Adaptation: Downside Exposure" to calculate the downside exposure assuming your portfolio consisted of only those three stocks. Refer to Table 7-4.

3. Consider how you might lower the risk of your portfolio; consider how you might increase the potential reward of your portfolio.

PART 3

Creating Your Portfolio Objectives and Strategy

What are your financial goals? Although this may seem like an overly simplistic question, coming up with a solid answer will guide your decisions when you manage your portfolio.

In Chapter 8, we'll examine the three main goals you might have for your portfolio: growing your assets, producing income, or preserving capital. We'll review the assets that you can use to achieve those three outcomes.

Then in Chapter 9, we'll examine different types of investment objectives, and I'll show you how your objectives shape your portfolio, which in turn will determine your results. I'll discuss the essential difference between having a portfolio and just having a collection of investments. We'll also look at the objectives of three hypothetical investors at different life stages and how they manage their portfolios accordingly.

In Chapter 10, we'll discuss how to choose a portfolio strategy suited to your circumstances and objectives. With a strategy in place, you'll be less likely to react to market swings, friendly advice, or sales pitches and thereby stay the course toward meeting your financial goals. I'll share an anecdote of a hypothetical investor, "George," who relies on periodically selling off his investments whenever he needs cash. I'll point out the risks to using this method, and we'll discuss the differences between his "total return" strategy and a "demand-based" approach. You'll learn which of these strategies may best suit you.

CHAPTER 8

How to Use Different Assets for Different Purposes

What's in It for You?

This chapter will help you understand the effectiveness of various types of financial instruments to meet different objectives.

Contents

What Can Your Investments Do for You?

Keeping in mind that portfolio management is goal directed, the starting point is to focus on the end result that you want to achieve. There are three basic results that you can achieve.

1. Grow your assets
2. Produce income (interest and dividends) to withdraw periodically or to reinvest
3. Preserve your capital

If you think of investments in these terms, you can categorize the collection of investments that you own based on expectations—that is, based on what they can do for you. Think of them as tools.

You could use *any* instrument of the market to grow a nest egg in preparation for retirement or to create monthly cash flow after retirement to replace your salary, but some will be more effective than others. If you understand the use to which you can put different assets, you can make sound judgments about the best types of investments for your portfolio, a subject we'll discuss in more detail in the chapters to follow.

Using Tools

Just as there are optimal uses for ordinary tools such as hammers, can openers, and tire jacks, there are optimal uses for different types of financial assets. Say you wanted to hammer a nail into a wall and you had the option of using a hammer or a can opener. While a can opener might do the job, the hammer will do a better job. Similarly, a bond ladder (defined below) spinning off monthly cash flows, may be more effective in producing cash flow for retirement than growth stocks.

A bond ladder is a construction of a series of bonds with staggered maturities, with longer maturities (typically) offering higher yields. As time goes on and shorter-term bonds mature, they are replaced by bonds with longer maturities. Meanwhile, interest is paid to the investor, usually semiannually. If an investor needs monthly income, bonds of different payment dates can be purchased so that the investor receives interest monthly.

There are more effective and less effective uses for financial assets, all of which depend on what you are trying to achieve.

Managing Your Goals

It's best to divide your portfolio into components, one for each purpose you are trying to achieve.

Capital Appreciation

When you invest for capital appreciation, the underlying assumption is that you will buy an investment today with the expectation that you will make a profit at some future date when you sell it. To achieve capital appreciation, or growth, you need to use the tools of the marketplace that are most effective for that purpose. Individual stocks serve this goal (discussed in Chapters 13, 16, and 17), as do instruments that package products, such as stock mutual funds (discussed in Chapter 19), stock unit trusts, or exchange-traded stock funds. A stock unit trust is an investment company that purchases a fixed portfolio of stocks. Exchange-traded funds (ETFs) are mutual funds that are traded like stocks.

Stocks represent ownership interest in the companies that issued them; there are no return promises attached to them. Stocks are not guaranteed by anyone to grow your assets. Companies that declare and pay dividends on their common stocks actually have no legal obligation to do so. Instead of promises, guarantees, or contractual responsibilities, the investor makes do with the underlying hope and expectation that he will sell the stock to someone else at a higher price than his purchase price.

Income Production

Let's say you have been investing in stocks for the length of your working career and now are retired and need $5,000 a month to pay for living expenses. You can try to do this by selling stocks out of your portfolio each month as you need money. What do you do if some of your stocks drop dramatically in price, as many stocks do from time to time? Do you stop paying your bills? Imagine trying to determine which stocks you should sell each month under those circumstances.

The premise here is that you can generate cash flow by selling some of your investments. But, by doing so, you use up precious principal. Isn't it better to use earnings distributions (dividends or interest) rather than principal? (We will return to these two methods of producing cash in Chapters 10 and 11.)

Indeed, interest-bearing bonds and dividend-paying stocks pay earnings distributions. As mentioned, some stocks and stock mutual funds pay dividends, which are a form of cash flow that you can spend for living expenses. Bonds pay interest, and bond mutual funds pay dividends, both of which you can also spend when you need your portfolio to produce cash for you.

For cash-flow purposes, bonds and other fixed-income instruments of the market are a better choice than stocks. First, bonds tend to pay higher distributions than stocks. Second, bond distributions for a particular bond are generally fixed in amount; stock distributions are not. Third, bond distributions are set for a period of time (until the maturity date of the bond), offering the opportunity for planning.

As we'll discuss in Chapter 14, bonds generally promise two things: return of principal at some specified future date when the bond "matures" (terminates or expires) and interest payments from the date of issue until maturity. The issuer of the bond, however, generally guarantees neither the repayment of principal nor interest payments. Both depend on whether the issuer can stay in business. If the issuer does close its doors, the bondholder can lose both the income stream and, in the worst case, all the principal. Local, state and federal governments issuing bonds can also go out of business.

Preservation of Capital

Sometimes you want your money to be safe above all else; your goal is to preserve capital. The best financial tools to achieve stability of principal are short-term money market instruments, such as U.S. Treasury bills, certificates of deposit, and money market mutual funds. With money market instruments, your assumption is that you will receive your original investment back and no less, plus interest. Money market instruments are discussed in Chapter 15.

Summary

Different instruments of the market, such as stocks, bonds, and Treasury bills, serve different investor needs. In Chapter 9, we'll take a closer look at the three essential investment objectives we discussed in this chapter.

Key Points

1. It helps to think of assets as tools that can be put to use in your portfolio for specific purposes.
2. Approach each investment choice from the vantage point of understanding what it can do for you.
3. If you have multiple investment goals, as most people do, it's best to split your portfolio into components and to deal with each goal distinctly.

Steps to Take

1. Review all your holdings in all of your accounts, and don't leave out retirement plans at work.
2. Determine the percentage of your overall portfolio that is represented by growth, income, and preservation of capital objectives.
3. Consider if you are using your assets effectively.

Portfolio Objectives and How to Set Your Own

What's in It for You?

Investment objectives determine the composition of your portfolio, which means they determine your results. This chapter will show you different types of investment objectives and help you to formulate your own.

Contents

Defining Your Goals: A Critical Step

Investment objectives are goals. The big difference between merely having a collection of investments and having a portfolio is pursuing goals.

If you haven't given your investment objectives much thought, you might be working with an unstated and perhaps unmanageable goal such as: "My objective is to make as much money as possible as quickly as possible." While this might be a valid objective for a speculative trader, you need to think long and hard before making it your own goal, because it can lead you to take on more risk (perhaps too much) and make you easy prey for unscrupulous salesmen who see you as an easy mark.

In this chapter, we'll discuss how to set investment objectives and how to construct a portfolio using a primary (highest-priority) and secondary (lower-priority) objective. Without a process, all you have is a collection of investments. Without objectives, your investment activity is not directed toward any particular goal—and an unstated goal can lead to making more risky choices.

Growth: Investing for the Future

Karen is 50 and employed full time. All of her expenses are covered by her paycheck, and she has money left over to invest.

Because Karen's current expenses are covered, she's investing for the future. Her primary objective will be "growth," and she will be investing in instruments of the market that offer growth of capital, such as stocks or stock mutual funds. Depending on other holdings and circumstances, she may have a secondary objective of income or preservation of capital to diversify her holdings across asset classes.

Investing for growth is usually a longer-term activity that occurs over a period of years. The exception is someone who is looking for a quick profit.

Income: Investing for the Present

Henry is 77 years old and is no longer working. His Social Security covers one-half of what he needs to live on, and he has $500,000 in liquid assets.

His primary objective is income production since he needs to generate cash flow for current living expenses. To accomplish this, he invests in instruments that produce income, such as bonds, bond funds, or stocks that pay dividends.

Henry also needs to continue to build capital by investing in stocks to offset future inflation, and as a result, his secondary objective is growth. Finally, he also wishes to use part of his portfolio for preservation of capital by investing in short-term money market instruments, such as Treasury bills.

Investing for income will be an objective for most people at some time in their lives, thus you'll need to know how to determine the portion of your portfolio that you'll dedicate to that objective. The percentage will be based on the cash-flow demands you will be placing on the portfolio, as explained in Chapter 10.

Preservation of Capital: Putting Assets on Hold

Never married, Doug is 65 and has a lifelong pension that not only fully covers all his needs, but also increases yearly to cover higher costs due to inflation. He has no investment experience. He has just come into a large inheritance that he does not want to jeopardize under any circumstances.

Preservation of capital is Doug's primary objective for his inheritance. By investing in instruments intended for preservation of capital, such as U.S. Treasury bills, he will be able to protect his inheritance from serious losses. He may also have a secondary objective of diversification with fixed income by buying some high-quality bonds.

Multiple Objectives

If you have multiple objectives, as do Karen, Henry, and Doug, you'll want to split your portfolio into parts that you use for each goal. This will help you with monitoring your portfolio to make sure that each objective is being met.

You can have a portion that produces income, another portion invested for growth, and a third portion invested for preservation of capital to stabilize your portfolio and protect your principal. As you'll see in the next few chapters, how much of the portfolio you use for each objective will depend upon your needs. The biggest demands for most investors nearing retirement will be the need for regular cash flow as well as continued growth to offset inflation.

Other Objectives

The three objectives that we have been discussing are the basics. There are many variations on the theme. Your growth objective could be "conservative growth," or "aggressive growth," or even "speculation."

As we discussed, one technique to manage these nuanced objectives is to split your portfolio by objective, you so can monitor performance and make adjustments as necessary (we will discuss monitoring in Chapter 21).

Primary versus Secondary Objective Illustrated

Should everyone have a primary and a secondary objective? Most likely. But, there are situations in which you can live with just one.

Say Amy has a 20-year-old daughter, Beth, who lives at home. Beth earns money at a part-time job and with the earnings socks away up to $5,000 into a Roth IRA. Beth can easily have a single objective—growth.

Or, say your retirement portfolio is not as large as you would like, you have no need for current income, and you are used to investing through monthly payroll deductions. This was the situation with Susan, a reader of my weekly financial column. At age 45, single, and employed with a large company, Susan was 100 percent invested in stock mutual funds through her company 401(k) plan. She lived modestly and had money left over from her paycheck after expenses each month, which she put in a bank account.

Susan planned to work until age 65. She had no pension benefit coming to her, and her 401(k) was her only asset. She was experienced with investing in the stock market and was not concerned about market fluctuations. She had enough money in her bank account to cover six months of expenses in an emergency.

Investing 100 percent of her monthly 401(k) payroll deductions for growth is reasonable; because Susan is investing monthly in diversified stock mutual funds, when they drop in price as they will do from time to time, she purchases more shares. This is a form of "dollar cost averaging," which helps patient long-term investors acquire more shares in down markets. As Susan approaches retirement, however, she will need to add a secondary objective of income or preservation of capital in order to bring in some noncorrelated assets to diversify her holdings and thereby lessen the volatility of her 401(k) portfolio.

Depending on her circumstances after she retires, Susan may want to switch to a primary objective of income. As we'll explore in Chapter 11, there is a way to calculate how much Susan will need to set aside for income production when that becomes her primary objective after retirement.

Stocks versus Bonds

If you have not been saving enough and now find yourself trying to catch up, should your primary objective be growth? Should you add a secondary objective of income or preservation of capital? That will depend on these factors: your experience as an investor, whether you have a pension or other sources of retirement income, and how much time is left before retirement. None of these factors alone is determinative. You need to weigh all of them.

Experience

If you are an inexperienced investor, limiting yourself to stocks or stock mutual funds alone would be far too risky, since your portfolio will fluctuate as your holdings do. If you are unprepared, you might sell at the wrong time, which, as we saw in Chapter 3, individual investors tend to do.

It's best to add a secondary objective of income and a tertiary objective of preservation of capital for diversification. Generally—but not always—the volatility of your portfolio will decrease with the addition of bonds and money market funds. For example, you may have 50 percent stocks and 40 percent bonds, and 10 percent money markets. Or for even more safety, you may put 50 percent toward growth, with a secondary objective of preservation of capital for the remainder. In either case, if you need to grow your capital, your primary objective needs to be growth.

Pension

If you have a lifelong pension coming to you that will cover your expenses in retirement, you may not need to have a growth objective at all. Perhaps you want safety above all else, in which case you will have a primary objective of preservation of capital. If you want growth to leave money to your children, you might want to temper that objective by having a primary objective of growth and a secondary objective of income or preservation of capital. You could have 60 percent in growth and 40 percent in income or preservation of capital.

Time Horizon

The more time you have until retirement, the more time you have for compounding (the multiplier effect) to work in your favor. A long horizon gives you a chance to ride through just about any underperforming period in the stock market and could support the argument for you not to dilute your growth objective by adding bonds.

How long is long enough? Twenty, thirty years or longer, certainly. But what about ten years? This is where experience enters the picture again. As we saw in Chapter 4, the stock market as measured by the S&P 500 Index went nowhere in the first decade of 2000. However, an experienced investor, who knew how to invest for growth in sectors that outperformed the market, could think in terms of ten years.

If you have a long time on your side, you can be 100 percent invested in the stock market. You need some flexibility in terms of how and when you will be converting those assets to income, however. You do not want to find yourself needing to cash in a stock portfolio in a down market. Someone with a shorter horizon may have a strong rationale for investing a portion of his portfolio in bonds and money markets.

Summary

There are many personal factors to consider before deciding on stock and bond allocations, but most people can follow these general rules.

Invest in stocks for growth when you need to grow your assets, but be ready to ride out the fluctuations of the market—assuming you have done a good job with investment selection and portfolio construction.

Invest in bonds for income when you need money to live on or for diversification.

Invest in money markets to stabilize a portfolio at any age.

If your one and only objective is growth, add bonds or money markets if you want to lessen the risk of a 100-percent-stock portfolio.

In the next chapter, we'll talk about using investment objectives to establish an investment strategy to help you achieve your goals.

Key Points

1. Establishing investment objectives is a critical step to creating a personal portfolio.
2. Even if you want to grow your portfolio, think about adding a secondary objective of income or preservation of capital to help lower volatility.
3. If you have multiple investment objectives, split your portfolio into sections to handle them distinctly.

Steps to Take

1. Consider the illustrations in this chapter. Do you have multiple goals or only one?
2. Draft investment objectives that you can use for your current situation.
3. Draft a set of investment objectives that you might use after you retire.

What's Your Portfolio Strategy? How to Create Cash Flow

CHAPTER 10

What's in It for You?

Setting a portfolio strategy will put you on track toward achieving your goals despite market conditions, fads, sales pitches, friends' results, and other distractions that can undermine your success. In this chapter, we'll discuss how to go about the process of figuring out an appropriate strategy for your situation by comparing two approaches that generate cash flow—something that everyone who intends to retire someday will need to assess. We'll contrast the commonly used "total return" approach to creating retirement income with another technique that I'll call the "demand-based" strategy. This is an example of how to work through "doable alternatives" in the decision-making process we discussed in Chapter 2.

Contents

Stock Picking

If you talk with many investors as I do, you'll notice an interest in stock picking, rather than portfolio management. That's natural considering how people learn about investing. They might interact with a broker who makes a buy recommendation for a particular financial instrument. They might buy stocks through an online broker. Or, they might choose to invest in a company they read about in the paper. I think you'll agree that when friends and family dialogue about investing, they're talking about what stocks to buy, as opposed to portfolio management techniques.

As someone who plans and manages portfolios, I see stocks merely as tools to be used to accomplish objectives, all as part of a plan of action. Buying stocks before having a plan is like buying lumber to build a house before designing the house.

George's Story

For example, let's say a successful investor, George, buys stock based on his broker's recommendations. Later, after he retires, he needs money to pay his bills. He tells his broker he needs cash. The broker recommends selling some ABC stock, which George agrees to. Year after year, stock is sold to free up cash as needed.

George is happy, but only as long as his investments produce profits. Putting things into the context of decision making, a topic we discussed in Chapter 2, George's success requires a series of correct buy-low sell-high decisions. This is an unrealistic strategy in anything but a steadily rising market—something we know is simply not a reasonable long-term expectation.

Stock Picking versus Portfolio Approach

An effective overall strategy is the key distinction between random stock picking and managing a portfolio. The portfolio approach gives you the chance to make decisions based on longer-term goals instead of looking at each buy, sell, or hold decision in isolation.

In this chapter, I'll introduce what I call a "demand-based" portfolio strategy that helps you create cash flow from your investments to live on in retirement. We'll compare that strategy to a "total-return" approach (like George's), which calls for selling investments to produce cash flow.

Portfolio Approach

The more holistic portfolio approach to making investment decisions prioritizes your personal objectives over picking individual investments. Having a workable strategy to meet those objectives helps at all times, but probably most of all when events are occurring that may distract you, such as a correction or a spectacular move in a market. A good strategy that takes into account different types of markets will keep you from wandering from the goal, or worse, being drawn away by fear, a smooth-talking salesperson, or the breathless fervor of a speculative market.

Determining Your Strategy

To work, an effective strategy must produce desired results, be simple in concept, and be easy to execute. To produce desired results, start with the end in mind and work backward. What do you want to achieve? As we discussed in the last two chapters, you'll want to articulate that in your investment objectives.

Retirement Objectives

At some point in the future, most people will want their investment portfolio to pay them a stream of "pension" checks throughout their retirement, which may last for thirty years or longer. When you do retire, you will be using this stream of income to live on or to supplement your pension and Social Security retirement benefits.

Income Gap

First, let me introduce you to a cash-flow concept called the "retirement income gap." This is a term used by benefits specialists to indicate the gap between how much money an individual needs to live on and what he actually receives from his pension, Social Security, and other retirement plans.

You may also have a "current income gap." A current income gap can hit you at any age, usually as a result of a change of circumstances, such as a divorce, death of a spouse, disability, or loss of a job.

Demand-Based Portfolio Strategy

Families who enter retirement with a "retirement income gap" will need to use their portfolios to create their own personal pensions by using their assets in a planned and disciplined manner for the rest of their lives. The most conservative approach to doing so is to structure a "demand-based portfolio," a term I use to define a portfolio with two objectives. The primary objective is income: the goal is to have the portfolio generate enough interest and dividend income to cover current expenses and your income tax bill. The secondary objective is to invest for growth for the future to offset inflation and possibly to provide a legacy for heirs.

Total-Return Portfolio Strategy

The alternative to a demand-based portfolio is to structure a "total-return" portfolio. "Total return" is defined as interest plus dividends plus gains minus losses. A total-return portfolio works well for growth investors who have a long horizon. For example, if you are 30, 40, or 50, you will normally not need to withdraw money from the portfolio. But, if you are retired and need your portfolio to support you in retirement, caution is in order.

If you use a total-return philosophy, you need to calculate a reasonable withdrawal rate that would apply in your situation based on your assets, investments, risk, and time horizon. Be cautious about using someone else's withdrawal rate or relying on the often quoted figure of 4 percent (of your initial value). Your withdrawal rate will depend on your situation. Also be aware that using a total-return strategy, especially one that uses an unsustainable withdrawal rate, opens you up to the possibility of running out of money if you make poor investment decisions or hit down-market periods, especially if they occur in the early years of your retirement.

Demand-Based Portfolio Rules of the Road

Apply the following portfolio rules of the road if you are using a demand-based portfolio approach:

1. Live off the interest and dividend income produced by the portfolio.
2. Since it is easier to control your discretionary expenditures than it is to control the financial markets, lower your spending when income declines due to market conditions.
3. Avoid selling investments in order to raise cash to spend on living expenses.
4. Avoid withdrawing from tax-deferred accounts, such as IRAs and 401(k)s, until required to do so after age 70½.
5. If you have a multimillion-dollar tax-deferred account, such as an IRA, make sure you review your estate plan. At death, the combination of estate taxes and income taxes can be devastating. Income and estate tax planning will be essential in such cases.
6. Make appropriate accommodations for loss of purchasing power over time. Rising costs due to inflation need to be taken into account and offset with a strategy to add to the cash flow produced by the portfolio over a lifetime. You can accomplish this result in different ways, one of which is putting aside money for growth and later restructuring those holdings for income.
7. Plan your cash flows as if you'll live long, at least into your 80s or 90s.

8. Regularly monitor your portfolio withdrawals. If you are a conservative investor, you will not want your withdrawals to exceed the income generated by your portfolio.

9. Reassess your income needs yearly.

Summary

Investing with a plan means keeping your eye on the big picture. By seeing individual choices in the context of your overall strategy, you can avoid decisions that might get in the way of your long-term results. In the next two chapters, we'll go through examples of how to apply the demand-based strategy.

Key Points

1. An effective strategy is driven by your investment goals and helps you stay on track toward achieving them.

2. A total-return strategy for creating cash flow requires selling investments in good and bad markets; however, the strategy is risky in down markets.

3. A demand-based portfolio strategy creates cash flow from interest and dividends, thus protecting principal.

Steps to Take

1. Evaluate your current approach to managing your portfolio by making a list of your goals and expectations, along with any upcoming events in your life that may affect your financial circumstances (for example, having children, sending children off to college).

2. Use this list to create a strategy for managing your portfolio.

3. Create a doable alternative strategy for consideration.

Structuring Your Portfolio for Income and Your Retirement

If you're like most people, you'll be relying on your savings to see you through your retirement. But making sure your assets will last takes planning and a purposeful design. In Chapter 11, I'll demonstrate how to structure a portfolio for creating income. You'll learn how to assess your income requirements and determine how your portfolio can best generate that cash flow. We'll also cover income gaps and insufficient capital. We'll consider "Diane," who feared she would have to sell her home after her divorce. Diane's living expenses were exceeding her income. Through her example, I'll show you how to assess whether your assets can be structured to generate enough income to cover shortfalls you may encounter. I call the method of structuring a portfolio for income the "demand-based" portfolio strategy that I introduced in the last chapter.

In Chapter 12, we'll follow a soon-to-retire couple through the planning process of creating their own "personal pension" using this approach. You'll learn when this approach may be the best strategy to ensure that you don't outlive your assets. And we'll look at various factors that impact a retirement portfolio, including taxes, inflation, and risk.

CHAPTER 11

How to Structure a Portfolio to Create Income

What's in It for You?

If you currently think of your 401(k) and other retirement savings simply as a number—this chapter will lead you through the process of figuring out how you will need to *use* that money in your retirement. This chapter will help you determine how much cash you will need from your portfolio during times in your life when you need to supplement your income, and it will give you the tools to set up your portfolio to generate that cash flow.

Contents

Creating Income

When it comes to meeting different portfolio objectives, the most difficult to address is creating income after you stop working. In this chapter and the next, we'll take a closer look at how to structure a portfolio that satisfies that need.

Generating Cash Flow

In this chapter, we will be tackling the question of how to set up your portfolio to generate cash that you can spend. We will consider how to figure the amount you need from your portfolio at different times of life, including retirement, as well as how to structure your portfolio to produce that cash flow.

This discussion shows you a workable but simplified version of the process of structuring a portfolio based on expectations from different investment vehicles. The underlying assumption is that there is sufficient capital for cash flow to be generated from interest and dividends produced by income-producing investments. We will discuss how to account for taxes at the end of the chapter.

Income Gap

As we discussed in Chapter 10, many investors will need to generate cash flow from their portfolios because they face an income gap. While a retirement gap is illustrated in the next chapter, here is an example of a current income gap.

A year after her divorce, Diane was not sure how much she was spending, and she was afraid to find out. With some encouragement, she set up a system to track her spending over a three-month period. Diane collected all her receipts and canceled checks from the previous three months. She placed them into two stacks, one for (1) absolute *essentials* and fixed costs, such as housing expenses and real estate taxes; and (2) everything else, which included vacations and entertainment (*discretionary* expenses). Essential expenses take priority over discretionary expenses.

Calculating the Income Gap

After stacking up all the bills relating to housing, Diane realized that her essential expenses used up her entire $6,000 monthly alimony check. The largest expense was the cost of maintaining the large home the family had occupied before the divorce.

Nothing was left over. Nonetheless, she was spending an additional $2,000 a month for discretionary expenses—and running up her credit card debt by doing so.

This was an eye-opener for Diane. She realized she was running short $24,000 a year. With this knowledge, Diane realized her housing costs were too high for her to justify. She had some options: sell the home; supplement her income by getting a job; look to her other assets to generate additional monthly income.

Diane had received a $1 million divorce settlement. Her income gap was $24,000 a year. Could she structure a portfolio that filled the gap to enable her to stay in her current home?

Let's go through the basic calculation.

Capital Commitment

In this illustration, let's use 5-percent, 10-percent, and 2.5-percent interest rates in order to keep the math as simple as possible. In real life, you'll need to go to the market to explore current interest rates, and you'll also have to factor in the effect of taxes. Ask yourself how much of the $1 million principal you need to commit to produce $24,000 in annual income if your investment yields 5 percent, compared to 10 percent, and to 2.5 percent.

Remembering high school algebra, you find that $480,000 of capital invested at 5 percent gives you $24,000 of income before taxes. (Divide $24,000 by .05 to get $480,000.) The math tells you how much money you need in order to generate $24,000 a year before taxes if your investment pays you a cash flow of 5 percent.

If the yield is higher, you'll need less capital to produce the needed cash flow. At a 10-percent rate, you would need $240,000 of capital to generate

$24,000. (If you divide $24,000 by 0.10, you get $240,000.) You only need $240,000 of assets to free up $24,000 cash flow if your yield is 10 percent.

In comparison, you need almost $1 million of capital when you are working with a 2.5-percent yield.

Table 11-1 shows the capital needed to produce the $24,000 cash flow at different yields.

Table 11-1. Capital Required at Different Interest Rates to Produce $24,000 a Year

Desired Annual Cash Flow	Annual Yield	Capital Required to Produce Desired Cash Flow
$24,000	5.0%	$480,000
$24,000	10.0%	$240,000
$24,000	2.5%	$960,000

If the desired cash flow is $50,000 a year, you will need $1 million of capital if you earn a 5-percent yield, $500,000 at 10 percent, and $2 million at 2.5 percent, as you can see from Table 11-2.

Table 11-2: Capital Required at Different Interest Rates to Produce $50,000 a Year

Desired Annual Cash Flow	Annual Yield	Capital Required to Produce Desired Cash Flow
$50,000	5.0%	$1,000,000
$50,000	10.0%	$500,000
$50,000	2.5%	$2,000,000

By the way, if you are wondering whether you can find a 10-percent yield, the answer is "yes," but of course, at higher risk. While I don't recommend this, in just about every market, good and bad, you'll find some high-risk junk bonds (see Chapter 14) that promise to pay interest in the double digits.

Structuring the Portfolio

Recognizing that lower-risk investments offer lower yields, more capital must be committed to produce the desired cash flow. This gives investors a dilemma to solve when structuring a portfolio.

Assuming that the 5-percent figure is a mid-risk option at the time that Diane structures her portfolio, she will need to devote $480,000 of capital for income production, which is her primary investment objective.

She has $520,000 left of her $1 million to invest. She'll divide that up between her objective to grow capital and preservation of capital. How much should go to each of these objectives? That will depend on the rest of her story—her age, her ability to earn a paycheck, her future pension and Social Security, her future income needs, and her ability to manage her finances and her portfolio.

After considering all of these factors, Diane decides to allocate $100,000 of her remaining $520,000 for preservation of capital and $420,000 for capital appreciation.

This type of analysis can be the foundation for a plan. It will need to be implemented over a period of time, depending on current market conditions. Timing of purchases is one of the judgment calls that needs to be made based on experience.

Insufficient Capital

The illustration above may leave you with some concerns. What if you don't have the capital to produce the cash flow that you need from your portfolio?

Spending less and saving more is the best place to start. Even small amounts make a big difference over time. To see the math behind how compounding works in your favor over time, you might try out one of the many compounding calculators you can find online. (Go to the Savings and Investments Calculator available at *jacksongrant.us*.)

The longer you have, the less money you need to save to meet your goal. For example, if you are 40 years old and want to reach a goal of having an additional $100,000 by the time you turn 65, you need to invest a mere $145 a month, earning 6 percent a year. If you are 50 years old when you start saving, you'll need $347 a month to reach the same goal.

If you are too close to retirement age to build capital before you retire, don't forget that you still have a long life ahead of you that may last ten, twenty or thirty years or more—all enough time for compounding to work in your favor to build assets for use later in life. (In Chapter 6 of my book, *The AARP Retirement Survival Guide: How to Make Smart Financial Decisions in Good Times and Bad*, I provide a number of illustrations on how this method can build assets for later retirement decades.)

If you simply don't have the capital it takes to structure a portfolio using the demand-based method, you'll need to think about selling your holdings as you need money to pay for bills, a method that works well only when profits can be harvested. If you are in this position you will want to consider lowering expenses and delaying retirement. This is the reason why people with 401(k) plans need to think beyond the dollar value of the account to how they will use the 401(k) to generate cash flow after they retire.

The Demand-Based Formula

To see how much capital you need to generate a particular yearly cash flow at different interest rates, use the same formula discussed earlier. How much you need to put aside for income production at different interest rates is a function of cash-flow needs.

To find out how much you need to set aside to generate cash flow of $x, divide $x by the yield you are being offered, as we did in the illustration earlier in the chapter. For example, if the yield is 5 percent, as shown in Table 11-3 below, and you need $12,000 of yearly cash flow, you'll need capital of $240,000.

Table 11-3. Capital Required at 5-Percent Interest Rates to Produce Different Annual Cash Flow

Desired Annual Cash Flow	Annual Yield	Capital Required to Produce Desired Cash Flow
$12,000	5.0%	$240,000
$72,000	5.0%	$1,440,000
$120,000	5.0%	$2,400,000
$240,000	5.0%	$4,800,000

Desired cash flow divided by the annual yield gives you the capital (dollars) you need to invest at that rate of return.

What Should You Do First?

Determine the demands on your portfolio first. If you have a retirement (or current) income gap, determine the income you would need to take from your portfolio before you commit to any particular investment. Then you can think about the types of income-producing investments that would be best to generate that income (see Chapter 10).

The Tax Effect

In the illustrations in this chapter (and in the next), I have left out the impact of taxes to concentrate on how a demand-based portfolio works. In real life, we would also calculate the effect of taxes before structuring the portfolio. To give you an example of how that might work, let's go back to Diane's mid-risk option.

We figured that Diane would need $480,000 of capital invested at 5 percent to produce $24,000 of income. This assumes Diane pays no taxes on the income, which is possible if she invests in tax-free bonds.

Now, let's assume the income is generated by taxable bonds, which is a more likely scenario. Let's see how that capital commitment would change after accounting for taxes.

Let's use 25 percent as Diane's effective income tax rate. Here is how the math would work. To account for a tax of 25 percent, Diane would need to generate income of $32,000 to be able to spend $24,000. (You arrive at this number by dividing $24,000 by 0.75, which is 1.00 minus the tax rate of 0.25.)

The difference ($32,000 – $24,000 = $8,000), will be your tax bill on the interest income produced by the taxable bonds. Now, you solve for $32,000 of income at 5 percent. Dividing $32,000 by 5 percent (0.05), you get $640,000, which is the amount Diane would need to invest to produce $32,000, leaving her $24,000 to spend after she pays taxes of $8,000. That leaves $360,000 of her $1 million to invest for growth and preservation of capital.

Summary

It is essential that you know how much you need to generate from your portfolio for living expenses. If you know the size of your personal income gap, you can make sound strategic decisions today that will fill the gap into retirement. If you do not know the size of the gap, your ability to fill it in the future will depend entirely on luck. In the next chapter, let's see how this approach can be used by a retired couple.

Key Points

1. Generating cash flow is the most difficult portfolio objective to address.
2. The first step to creating a cash-flow plan is to calculate your income gap.
3. In order to structure your portfolio to meet your cash-flow needs, you must first determine the demands on your portfolio.

Steps to Take

1. Review your finances to see if you have a current or retirement income gap.
2. If you conclude that you need to produce cash flow from your portfolio, create a table, like Table 11-1, to help you determine whether you have sufficient capital to generate this cash flow.
3. List the demands on your portfolio, including taxes, to help you find the most suitable income-producing investments for your goals.

CHAPTER 12

Creating Your Own Personal Pension

How to Structure a Portfolio for Retirement Income Using the Demand-Based Portfolio Approach: A Case Study

What's in It for You?

By using a soon-to-retire couple's situation to illustrate the concepts we've discussed earlier, this chapter will help you apply the same methods to your own situation. The illustration, which is a composite of the types of circumstances I see in my practice, will help you identify some planning points for you to consider as you develop your retirement income strategy. This illustration uses the more conservative demand-based portfolio approach introduced in Chapter 10 and discussed in Chapter 11, as opposed to a total-return approach, which works best in rising, not falling, markets.

Contents

About to Retire

Michael and Ann, both age 65, are getting ready to retire. They have no pensions. While their Social Security income is the maximum retirement benefit, their living expenses exceed that income by $10,000 a month ($120,000 a year).

Now, they need to structure a portfolio that will not only support them in retirement, but also leave a legacy for their children and grandchildren.

Where to Start

The first question to ask is how Michael and Ann want to live after they retire. What changes do they anticipate in their lifestyle?

Since they enjoy traveling, they plan on doing so at least until age 75, another ten years, when they expect to slow down a bit. They are expecting to live a quiet life near their friends and family, with no big changes in their current way of doing things. With grandchildren living in the area, they are certain they do not want to move to a retirement community in a warmer state.

When asked, they are not sure about how much they currently spend on living expenses. But, after reviewing them over a weekend together, they discover that their lifestyle calls for about $120,000 a year or $10,000 a month more than they will receive in Social Security retirement income. That number includes real estate taxes but not the income tax bill. They figure that only about a quarter of these expenses are discretionary items, such as vacations, charitable gifts, and entertainment.

Taxes?

At this stage of the inquiry, it's a good idea to exclude income taxes, since portfolio allocation decisions may result in taxable, tax-deferred, or tax-free investments. Factoring in taxes too early in the analysis might result in an inaccurate estimate of expenses. We'll come back to them later in the chapter.

Sources of Income

Michael and Ann have no pension income to rely on, and only modest Social Security income compared to their needs. As a result, they are looking to their $5 million in savings for retirement income.

Using Assets to Cover Retirement Expenses

Let's stop here for a moment to review some basic concepts about cash-flow needs and how to use assets to meet those needs throughout retirement.

You need to know how much you will be spending on living expenses each year during your retirement to see if you will need to supplement your Social Security and pension benefits with your savings and investments.

If you fall within the norms published by the U.S. Department of Labor, you can expect that you will spend 30 percent less in the first year of retirement than you do your last year of work. For example, if you are about to retire and spend $100,000 a year for living expenses, you can expect to spend 70 percent or $70,000 in your first year of retirement, assuming you don't plan to change your lifestyle much after retirement.

This rule of thumb does not apply in all situations, of course. For example, if you plan on traveling more after you retire, you will need to increase your estimate. Also, the estimate is based on today's dollars. You will need to adjust it for year-to-year increases in the cost of living due to inflation, which can complicate matters when trying to do those calculations on your own.

How do you estimate future expenses? See the following paragraphs for a strategy and things to consider.

Inflation

Based on history, you can reasonably assume that inflation during your retirement will average somewhere between 3 percent and 6 percent per year, as measured by the CPI (Consumer Price Index). (In 2007, inflation was 4.1 percent; only 0.1 percent in 2008, and 2.7 percent in 2009.)

Assuming 3-percent annual inflation throughout your retirement, if you are 65 today, by the time you are 89, your cash will have one-half the buying power it does today. That is, at 89 you will need twice as much cash to pay for the same level of expenses you incurred when you were 65. For example, if your expenses were $10,000 at age 65, you would need $20,000 at age 89 if inflation averaged 3 percent per year during that period. Using the same example of $10,000 of expenses at age 65, now assume inflation is 6 percent per year. At that rate, you will need $20,000 when you are 77 and $40,000 when you are 89.

Income from Pension and Social Security Benefits

You'll also want to estimate your income from pension and Social Security payments. Remember that while Social Security benefits are indexed to inflation, most pensions (unless you work for the government) are not. Adding together the pensions and Social Security benefits you and your spouse will receive in your first year of retirement will give you a sense of your "guaranteed" sources of income. (Don't consider your investments just yet.)

Calculate Your Retirement Income Gap

Now, compare your income to your expenses. Some people will cover their expenses with income from Social Security and pensions. Their biggest challenge, unless their pensions are indexed to inflation, will be to offset inflation in future years.

Others, who have a retirement income gap (when pensions and Social Security do *not* cover current expenses), will have an additional hurdle to overcome: how to convert assets to income now and in the future as those expenses rise due to inflation. They will have to earn enough from their portfolios to be able to withdraw what they need for expenses. They'll also need enough to pay for income taxes on their taxable income to cover the gap between what they are taking in (their pension and Social Security income) and what they are spending (their living expenses).

Monte Carlo Projections

At this point, you might think you need to project income and expenses into the future. You can create a spreadsheet to make these projections using what you consider to be reasonable assumptions for spending, inflation, rates of return on your portfolio, and taxes.

The problem you will face is the variability of assumptions. Consider using a Monte Carlo simulation, a program that randomizes assumptions and produces a probability of success (or ruin) for different assumptions. You can find different online programs that help you do this, such as Palisade's @ RISK, (available at *www.palisade.com/risk*) or Frontline Systems' Risk Solver (available at *www.solver.com/risksolver*), both add-ons for Microsoft Excel.

Be alert to projections that are based on faulty reasoning or missing assumptions. For example, I once reviewed a projection run by a financial institution for a widow concluding that her biggest problem would be a large estate tax bill. The projection was wrong because it failed to account for the substantial monthly withdrawals she would need to make for living expenses.

Portfolio Goals

The portfolio goal for the retired couple in our example is to be able to withdraw $120,000 a year, increasing by inflation, for as long as they live, plus provide an inheritance for their heirs, all within acceptable risk parameters, defined in part by the couple's experience with investing.

Their primary investment objective would be income production; the secondary objective would be growth over the long term to offset future inflation, and the tertiary objective would be capital preservation.

Based on these objectives, how would this couple allocate their assets?

Using the demand-based formula, we need to start with cash-flow needs.

Let's find out how much should be allocated to income production based on the need for $120,000 a year.

Let's assume that the lowest-risk investment yields 2.5 percent. For mid-level risk, let's use 5 percent. And, for high risk, let's assume a yield of 10 percent.

How much capital would you need to put to work to produce the desired annual cash flow at these three yields?

For the lowest risk choice, you would need the most capital: $4.8 million ($120,000 divided by 2.5 percent = $4.8 million). For mid-risk, you would need $2.4 million ($120,000 divided by 5 percent = $2.4 million). For the high-risk option, you would need the least amount of capital ($1.2 million = $120,000 divided by 10 percent). Table 12-1 summarizes these calculations.

Table 12-1. Cash Flow at Three Yields

Desired Income Required	Risk Level	Annual Yield	Capital
$120,000	Low	2.5%	$4.8 mil
$120,000	Mid	5.0%	$2.4 mil
$120,000	High	10.0%	$1.2 mil

Risk

As we discussed earlier, no one wants to assume more risk than is necessary to achieve desired results. Yet, as we review these figures, you can't help noticing that the lowest-risk alternative uses up the most amount of capital, leaving little for the secondary (growth) and tertiary (preservation of capital) objectives.

On the other hand, no one wants to assume the highest risk option in order to achieve cash flow, since the couple needs to conserve principal in retirement. Accordingly, the mid-risk option may be the best alternative in this example.

Reincorporating Income Taxes

We figured that Michael and Ann needed $2.4 million of capital invested at 5 percent to produce $120,000 of income. This assumes they pay no taxes on the income, which is possible if the couple invests in tax-free bonds.

We'll assume that the income is generated from corporate bonds to get a sense of how taxes might affect the capital commitment.

Let's use 25 percent as the couple's effective income tax rate. Here is how the math would work. To account for a tax of 25 percent, the couple would need to generate income of $160,000 to be able to spend $120,000. (You arrive at this number by dividing $120,000 by 0.75, which is 1.00 minus the tax rate of 0.25.)

The difference ($160,000 minus $120,000 = $40,000) will be the tax bill on the interest income produced by taxable bonds. Now, you solve for $160,000 of income at 5 percent. Dividing $160,000 by 5 percent (0.05), you get $3.2 million, which is the amount the couple would need to invest to produce $160,000, leaving $120,000 to spend after taxes of $40,000.

Starting with $5 million of savings, using $3.2 million for income, leaves $1.8 million to invest for growth to offset inflation and preservation of capital—a good place to be.

Demand-Based Allocations

This type of analysis illustrates whether it is possible to use the demand-based approach to portfolio construction; some will not have sufficient savings to cover current expenses with income-producing instruments and future expenses by growing the portfolio. How the growth portion of the portfolio is constructed will determine the overall risk of the portfolio.

Summary

You, too, can review your situation and your holdings to plan your own portfolio. This account of Michael and Ann is an example of how to approach the project. Take one step at a time, and a picture of what you need to do will unfold as you consider your situation.

Key Points

1. If you're getting ready to retire, consider how you want to live and what your projected income and expenses will be in order to come up with a financial game plan that will enable you to meet your goals.
2. If you have adequate assets, using the demand-based asset approach to create income to cover expenses will protect your assets while allowing for growth.
3. When designing your retirement portfolio, it's important to factor in projected inflation, taxes, and to account for the lower tolerance for risk necessary for retirees.

Steps to Take

1. Review your current expenses, and, based on them, project your retirement expenses.
2. Assess your sources of retirement income including Social Security, pensions (if any), and all other assets.
3. If you have adequate assets, specify your portfolio goals including primary, secondary, and tertiary (if applicable) objectives, in order to begin the process of designing your demand-based asset allocations.

Investing for Three Different Goals

As we discussed in Part 2 of the book, there are three basic expectations an investor can have for his investments: capital appreciation, growth of income, or preservation of capital. In Part 5, I'll show you which types of investments can help you achieve each of these outcomes.

We'll begin with investing for capital appreciation in Chapter 13. As this goal requires investing in the stock market, we'll look at two popular investment styles: value and growth. And I'll demonstrate a less mathematical approach to managing risk than calculating CAPM, which we covered in Chapter 6. We'll also see what Warren Buffet says about monitoring your portfolio's performance.

In Chapter 14 you'll get a crash course in bonds, which can be a good investment choice if you are investing for income. We'll review interest rates, length of maturity, and call features. We'll also look at bond ratings and their reliability, and bond performance over the short and long term. Chapter 14 also includes a special section on municipal bonds and a section on how to find and buy bonds.

Sometimes simply preserving capital is your goal. But is playing it safe always a good strategy? In Chapter 15 we'll talk about when investing for preservation of capital makes sense and when it may put your portfolio at risk. As an example, we'll explore whether "Gloria," a new widow with no investment experience, made a wise decision when she chose to invest her husband's life insurance death benefit. Then we'll take a look at which instruments are the safest bet.

CHAPTER 13

Investing for Capital Appreciation

What's in It for You?

How do you approach meeting your investment objective for capital appreciation? This chapter helps set the stage for investing in stocks, a subject we'll cover in Chapters 16 through 19. Here, we'll discuss your goals, the effort it takes to reach those goals, and how to get a sense of the market.

Contents

Objective: Capital Appreciation

If your objective is capital appreciation, you will be looking to the stock market to meet that goal. There are hundreds of sources of information about stocks and stock selection, including hundreds of books; scholarly works; guides; newsletters; research reports; screening software; Internet sites; and television, cable, and radio news programs, all with advice for the individual investor. Add to that the people who are willing to give advice, and what you have is a mad mix of gurus hankering for your attention.

In fact, so much information is available that the best advice is to decide on a few sound sources and to ignore the rest. Ultimately, you will have to determine what resources are best for you considering your interests, time, and background. To give you a start in the right direction, we'll discuss some resources and how to use them in Chapters 16 through 19, and in the resources section in the back of the book.

This chapter provides a general overview of three factors that might affect your approach to investing for capital appreciation: (1) the effort you are willing to devote, (2) whether your goal is to "beat the market," and (3) your style. These preliminary issues really come down to a question of how much time you want to spend researching stocks and monitoring your results.

Effort and Attention

Benjamin Graham, coauthor of the classic investment text *Security Analysis: Principles and Techniques* and author of *The Intelligent Investor*, is recognized for having articulated reasoned investment principles for the individual investor. It is helpful to see the investment process from Graham's perspective, especially when comparing the effort and attention an investor must expend to achieve certain outcomes.

Graham separates investors into two categories. "Defensive investors" emphasize avoidance of serious mistakes, as well as freedom from "effort, annoyance, and the need for making frequent decisions." In contrast, "enterprising" or "aggressive investors" are willing to devote time and care to the selection of securities that are both sound and more attractive than average.

The expectation is that the aggressive investor, who puts more time and effort into investing, is likely able to outperform the defensive investor.

To be successful, Graham suggests, the aggressive investor must make sure his results will not be worse than the defensive investor's—otherwise the effort is unwarranted.

Indeed, if you think in terms of the nature of long-term investing as making a series of correct decisions (Chapter 2), you'll agree with Graham's point. If you think of the effort that it takes to search for, select, and manage a large number of individual stocks, there better be a payoff in terms of higher profits than can be achieved with less activity. If you pursue an aggressive course of action and find that your outcomes are *not* rewarding, it's best to shift to a defensive strategy in which the goal is to avoid mistakes.

That brings us to the question of what you should be shooting for.

Beating the Market

When structuring the growth portion of a portfolio, one of the first questions to ask is, are you trying to "beat the market"? Beating the market means you have your sights set on returns that outperform the market as measured by the S&P 500 Index.

If the answer is "yes," then you'll need to take on more risk. For example, you can choose stocks with higher betas and higher standard deviations. You can concentrate in sectors that are rotating into favor due to the economic cycle, or, you can use leverage to boost returns—all subjects we've discussed in this book.

To be successful using these portfolio enhancement techniques, you need to have a lot of experience in the markets, have money that you can afford to lose, and be skilled not only in selecting and monitoring your investments, but also in taking profits and cutting losses.

If you do not have years of experience already, you will need to build confidence through researching stocks, placing "paper" trades (which you can do with stock simulation programs such as *stocktrak.com*), and learning what works and what doesn't through that process. You don't want to practice with real money.

To meet your capital appreciation, or "growth," objectives, you will want to select stocks or stock mutual funds that give you the potential for growth over a defined period of time at acceptable levels of risk. Risk is a key determinant. When you monitor your results, as we'll discuss in Chapters 20 and 21, you'll know whether you made a good choice. If not, you'll replace the stock with a better choice.

Caution About Optimism

Be aware that good outcomes depend in part on the general direction of the market. As Warren Buffett said of performance in the 1997 annual report for Berkshire Hathaway:

> Given our gain of 34.1%, it is tempting to declare victory and move on. But last year's performance was no great triumph: Any investor can chalk up large returns when stocks soar, as they did in 1997. In a bull market, one must avoid the error of the preening duck that quacks boastfully after a torrential rainstorm, thinking that its paddling skills have caused it to rise in the world. A right-thinking duck would instead compare its position after the downpour to that of the other ducks on the pond.
>
> So what's our duck rating for 1997? . . . though we paddled furiously last year, passive ducks that simply invested in the S&P Index rose almost as fast as we did. Our appraisal of 1997's performance, then: Quack.

As Buffet points out, sometimes investment success can be attributed in large part to the general direction of the market. Be alert to that fact as you monitor your performance and plan for the future.

Your Personal Style

Before you set a course of buying stocks to meet your growth objective, consider whether you want to adapt a "value" approach, which is typically for more conservative investors with a long horizon, or the more aggressive approach of a "growth" investor.

Styles of Investing: Value versus Growth

Warren Buffett is viewed as a value investor, one who buys the undervalued stock of a well-managed company that one can hold for the long term for its potential rise in price.

Value investors tend to buy a stock when it is priced right (that is, when it is viewed to be cheap) and to hold the stock, sometimes indefinitely. As Buffett says, "Whether we're talking about socks or stocks, I like buying quality merchandise when it is marked down." (Berkshire Hathaway 2008 Annual Report.)

Relative Value: Is the Price Right?

While many people use the price to earnings ratio (P/E) to assess whether a stock is pricey, we'll also look at the price to book ratio (P/B). Earnings are just that—what the company earned after expenses and taxes (profits) over the last twelve months. Book value is stockholder equity (assets minus liabilities and preferred stock). To calculate these ratios, you divide the market price of the stock into the stock's earnings per share (for the P/E) or the stock's book value per share (for the P/B)—or simply look them up in any number of resources, such as Value Line or Morningstar. If the stock has a low P/E or P/B, it may attract the attention of value investors. Of course, even if a stock is a bargain, it can drop more and become an even better bargain—or wind up being a bad investment. Lower relative price of a stock is only one measure that value investors use to determine which stocks to buy; the stock has to represent a company with a good business judged by some of the metrics presented in Appendices A through D. Part of the assumption of the value investor is that you have to wait to reap your rewards. Again, value investing tends to be a long-term strategy.

Growth

If you are a growth investor, you may be willing to pay a higher price than a value investor for a stock since you are looking for stocks that are in rapid growth stages with the potential for a quicker profit than you would expect with a value stock. Growth investors would rather look for current success and quicker profit potential. They tend to buy stocks that are exhibiting growth trends as measured by earnings growth and sales growth, irrespective of relative price measures. And indeed, a stock that is overvalued (high P/B or high P/E) to a value investor may be attractive to growth investors if it exhibits potential for growth.

Time Horizon

Your time horizon needs to be considered before making a growth investment. Unless you are a skilled stock trader, it is better to take the safer route and lessen the risk level of your portfolio if you might need your principal a relatively short time after you invest it. If you can see yourself as someone who wants to buy for long-term potential, you would want to select value stocks that you can buy and hold for as long as it takes for the market to catch up to the value that you think the stock will attain. (Target price is discussed in Chapter 6.)

If you want to buy for short-term profit taking, you might look to growth stocks. The discussion of selection tools in Chapter 17 includes some examples of growth and value stocks and how to find them.

Is the Market as a Whole Cheap or Pricey?

Whether an investor is a growth or value investor, or a little of both, it's always helpful to get a sense of the playing field—just how pricey is the market right now?

To get a feel for the market as a whole, you can take an average P/E and P/B of the 500 stocks in the S&P 500 Index and compare different time periods to the present. This will give you a sense of relative values, which can affect your buy, sell, and hold decisions, as well as a starting point to compare your own stocks to the broad market.

Price to Book

As shown in Table 13-1, the P/B of the stocks comprising the S&P 500 Index was 6.7 at the start of the decade (a market top). By the end of 2002, the P/B had dropped to 3.5. Then, in 2007, it rose as the market rose to 5.0, finally falling to 2.8 at the bottom of the market in 2008.

Table 13-1 shows each year in the decade, along with the annual return for the S&P 500 Index for the year in question, the P/B, and the P/E. Keep in mind that the ratios are calculated as of December 31 of the year shown.

Table 13-1. P/B and P/E for S&P 500 Index Stocks for the Years 1999 through 2010

(Source: Morningstar Principia)

Yr Ending	P/B	P/E	S&P 500 Total Return
1999	6.7	38.8	21.0%
2000	5.2	32.0	−9.1%
2001	5.3	41.7	−11.9%
2002	3.5	34.7	−22.1%
2003	4.4	29.0	28.7%
2004	4.2	24.4	10.9%
2005	4.0	22.9	4.9%
2006	4.2	22.5	15.8%
2007	5.0	24.0	5.5%
2008	2.8	22.1	−37.0%
2009	3.3	32.5	26.5%
2010	3.4	25.3	15.1%
Average	4.3	29.2	
Median	4.2	27.2	
Maximum	6.7	41.7	
Minimum	2.8	22.1	

Table 13-2 (and Graph 13-1) compares the percentage change of the P/E and the P/B from year to year. As you can see, year-over-year percentage changes in P/E and P/B are not always in sync (see 2003 and 2006).

Table 13-2. P/B and P/E % Change from Previous Year

(Source: Morningstar Principia)

Yr Ending	P/B % Change from Previous Year	P/E % Change from Previous Year
2000	−22%	−18%
2001	2%	30%
2002	−34%	−17%
2003	26%	−16%
2004	−5%	−16%
2005	−5%	−6%
2006	5%	−2%
2007	19%	7%
2008	−44%	−8%
2009	18%	47%
2010	3%	−22%

A natural question is whether historical P/E or P/B can predict the future direction of the market. And the answer is, "not with any certainty."

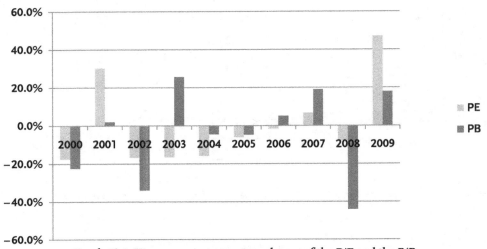

Graph 13-1. Year-over-year percentage change of the P/E and the P/B.

From Graph 13-1, you can see that the P/B and P/E, while both value measures, do not provide identical results. Some analysts believe that P/B is the more reliable measure of the two, in contrast to P/E since earnings are influenced by accounting practices and may vary from company to company. Book value does not.

You can compare your own stocks to these broad market measures for a quick read on where your stocks stand in terms of relative value. And you can do the same for the total stock portion of your portfolio.

Relative value alone will not determine whether you should buy (or hold or sell). It will just tell you that a stock is relatively cheap or costly; you will need to further evaluate the stock based on how the company's business is currently faring. How to do such an analysis is described in materials provided by the American Association of Individual Investors (AAII) (see Appendices A through D).

Summary

When buying stocks for your portfolio, your goal is to make money at some future date when you will sell the stock for a profit. You can also buy stocks that pay dividends for income purposes. You'll want to sell stocks that don't provide the results you are looking for.

When setting goals for yourself, be especially careful not to be influenced by an upward move in the market. Avoid the natural tendency to become more aggressive than you normally are or should be.

There are many ways to approach stock investing, some of which will have more appeal to you than others due to your own personal preferences and the amount of time you want to commit to the effort.

There are thousands of domestic and foreign stocks from which to choose as well as thousands of mutual funds that invest in stocks.

How should you go about the selection process? How long should you hold on? How do you know you're on track to meeting your objectives? These are the subjects we'll discuss in Chapters 16 through 19.

Key Points

1. For capital appreciation, you will want to invest in the stock market.
2. Defensive investors protect the downside. Aggressive investors shoot for the moon.
3. Value investors look for bargains, have a long time horizon, and wait for the market to catch up. Growth investors are less concerned with buying at a discount, focusing instead on whether the stock's earnings and sales are advancing.

Steps to Take

1. Consider whether you see yourself as a defensive or aggressive investor.
2. Consider your time horizon and risk tolerance. Does value or growth investing seem a better fit for you?
3. Consider your goals: are you are trying to beat the market? If so, review the techniques you use to limit risk, and think about selling rules, a subject we'll discuss in Chapter 18.

CHAPTER 14

Investing for Income

What's in It for You?

Though most people will have to invest for income at some point in their lives, few people have any experience doing so until after they retire. This chapter will help you assess bonds as income-producing instruments.

Contents

Creating Income

Most people will need to create income from their portfolios at some point in their lives, especially if they have substantial wealth and insufficient pension income to support themselves in retirement. While many people know how to buy stocks for growth, knowing how to turn assets into income is a far less familiar concept.

When I first came to Wall Street shortly after graduating from law school, I thought of all investments as having one goal: to make a profit. When I started working with portfolio managers in order to write mutual fund prospectuses, I started seeing that "profit" was really "total return," comprised of two components: one measuring capital appreciation or depreciation, the other measuring interest and dividends.

You could measure a bond based on how much the bond's principal fluctuated in price over time, and you could also measure the bond's interest payments.

Since you had two different components that you could measure, you could also put them to different uses or objectives—in this case income production (interest from bonds or dividends from bond mutual funds) and growth (if the price moves up).

To make a profit, you could buy a bond (or bond fund) with the intention of selling it at a higher price if conditions were right, much like a growth investment. Or, you could buy a bond and hold onto it until maturity, while receiving interest payments that you could spend, which would fall under the category of "income production."

Mutual Fund Managers Follow Objectives

Working on prospectuses forced me to think about different types of instruments of the market in terms of how investors could use them. The managers of the mutual funds who bought investments for their funds were following a set plan. They sought to achieve a certain result, such as growth of capital, production of income, or preservation of capital. This helped crystallize in my mind the real difference between a growth investment that you would normally buy to make a profit at a future date, versus an income investment that you would purchase for income production.

While some investors do buy stocks and sell them when they want cash for living expenses, the problem with this strategy is that bad stock choices and down markets put your capital at great risk. A less risky strategy would be to structure an income portfolio using income-producing investments from which you can earn interest (or dividends) instead of having to sell off principal.

You still have to deal with risks, but if this is done correctly, you can avoid selling off principal to meet your cash-flow needs and continue to grow your portfolio with stock investments in the growth portion of your portfolio. (In Chapters 11 and 12, we discussed how to determine the amount of money you need to invest in bonds to produce the amount of cash flow that you need for your living expenses in retirement.)

Bonds

Certain financial instruments are designed to pay the investor a set amount of money (interest) for a specific length of time and to repay the original amount of the investment (principal) at the end of that time (maturity date). Called "fixed-income instruments" or "bonds," they work just like an IOU. The investor is the lender. The borrower ("issuer") can be the federal government, the state you live in, your municipality, or a corporation. Thus, you could have U.S. bonds, state bonds, municipal bonds, bonds issued for a specific purpose, such as raising money to build a hospital or a road, or corporate bonds.

If you buy a U.S. government bond, you are actually lending money to the federal government in exchange for two promises: to pay you regular interest payments in accordance with the terms of the bond and to repay the amount the government borrowed from you at the agreed upon time. The bond is the government's IOU promising to pay you back when the loan comes due, plus interest during the time the loan is outstanding. You can buy government bonds directly from the Federal Reserve Bank or through your local banker or broker.

Interest Rates

An important element of the IOU is the interest rate, which is usually fixed for the life of the loan (fixed rate). If the "coupon" (interest rate at issue) on your 30-year U.S. bond is 5 percent, the lender, the federal government, agrees to pay you 5 percent per year for thirty years, not more, not less. Some bonds do have variable interest rates, and some pay interest only at maturity.

At the time you consider purchasing a bond, you need to know the interest rate features and whether they are fixed, floating, or accreted. A floating rate changes over time in accordance with the terms of the bond. Interest is accreted in bonds such as zero-coupon bonds, which are issued at a discount from face value with interest paid only at maturity.

An important aspect of an IOU is that the borrower has no obligation to repay you until the maturity date. If you buy a $10,000 30-year U.S. Treasury bond that matures in the year 2042 and you want your money back from the borrower in 2030, you are out of luck. The Federal Reserve Bank has no obligation to repay the loan until 2042. While you won't be able to get your money back from the government before maturity, nothing prevents you from selling the bond to anyone who wants to buy it. Let's talk about how that might work.

Selling Your Bonds

If you wanted to sell your U.S. bond for the price you paid for it, would you be able to do so? Perhaps, perhaps not. It all depends on the bond's income stream and how it compares to current rates for a bond.

Let's walk through an example together. You would like to sell the $10,000 30-year U.S. bond you bought 10 years ago. Your bond matures in 20 years and pays interest of 5 percent ($500) per year. Your next-door neighbor, Emily, happens to be in the market for a $10,000 20-year U.S. bond.

You bought the bond for $10,000, the face value of the bond. If Emily bought the bond from you, at maturity, Emily would receive $10,000. Does that mean $10,000 is a fair price? Perhaps, perhaps not. The answer will depend on current yields for like bonds.

Let's go through three scenarios, illustrated in Table 14-1. New 20-year U.S. bonds are offering the same rate as your bond (5 percent—"A" in Table 14-1), a higher rate (10 percent—"B"), and a lower rate (2.5 percent—"C").

Table 14-1. Scenarios A, B, and C

A	5% Coupon	5.00% Current Market Rate	B	5% Coupon	10% Current Market Rate	C	5% Coupon	2.50% Current Market Rate
Year	Interest Payments on Your Bond	Present Value at Market Rate	Year	Interest Payments on Your Bond	Present Value at Market Rate	Year	Interest Payments on Your Bond	Present Value at Market Rate
1	500	476.19	1	500	454.55	1	500	487.80
2	500	453.51	2	500	413.22	2	500	475.91
3	500	431.92	3	500	375.66	3	500	464.30
4	500	411.35	4	500	341.51	4	500	452.98
5	500	391.76	5	500	310.46	5	500	441.93
6	500	373.11	6	500	282.24	6	500	431.15
7	500	355.34	7	500	256.58	7	500	420.63
8	500	338.42	8	500	233.25	8	500	410.37
9	500	322.30	9	500	212.05	9	500	400.36
10	500	306.96	10	500	192.77	10	500	390.60
11	500	292.34	11	500	175.25	11	500	381.07
12	500	278.42	12	500	159.32	12	500	371.78
13	500	265.16	13	500	144.83	13	500	362.71
14	500	252.53	14	500	131.67	14	500	353.86
15	500	240.51	15	500	119.70	15	500	345.23
16	500	229.06	16	500	108.81	16	500	336.81
17	500	218.15	17	500	98.92	17	500	328.60
18	500	207.76	18	500	89.93	18	500	320.58
19	500	197.87	19	500	81.75	19	500	312.76
20	10500	3,957.34	20	10500	1,560.76	20	10500	6,407.84
Market Price	Total	10,000.00	Market Price	Total	5,743.22	Market Price	Total	13,897.29

If the income streams of new bonds and your bond are identical (A), you'll be able to sell the bond at your purchase price (see Market Price at the bottom of Table 14-1). Note that row 20 of the table shows the principal repayment and the final interest payment. If the bond you are selling offers the buyer lower income streams, you'll have a loss (B). In this example, your selling price will be $5,743 for a loss of over 40 percent. If the bond you are selling offers the buyer higher income streams than he can get in the current market, you'll make a profit (C) of $3,897.

An investor who could buy a 10-percent U.S. government bond maturing in 20 years for $10,000 would not pay $10,000 for a 5-percent bond. After all, a $10,000 investment in a 10-percent bond creates $1,000 of interest each year while the same investment in a 5-percent bond pays interest of only $500 a year.

To make your lower-yielding 5-percent bond attractive enough for someone to buy it from you when they can get a 10-percent bond from the issuer, you would have to be willing to sell your bond for much less than the face value so that Emily gets the same income stream she would get with a new bond.

Since bond prices and interest rates are inversely related, when interest rates go up, bond prices go down, as you can see from the preceding example. Similarly, if interest rates go down, bond prices go up.

Keep in mind, however, that if you had purchased the bond for income purposes, you would have had to use your proceeds, including the profits, to buy another bond to replicate your $500-a-year income stream.

You may be thinking that interest rates on U.S. government bonds can't fluctuate all that much, since you don't hear about people losing money if they sell their government bonds before maturity. This is not always the case.

Let's go back a few years in history to a period of rising interest rates. If you had purchased a 20-year U.S. government bond in October 1972, your coupon would have been 6 percent. If you wanted to sell that bond in February 1980, you would have lost 50 percent of your principal, since bond interest rates had risen to over 12 percent. Similarly, the price of even the highest-quality corporate bonds fell more than 50 percent in value in the early 1980s when interest rates rose, meaning that investors who had to sell their bonds would have locked in their losses due to market forces.

Length of Maturity

Fixed-income instruments are issued in periods ranging from the very short (under one year) to the very long (thirty years or longer). The longer the maturity (and thus the income stream), the greater the impact on price in changing interest rate environments. And, the longer the maturity of the bond, the greater likelihood that interest rates will change during the holding period. That translates into higher risk. The shorter the maturity of the bond, the lower the chance that interest rate fluctuation will impact the bond's market price should you have to sell before maturity.

Creditworthiness

Another element to consider is the borrower's ability to keep its promises to you. An IOU is an unsecured debt, which means there is no collateral for you to sell in the event of a default. If you borrow money from a bank to buy a home, the bank has a collateral interest in your home to protect itself if you stop paying the mortgage. That is, the bank has the right to foreclose on the mortgage and sell your house to collect on the loan if you default. In the case of a bond, you are the lender, but you have no collateral to sell if the borrower defaults. All you have is the promise of the borrower to pay you in accordance with the terms of the bond.

U.S. government bonds are backed by the full faith and credit of the United States, which makes them the most creditworthy bonds you can buy. The creditworthiness of the borrower ("issuer") is an important factor to consider when you are lending money by buying a bond because there is no collateral to sell if the issuer defaults on the loan.

Ratings

If you want to get some independent guidance on whether an issuer can make good on its bond promises, you can look at one of the rating services, such as Standard & Poor's (S&P), Moody's Investor Service, or Fitch's. Rating books published by these companies are available in the library and by subscription. Ratings are available for free on their websites if you register as a user. The highest rating assigned for corporate bonds by S&P is AAA, which means the issuer's capacity to pay interest and repay principal is "extremely strong." BBB-rated bonds have "adequate capacity" to pay interest and repay principal. However, "adverse economic conditions or changing circumstances are likely to lead to weakened capacity to pay interest and repay principal." B-rated bonds have the current capacity to pay interest but have "greater vulnerability to default." C-1 is not paying interest currently. Debt rated D is in payment default. (See "A Warning About Ratings" below.)

Lower-Rated Bonds

If some borrowers that issue bonds are more likely to pay you interest and repay your principal and others are less likely to do so, why would you ever invest in the latter? People buy lower-rated bonds for one reason: higher yields. To compete for capital, companies that are less creditworthy need to pay a higher yield to attract investors.

Depending on the issue and the market, you may find a difference in yield of 3 to 4 percent between a high-rated bond and a low-rated bond. If you are trying to generate income from bonds and high-quality bonds are paying, say, 3 percent and low-quality bonds are paying 6 or 7 percent, you may find yourself buying the higher-yielding, lower-rated bonds. A 3-percent yield spread on a $1 million bond portfolio means an extra $30,000 a year of interest payments.

Should investors buy high-risk, high-yielding bonds? When people need cash flow for retirement, they sometimes search for higher yields, many times to their detriment. I would not normally recommend buying individual high-yield bonds because of the default risk. Some high-yield bonds stop trading when no one wants to buy them. Some companies go out of business.

However, in the right circumstances, a diversified mutual fund investing in high-yield bonds may be appropriate for some more aggressive investors, keeping in mind that higher yields inevitably translate to more dramatic price swings. How to select high-yield bond funds will be an important skill for those investors. Chapter 19 will give you some general guidance on selecting funds.

A Warning About Ratings

You should be aware that you can't choose bonds based on ratings alone. Ratings are opinions issued by rating agencies when the issuer initially comes to market. As a result, they call on analysts to forecast far into the future for a longer-term bond.

As former bond analyst Annette Thau explains in her book, *The Bond Book*:

> When forecasting economic conditions for the next six months or for perhaps one year, experts stand on reasonably secure ground. But the further they predict into the future, the more imprecise and unreliable their forecasts become. Any prediction of economic conditions that goes out more than five years becomes guesswork. Bear in mind, however, that the rating extends over the entire life of the bond, even if that is 30 years.

Credit ratings are updated by agencies over time on an as-needed basis. You'll need to be alert to the rating changes of your bonds. If a bond falls below investment grade, which it can, the analyst thinks your chances of default may increase. Lower-quality bonds have a higher incidence of defaults. Moreover, credit agencies aren't infallible. Their ratings are not buy recommendations nor guarantees about the creditworthiness of the issuer. You should also be aware that rating agencies were criticized for not adequately addressing the default risk of financial bonds during the credit crisis in 2008.

Given this knowledge, it's still worth it to use ratings as a starting point for further research. We'll talk about how to do bond research shortly.

Redemption or Call Features

Some bonds are issued under an agreement that gives the issuer the right to repay the principal before the maturity date. Known as a "call" feature, in falling interest rate environments, this gives the issuer (who is borrowing money from you) the ability to pay off high-interest debt and issue new bonds at lower rates. The call feature is a benefit to the lender and a detriment to you the investor, since you will be in the position of having to replace the income stream you have been relying on in a lower-yielding market. Also, the federal government has from time to time instituted a repurchase program to buy back your U.S. government bonds before maturity.

Lowering Risk

To lower the risks of bond investing, your most important considerations will be creditworthiness, length of maturity, and call features. First, if you are buying a bond to generate income, buy higher-quality bonds with solid creditworthiness. Second, "ladder" the bonds so that some mature every year or two, which will lessen your exposure to market risk. As we discussed in Chapter 8, a bond ladder involves buying a series of bonds with shorter to longer maturities. Third, if you can't afford quality because you need more income than high-quality bonds can give you, be absolutely certain to diversify the higher-risk bonds you might be considering.

How to Research Bonds

The bond market was one of the least transparent markets for individuals until 2005, when the Trade Reporting and Compliance Engine (TRACE) became available through FINRA (Financial Industry Regulatory Authority; previously the National Association of Securities Dealers, Inc., NASD). Because bonds are marked up by dealers when they are sold out of their inventory to customers, buyers can't tell if they are getting a good deal. The same holds true when bonds are sold by customers—the dealer prices the bond with an undisclosed markdown.

TRACE now captures transaction reports from all FINRA-registered firms on more than 30,000 corporate bonds. You can access the information captured by TRACE through *BondInfo,* at *www.BondInfo.com.*

You can use TRACE to find any kind of bond that you would like through its search tool. You can search for name, maturity, ratings, and recent trading activity, including time and sales. You can identify an individual bond and review the symbol, maturity date, type of bond, interest payment frequency, coupon type, call features, and composite trade information, which includes the net change in price from the previous trade. This page also carries the call schedule if the bond is callable.

Armed with this information, you can call your broker to ask for a quote, making sure you identify the bond by its symbol and maturity date. Based on the price and yield quoted by the broker, you can compare the last trade information you have from *BondInfo* and make a decision on whether you like the quote. You can pass it up if it is unfavorable or ask for a better deal. However, you'll need to keep things in perspective. If you want to buy only a few bonds, you won't get the same deal as a multimillion dollar trade that you might find executed on *BondInfo*.

You can also see the most actively traded bonds for the prior day, including stock-like reporting—the highest price recorded that day, the lowest price, and the price of the last trade of the day ("last price"). (The bond-trading day closes at 5:16 pm.)

Caution: If you look at yields under the most-active list, don't be tempted to buy the highest-yielding bond you see without further due diligence. (The yield shown is the most conservative potential yield, "yield to worst," considering call features and maturity date.)

On a recent search of the most-active list, I found a bond yielding 39.9 percent. Of course, the bond was rated Ca by Moody's, which translates into mega-risk. A Ca rating is speculative to a high degree, according to Moody's.

For additional information on how to buy bonds, visit "Smart Bond Investing" under "The Bond Learning Center" on the *FINRA.org* website. You can also use databases like the Morningstar Investing Classroom, which has a "curriculum" on bonds at *Morningstar.com*.

A Special Note About Municipal Bonds

The Electronic Municipal Market Access (EMMA) at *www.emma.msrb.org*, which is operated by the Municipal Securities Rulemaking Board (MSRB), is a resource for municipal bonds research. Another resource is *www. investinginbonds.com,* which is run by the Securities Industry and Financial Markets Association (SIFMA).

On EMMA, locate the Official Statement, which is a disclosure document required to be written by the issuer at the time the bond is issued. It contains a detailed description of the terms of the offering, including covenants of the issuer and bond counsel's opinion on the legality of the issue and an opinion on whether interest on the bond would be treated as taxable or tax-free, along with a copy of the bond insurance policy, if the bond is insured.

Since the Official Statement is current as of the issue date, if you are buying a bond in the secondary market you'll need to update this information with "Continuing Disclosure," which is also available through EMMA, namely: (1) disclosure required under SEC rules, such as annual financial information; (2) voluntary disclosures, such as more frequent financials and operating data (monthly or quarterly); and (3) advance refunding documents (applicable when an old issue of bonds is being refinanced with a new issue of bonds). (You'll also find continuing disclosure on the Securities and Exchange Commission [SEC] website at *www.sec.gov/info/municipal/nrmsir.htm.*)

Keep your eyes open for negative events, such as delinquencies in paying interest or principal on any obligations; other types of defaults; financial difficulties, which might be evidenced by unscheduled draws on credit; rating changes; adverse rulings from the IRS; litigation; notices to bond holders; and, of course, insolvency and bankruptcy. Once you are satisfied, you'll also want to review trading data, which you can also access daily on EMMA and *investinginbonds.com.*

To help you build a foundation on municipal bonds, spend some time with Morningstar's online resources, called "Morningstar Investing Classroom," an excellent basic resource to put you on the path toward sound municipal bond investing.

Summary

If you want your investments to generate cash flow for you to live on, you will probably find that bonds are better than stocks for that purpose. Generally, but not always, dividends paid by companies on stocks tend to be lower than interest on bonds. Bonds are also useful to diversify your stock portfolio, as discussed in Chapter 8.

Be mindful that some financial advisers don't believe in buying bonds for income purposes. Instead, they believe that you can buy stocks and sell them when you need money to live on. This strategy works best when the stock market is going up, and it can put you out of business very quickly when it is going down.

Key Points

1. When investing for income, consider bonds as a means of income production.
2. To minimize the risk of buying bonds for income, buy high-quality bonds and "ladder" them so that they mature every year or two.
3. Consider bond creditworthiness, length of maturity, and call features.

Steps to Take

1. Review your accounts to look for how you are generating income now.
2. If you are selling positions to generate cash to live on, consider adding a bond component to your portfolio that will generate interest.
3. Use some of the resources we discussed to find the current yields on high-quality bonds maturing in three, five, ten years and longer.

Investing for Preservation of Capital

CHAPTER 15

What's in It for You?

When is treading water (preservation of capital) better than taking a swim (investing for growth)? This chapter will help you understand how and when preservation of capital might be an appropriate objective. As you will see, inflation will be a concern for anyone who invests for preservation of capital for any length of time.

Contents

Of the three investment objectives we have been discussing—growth, income, and preservation of capital—the last is the least risky. Investments that preserve your capital keep it safe against market losses. Even those with no experience buying stocks, bonds, or mutual funds have opened savings accounts and certificates of deposit (CDs) and bought U.S. savings bonds. When you invest this way, you are actually investing for "preservation of capital," not for growth, nor income.

In this chapter, let's talk about expectations if you invest for preservation of capital, circumstances in which preservation of capital should and should not be your goal, and the best instruments to use for this purpose.

The Rewards—and Risks—of Preservation of Capital

No one wants to lose money. Investing for preservation of capital is the safest way to invest. In case you might think that you should put all your money toward this objective, let me point out why you should not. When you invest for preservation of capital, you are protecting your principal against steep declines due to market fluctuations. But, as with any investment, there is a cost. The cost is a lower return. Since you are investing for safety, your real return will be low—or negative—after accounting for inflation and taxes.

Let's explore real return for a moment. U.S. Treasury bills, which are money market instruments appropriate for preservation of capital, returned 3.6 percent per year on average for the period 1926 through 2010. After inflation is taken into account, the return drops to 0.6 percent per year, which is the real inflation-adjusted return. (The data for the period 1926 through 2010 is provided by Ibbotson Associates.) If you also subtracted your income tax liability, this would reduce your real return even further.

In contrast, the total return on long-term government bonds for the same period was 5.5 percent before inflation and 2.4 percent after inflation. The total return on corporate bonds was higher: 5.9 percent before inflation and 2.9 percent after inflation.

Stock returns were even higher. Stocks of large companies, as represented by the S&P 500 Index, returned 9.9 percent per year before inflation for the period 1926 through 2010, and 6.7 percent in real terms (inflation-adjusted). This comparison underlines the need to consider the risk-reward relationship of different investments before structuring a portfolio—concepts discussed in earlier chapters.

Longer Horizons

When investing for longer periods of time, inflation becomes an important consideration. Spend a few minutes with Table 15-1 below, which provides data before and after inflation for twenty-year periods starting in 1926 (20 years ending 1945) through 2010.

Table 15-1. Average Annual Total Returns for All 20-Year Periods between 1926 and 2010 Shown Before and After Inflation

(Source: Ibbotson)

	Before Inflation (%)	Inflation-Adjusted (%)
S&P 500 Index	9.9	6.7
Long-Term Corporate Bonds	5.9	2.9
U.S. Long-Term Government Bonds	5.5	2.4
U.S. Treasury Bills (30-day)	3.6	0.6

Pay particular attention to U.S. Treasury bills. Before inflation is taken into account, the return is 3.6 percent per year on average for all twenty-year holding periods between 1926 and 2010. But, after accounting for inflation, the return is less than 1 percent (0.6 percent). As you can see, the S&P 500 Index has the highest inflation-adjusted returns at 6.7 percent, and indeed, that's one reason that stocks are seen as inflation hedges.

When Investing for Preservation of Capital Makes Sense

There are times when assuming the least amount of market risk is an absolute necessity. Gloria, a widow, was referred to me by her insurance agent a few weeks after her husband's sudden death due to a heart attack. The agent had delivered a check to Gloria for $1 million, which was the death benefit on her husband's insurance policy. Gloria had never invested and, in fact, had never gone to the bank or even written a check; her husband had closely controlled the finances in the family, leaving Gloria totally in the dark. Not surprisingly, Gloria was frantic. She had three teenagers to raise alone. And, she had to make financial decisions for herself for the first time in her life.

My recommendation to Gloria was to invest for preservation of capital for an entire year, by investing the entire $1 million into U.S. Treasury bills. This strategy would allow her to protect her principal from risk of loss and give her time to settle into a routine at home without worrying about losing her money. It would also allow her to learn about the risks and potential rewards of different market instruments at her leisure over the next year, rather than under the pressure of having to make a quick decision that might involve a risk she could not reasonably assess in her current circumstances. Then, after a year, Gloria could make better decisions based on her understanding of the risk-reward trade-offs the market offered her.

There are other times when you might invest for preservation of capital. You may wish to set aside a portion of your overall portfolio for this purpose for emergencies, or to stabilize your portfolio, or for a temporary parking place while you assess what you want to do with your money. For emergencies, some recommend setting aside enough to cover six months of living expenses.

Instruments

The financial instruments of the market that are most suited for preservation of capital are money market instruments, which are short-term (under one year) debt instruments. Debt instruments are IOUs, as discussed in Chapter 14. Money market instruments are not expected to fluctuate in price due to market conditions, in part due to their short maturity, or due to how they are structured. For example, if you buy a 1-year certificate of deposit (CD), by definition you will get your original investment at the end of the holding period irrespective of interest rate changes or market action. You will also get your agreed-on interest payment.

Another example is a money market mutual fund, which allows your principal to remain stable, with only the dividend fluctuating in response to interest rates. Although money market mutual funds are considered an extremely safe investment, on two occasions individual funds have "broken a buck," or had their net asset value dip below $1 per share. The last time this happened was in September of 2008 and was related to Lehman Brothers filing for bankruptcy. The U.S. Treasury Department stepped in and guaranteed these funds, thus avoiding losses for investors.

U.S. Treasury bills are also money market instruments; however, unlike CDs or money market mutual funds, the price of Treasury bills does fluctuate with interest rates. The shorter the maturity, the less likely the impact of price fluctuations. For example, a 3-month bill will be less volatile than a 12-month bill if interest rates change. If you intend to buy a bill and to hold onto it until it matures, the fluctuation will not affect you in any way.

When you buy a Treasury bill, you pay less than the face value, "par," and your interest is "accreted," meaning you get the interest when you redeem the bill. The difference between the purchase price and the amount you get at maturity is the interest you earn on the bill. You can buy U.S. Treasury bills directly from the Federal Reserve Bank. You can do this by mail or online at *www.treasurydirect.gov*.

Money market instruments generally do not pay distributions (interest or dividends) that are much higher than the current rate of inflation. From time to time, money market rates may seem high, as they did in the early 1980s, when you could have earned double-digit returns.

When U.S. Treasury bills earned interest of 13, 14, and even 17 percent per year during 1980 and 1981, the Consumer Price Index (CPI), which measures inflation, was 12 and 13 percent. If you wanted to get a thirty-year mortgage to buy a home at this time, you would have had to pay interest in the 12 percent to 18 percent range. Remember to keep that in perspective.

Summary

Preservation of capital is a valid investment objective for at least a part of your portfolio during certain times of your life, for example in retirement. It can be a valid purpose for your entire portfolio under certain scenarios, such as when you need to sit on the sidelines for a while or when you have no need to grow your assets or produce any income from your assets for living expenses. Keep in mind, however, that inflation and taxes will negatively impact your returns over longer holding periods.

Key Points

1. Preservation of capital can be an appropriate investment objective under certain circumstances, such as safeguarding a portion of your portfolio or temporarily sitting out of the market.
2. Money market instruments are the best choices for preservation of capital.
3. Money market instruments have short maturities, lower risk, and lower returns than other instruments, and over time, do *not* outpace inflation.

Steps to Take

1. Review your portfolio to determine which investments, if any, are functioning to preserve capital.
2. Make a list of situations under which you would want to invest for preservation of capital.
3. Given your goals, what proportion of your portfolio should be invested for preservation of capital now?

6

Utilizing Independent Research: Choosing Stocks

Given that there are thousands of stocks, how to choose wisely can seem overwhelming. Let's look at tools that can help you narrow your search.

One way to classify stocks is to divide them into industry sectors, as we'll discuss in Chapter 16. We'll take a look at the ten broad sectors that Standard & Poor's uses to categorize stocks. I'll show you why it's important to know which sectors your stocks fall into, and we'll explore the concept of sector rotation. We'll also discuss how you can compare sector characteristics like dividend yields to help you maximize income in your portfolio. In addition, we'll review how sectors have performed in recent years.

In Chapter 17 we'll examine another way of classifying stocks: Morningstar's "types." Ranging from "distressed" to "slow growth," Morningstar screens thousands of stocks to predict how each may behave going forward. This is another tool to help you assess the risk and reward of potential investments as well as choose stocks most likely to meet your growth objectives.

Then in Chapter 18, we'll talk about the importance of developing your own selling discipline. Many investors fail to realize gains or limit their losses because they lack a set of rules that help determine the time to sell. I'll show you two methods—one based on price, the other based on selection criteria. We'll use another independent research source, Value Line, to create a model investment policy that includes both selection (buy) and deselection (sell) criteria.

In Chapter 19, we'll investigate mutual funds. I'll show you how mutual funds can help you meet your investment objectives. I'll also highlight some mistakes investors make when selecting funds. This chapter will give you the foundation you'll need to make informed decisions for both buying and selling mutual funds. Finally, this chapter will highlight red flags to look out for and identify key characteristics of good mutual funds.

CHAPTER 16

Sectors

What's in It for You?

There are thousands of stocks that you can potentially buy. How do you begin to search for the stocks that are right for you? After sharing some thoughts about stock research, I'll review with you the most basic of classifications, the sectors of the 500 stocks represented by the S&P 500 Index. We'll also look at stocks that pay dividends.

Contents

As you might imagine, if you are trying to get a handle on thousands of stocks, you have to start with some sort of classification system based on shared characteristics. Classifications alone will not tell you what to buy; however, understanding commonalities has two benefits. First, groupings will assist you in comparing the stocks you are considering to other similar stocks. Second, they will help you assess stocks in terms of how well they might fit and interact with each other in your portfolio, based on diversification and risk considerations.

Brokerage Research

You may invest in stocks recommended by your stockbroker, who in turn relies on research published by the brokerage firm that employs him. Many times the research is condensed into a "focus list," which is a short list of stocks recommended by the firm.

Brokerage firm research ("in-house research") grew dramatically after brokerage firms realized they needed to add value when competing for clients, especially after the 1975 deregulation of securities commissions and the advent of discount brokerage. Typically, discount brokerage firms do not hire their own analysts. Instead, they usually provide their clients with independently published research.

Independent Research

In this chapter we'll take a look at an independent resource, Standard & Poor's, whose history goes back to 1860 when Henry Varnum Poor, a founder of the financial information industry, published a history of the railroads. Standard Statistics merged with Poor's Publishing Company in 1941, creating Standard & Poor's, the firm that every investor recognizes as the publisher of the S&P 500 Index, representing the U.S. stock market. Standard & Poor's also publishes "The Outlook," which is a weekly market overview for individual investors. You will also find *marketsmith. com* helpful (published by William O'Neal and Company, Inc.) as well as TC2000 by Worden Brothers, Inc.

In the next chapter, we'll consider Morningstar, an independent research firm that started out in 1984 as a publisher of mutual fund information. And, in Chapter 18, we'll take a look at Value Line, started by Arnold Bernhard in 1931 specifically for the individual investor, the oldest independent source of stock research.

Sectors

The S&P 500 Index, which is limited to the largest stocks in the U.S. stock market, represents approximately 75 percent of U.S. stocks by capitalization. Standard & Poor's divides these stocks into ten GICS (Global Industry Classification Standard) sectors, which we will discuss here, as well as 24 industry groups, 68 industries, and 154 sub-industries.

In this chapter, we'll focus on these 500 stocks and the ten sectors: Consumer Discretionary, Consumer Staples, Energy, Financials, Health Care, Industrials, Information Technology, Materials, Telecommunication Services, and Utilities. You can find current data on sectors on Standard & Poor's website for free by registering online at *standardandpoors.com*. (Note that Morningstar uses twelve sectors.)

Why Sectors?

You need to know the sector of each stock that you are choosing for your portfolio. Stocks in a sector tend to move in similar fashion—for example, a severe decline in one bank stock may affect other bank stocks, so that the entire sector moves down, sometimes in sympathy, sometimes for fundamental reasons.

Owning stocks in different sectors helps diversify a portfolio. As some sectors move up, others might move down, and vice versa.

There is no question that the market favors different sectors at different times. Notice the sectors represented by the largest stocks in terms of market capitalization at the beginning of the 2000 decade (end of 1999), a market high, in Table 16-1. We'll also look at the top ten stocks for the market bottom of March 2009 (Table 16-2) and the end of 2010 (Table 16-3). Notice the differences in the stocks as we move through time.

Table 16-1. Market Capitalization of the Ten Largest Stocks at the End of 1999
(Source: Morningstar Principia)

	Company	Market Cap ($ Millions)	Percentage of Top Ten Market Cap	S&P Sector
1	Microsoft (1,2,3)	602,433	19.8%	Information Technology
2	General Electric (1,2,3)	507,217	16.7%	Industrials
3	Cisco Systems	366,499	12.1%	Information Technology
4	Wal-Mart (1,2,3)	307,865	10.1%	Consumer Staples
5	Intel	275,008	9.1%	Information Technology
6	Lucent	229,798	7.6%	Information Technology
7	Exxon (1,2,3)	195,590	6.4%	Energy
8	IBM (1,2,3)	194,456	6.4%	Information Technology
9	Citigroup	187,761	6.2%	Financials
10	America Online	169,618	5.6%	Information Technology
	Top 10 Total	**3,036,245**	**100.0%**	

(1) Indicates that the stock appears in Table 16-1.
(2) Indicates that the stock also appears in Table 16-2.
(3) Indicates that the stock also appears in Table 16-3.

At the height of the Internet bubble, the number 1 spot, Microsoft, claimed almost 20 percent of the total capitalization of the top ten. Six of the ten stocks, representing 60.5 percent of the top ten at the end of 1999, were technology stocks.

The next table (16-2) sets out the ten largest stocks at the market bottom of March 2009. The largest stock is ExxonMobil, an energy stock. Exxon, together with Chevron, represent just under 30 percent of the top ten.

Technology is the next largest sector with 24.7 percent representation, down from six stocks to only three. Microsoft has dropped from first place to fourth, with market capitalization falling dramatically from $602.4 billion in 1999 to $163.3 billion in March 2009.

Table 16-2. Market Capitalization of the Ten Largest Stocks at March 2009

(Source: Morningstar Principia)

	Company	Market Cap ($ Millions)	Percentage of Top Ten Market Cap	S&P Sector
1	ExxonMobil (1,2,3)	336,525.00	20.6%	Energy
2	Wal-Mart Stores (1,2,3)	204,365.00	12.5%	Consumer Staples
3	AT&T	163,679.80	10.0%	Telecommunication Services
4	Microsoft (1,2,3)	163,319.60	10.0%	Information Technology
5	Johnson & Johnson	145,481.30	8.9%	Health Care
6	Procter & Gamble (2, 3)	138,012.60	8.5%	Consumer Staples
7	Chevron (2,3)	134,786.60	8.3%	Energy
8	IBM (1,2,3)	129,995.20	8.0%	Information Technology
9	Google (2,3)	109,741.10	6.7%	Information Technology
10	General Electric (1,2,3)	106,765.90	6.5%	Industrials
	Total Top Ten	**1,632,672.10**	**100.0%**	

(1) Indicates that the stock also appears in Table 16-1.
(2) Indicates that the stock appears in Table 16-2.
(3) Indicates that the stock also appears in Table 16-3.

The final table (16-3) is a list of the ten largest stocks at the end of 2010. The largest stock remains Exxon. Exxon, together with Chevron, represent 25 percent of the top ten. The technology sector is the largest sector with four of ten stocks or 41.0 percent of the top ten at the end of 2010.

Table 16-3. Market Capitalization of the Ten Largest Stocks at the End of 2010

(Source: Morningstar Principia)

	Company	Market Cap ($ Millions)	Percentage of Top Ten Market Cap	S&P Sector
1	Exxon (1,2,3)	368,711.7	16.7%	Energy
2	Apple	295,886.6	13.4%	Information Technology
3	Microsoft(1,2,3)	238,784.7	10.8%	Information Technology
4	General Electric(1,2,3)	194,874.8	8.8%	Industrials
5	Wal-Mart Stores(1,2,3)	192,098.4	8.7%	Consumer Staples
6	Google (2,3)	189,936.8	8.6%	Information Technology
7	Chevron (2,3)	183,634.1	8.3%	Energy
8	Procter & Gamble (2,3)	182,599.1	8.3%	Consumer Staples
9	IBM (1,2,3)	182,328.9	8.3%	Information Technology
10	Berkshire Hathaway	180,686.1	8.2%	Financials
	Top Ten Total	**2,209,541.2**	**100.0%**	

(1) Indicates that the stock also appears in Table 16-1.
(2) Indicate that the stock also appears in Table 16-2.
(3) Indicates that the stock appears in Table 16-3.

If you study these tables, you'll notice that sector representation among the top ten companies changed dramatically from one period to another. Table 16-4 summarizes the capitalization of the technology sector.

Table 16-4. Technology Representation in the Top Ten Stocks Capitalization ($ Millions)

	Dec-99	Mar-09	Dec-10
Technology Market Cap	1,837,811	403,056	906,937
Total Market Cap	3,036,245	1,632,672	2,209,541
Percentage Technology	60.5%	24.7%	41.0%

Sector Rotation

Some theorize that you can predict the movement of different sectors based on the economic cycle ("sector rotation"). For example, when the economy is declining, stocks of companies may move up in price if the company sells products that people must have even in tough economic times, like toothpaste. Presumably, companies that sell jewelry would decline in such markets and recover when the economy is in an upswing. There are a number of services based on the premise that you can predict future stock prices by anticipating the sectors the market will favor based on the cycles of the economy.

Sector rotation is intuitively and logically sound. The problem however, challenges Benjamin Graham, coauthor of the classic investment text *Security Analysis: Principles and Technique*, is that it "is not as easy as it always looks in retrospect." Graham concludes that "obvious prospects for physical growth in a business do not translate into profits for investors." Even experts have no "dependable ways of selecting and concentrating on the most promising companies in the most promising industries."

While it is always best to choose stocks from the best companies in a sector based on how well the company runs its business (metrics are provided in Appendices A through D), it is another matter to find the best company within a sector that is itself most likely to grow in the future. If you are interested in learning more about sector rotation, Standard & Poor's is a good resource.

Dividend Contributions and Yields by Sector

Anyone who wants to invest for income will be interested in stocks that produce dividends. Let's spend a few minutes with Table 16-5, which shows the stocks in the S&P 500 Index by sector and each sector's "dividend contribution," "dividend yield," and the number of "dividend-paying issues" in each sector.

As we can see from Table 16-5, 373 of the 500 companies in the S&P 500 Index paid dividends in 2010. The average dividend yield was 1.9 percent. The dividend yield for the Consumer Staples sector was 3.0 percent, and this sector was the largest contributor (16.9 percent) of dividends paid in 2010 by the 500 companies in the S&P 500 Index, even though only thirty-nine companies paid dividends in the sector. Some sectors outpaced the average yield (1.9 percent) by quite a bit. The highest-yielding sector was Telecommunication Services with a dividend yield of 5.2 percent, representing only six companies. The next highest-yielding sector was Utilities, with a yield of 4.4 percent for 2010, representing thirty-two companies.

Table 16-5. Dividend Contributions and Yield of Sector for 2010
(Source: Standard & Poor's)

Sector	Sector Dividend Contribution	Sector Dividend Yield	Number of Dividend-Paying Issues
Consumer Discretionary	7.9%	1.4%	59
Consumer Staples	16.9%	3.0%	39
Energy	11.6%	1.8%	31
Financials	9.1%	1.1%	69
Health Care	13.0%	2.2%	22
Industrials	12.4%	2.1%	55
Information Technology	9.3%	0.9%	32
Materials	3.6%	1.8%	28
Telecommunication Services	8.6%	5.2%	6
Utilities	7.8%	4.4%	32
S&P 500	**100.0%**	**1.9%**	**373**

Dividends are not guaranteed—they are declared by the company's board of directors based on a number of factors, most importantly whether the company is earning money. As you can see from Table 16-6, there was a big jump in the number of companies that decreased their dividends from 2007 (eight) to 2008 (68) to 2009 (68), as you would expect during recessionary periods. In 2010, only four reduced their dividends.

Table 16-6. Dividend Actions
(Source: Standard & Poor's)

	Number of Issues Increasing Their Dividend	Number of Issues Decreasing Their Dividend
2010	243	4
2009	151	68
2008	236	40
2007	287	8
2006	299	7
2005	306	9
2004	271	3

During the same time period, however, many other companies increased their dividends. As you'll notice in Table 16-6, the fewest increases ocurred in 2009 (151), the same year the largest number of companies decreased their dividends (68). Stocks that increase dividends over time are attractive to investors who want both income and price appreciation.

Dividend Aristocrats

Income investors will be interested in companies that have increased dividends steadily over the last twenty-five years, as represented by the S&P's Dividend Aristocrats Index. Table 16-7 provides a list of these dividend aristocrats as of April 2011. You can find a more current list on the Standard & Poor's website at *standardandpoors.com*. This list is a good starting point for further research.

Table 16-7. S&P Dividend Aristocrats List
for April 2011
(Source: Standard & Poor's)

Company	Ticker	Sector
3M Co.	MMM	Industrials
Abbott Laboratories	ABT	Health Care
AFLAC Inc.	AFL	Financials
Air Product & Chemicals	APD	Materials
Archer-Daniels-Midland	ADM	Consumer Staples
Automatic Data Proc.	ADP	Information Technology
Bard (C.R.)	BCR	Health Care
Becton, Dickinson	BDX	Health Care
Bemis Co.	BMS	Materials
Brown-Froman 'B'	BF.B	Consumer Staples
CenturyTel Inc.	CTL	Telecommunication Services
Chubb Corp.	CB	Financials
Cincinnati Financial	CINF	Financials
Cintas Corp.	CTAS	Industrials
Clorox Co.	CLX	Consumer Staples
Coca-Cola Co.	KO	Consumer Staples
Consolidated Edison	ED	Utilities
Dover Corp.	DOV	Industrials
Ecolab Inc.	ECL	Materials
Emerson Electric	EMR	Industrials
ExxonMobil	XOM	Energy
Family Dollar Stores	FDO	Consumer Discretionary
Grainger (W.W.)	GWW	Industrials
Hormel Foods Corp.	HRL	Consumer Staples
Johnson & Johnson	JNJ	Health Care
Kimberly-Clark	KMB	Consumer Staples
Leggett & Platt	LEG	Consumer Discretionary
Lowe's Cos.	LOW	Consumer Discretionary
McCormick & Co.	MKC	Consumer Staples
McDonald's Corp.	MCD	Consumer Discretionary
McGraw-Hill Companies	MHP	Consumer Discretionary
PepsiCo Inc.	PEP	Consumer Staples
Pitney Bowes	PBI	Industrials
PPG Indus.	PPG	Materials
Procter & Gamble	PG	Consumer Staples
Sherwin-Williams	SHW	Materials
Sigma-Aldrich	SIAL	Materials
Stanley Black & Decker	SWK	Consumer Discretionary
Target Corp.	TGT	Consumer Discretionary
VF Corp.	VFC	Consumer Discretionary
Walgreen Co.	WAG	Consumer Staples
Wal-Mart	WMT	Consumer Staples

If you need to produce income *and* have the potential for growth, S&P Dividend Aristocrats are worth researching further.

Summary

When confronted with thousands of choices, classification systems, such as S&P's sectors and Dividend Aristocrats, will help you start to distinguish one stock from another. You'll be able to research individual stocks by using independent or brokerage research. In the next chapter, we'll discuss another way to look at stocks, using Morningstar's types. Then, in Chapter 18, we'll look at Value Line's approach to stock selection and explain how you can use its services to craft an investment policy for yourself that includes when to sell.

Key Points

1. Both individuals and firms rely on research to determine which stocks to buy to meet particular growth objectives.
2. Different sectors respond to economic movements.
3. Stocks of companies that increased dividends over the last twenty-five years are worth researching further if you are an investor who is looking for both capital appreciation and income.

Steps to Take

1. Log onto *www.standardandpoors.com* to explore their free services.
2. Review your current stock holdings to identify their current sector representations.
3. If you are interested in dividend-producing stocks, find the current "Dividend Aristocrats Index" on the Standard & Poor's website (*www.standardandpoors.com*).

How Do You Choose Stocks for Capital Appreciation?

What's in It for You?

Publishers of stock research group stocks into different categories. This chapter explores how an investor can benefit from Morningstar's "types." We'll explore Value Line in the next chapter.

Contents

Financial Categories

In the last chapter, we saw how Standard & Poor's groups stocks into ten sectors. You can also categorize stocks by how well (or how poorly) the companies that issued the stocks are running their businesses. This type of categorization helps investors compare companies based on whether the company might be a good investment opportunity.

In this chapter, let's consider how you might use Morningstar's "types" to make stock selections for your portfolio. Keep in mind that the companies shown here may move from one type to another as business conditions change, as we will explore together later in this chapter under "Different Market Periods." *Be sure to update your research before making any decisions based on what you read in this chapter.*

Morningstar groups stocks into eight "types," going beyond sectors to examine how the stock might act and thus how the stock might benefit the investors. As you read the descriptions below, you'll find that some types sound attractive to you and others don't. For example, in order to benefit from a "Distressed" stock, you need to wait for a business turnaround— something you may not want to do. Perhaps "Classic Growth" stocks, the type that value investor Warren Buffett might favor, will pique your interest. (We explored Buffet's method of picking stocks in Chapter 13.)

Distressed

When Morningstar determines how to group companies by type, it starts with the most risky part of the market, Distressed stocks. These are companies that Morningstar feels have operating problems, such as negative earnings, high debt, and low debt coverage.

Signs of distress could signal that the company may go out of business or they may turn around. Morningstar excludes rapidly growing companies (revenues growing faster than 50 percent) from this type but includes them under "Speculative Growth," which we will discuss shortly.

Distressed stocks numbered 2,016 stocks, at the end of December 2010, representing 17.8 percent of the 11,358 stocks in the Morningstar database at the time. Examples of Distressed stocks at the end of December

2010 are: My Healthy Access (symbol: MYHA), MicroVision, Inc. (symbol: MVIS), and Newport Gold, Inc. (symbol: NWPG).

An investor wanting to buy a Distressed stock would have to believe the company would turn around. For those investors, Morningstar does recommend some stocks in the Distressed type—at the end of 2010, four stocks out of 2,016 earned five stars, an indication that the stock was trading below "fair value" and was thus potentially desirable to an investor.

Fair value is essentially an estimate of what the stock is really worth, the assumption being that you would want to buy stocks that are cheaper than the analyst's fair-value assessment. Morningstar calculates fair value based on a proprietary discounted-cash-flow model that forecasts ahead to three different time periods. In the second stage, Morningstar analysts look to the predictability and sustainability of a company's future profits—to establish whether there is a wide or narrow "economic moat," which is a Warren Buffet term. A wide moat is desirable since it indicates that the company has a basis for keeping competition at bay.

In December 2010, for example, four Distressed-type stocks earned a five-star rating, including Sprint Nextel Corporation (symbol: S) and Lexicon Pharmaceuticals, Inc. (symbol: LXRX). At the end of December 2010, four stocks received a one-star rating from Morningstar, indicating that the current stock price was above fair value. Sixty-six stocks received two, three, or four stars, and the rest (1,942 of 2,016) were unrated. Two examples of one-star-rated Distressed stocks (indicating a stock that Morningstar does not recommend at the time of the rating) at the end of December 2010 were Altus Pharmaceuticals, Inc. (symbol: ALTUQ) and BankAtlantic Bancorp (symbol: BBX).

Conservative investors would probably exclude even highly rated, five-star Distressed stocks from their "buy" lists unless they were willing to accept the risk of Distressed stocks.

High Yield

Next, Morningstar checks the remaining stocks that it follows and screens for high-dividend-paying stocks, which it types "High Yield" (67 stocks of 11,358 [2.5 percent] of the December 2010 database).

These are stocks that pay a dividend that is more than twice the average dividend for large cap stocks. The higher dividend can be due to the company paying out earnings instead of putting them to work. Excluded from this type are limited partnerships and "Hard Assets," which is a separate type.

High Yield stocks might appeal to investors who want to receive dividend income and participate in slow growth at the same time. Barnes & Noble (symbol: BKS, yielding 7.1 percent), Earthlink, Inc. (symbol: ELNK, yielding 7.2 percent), and World Wrestling Entertainment (symbol: WWE, yielding 10.1 percent) were a few Morningstar High Yield stocks at the end of December 2010. At the time, none of 199 stocks in the High Yield type held a five-star rating, and only one rated two stars: Windstream Corporation (symbol: WIN, yielding 7.2 percent). Fifty-nine of the sixty-seven High Yield stocks were unrated at the end of 2010.

Hard Asset

Then, Morningstar screens the remaining stocks for the following industries: precious metals, oil and gas, real estate investment trust (REITs), and other real estate companies, leaving out Distressed types. These stocks fall under the "Hard Asset" type, representing companies that have a below-average correlation to the overall stock market, which would make them suitable for diversification purposes according to Morningstar. Morningstar analysts believe Hard Asset types can be used in a portfolio as inflation hedges because of their low correlation to the overall stock market.

At the end of December 2010, there were 648 Hard Asset companies in Morningstar's database, representing 5.7 percent of the total. Examples of Hard Asset stocks are Chevron (symbol: CVX), Halliburton Company (symbol: HAL), and U.S. Gold Corporation (symbol: UXG).

Cyclical

Next, Morningstar screens for the Cyclical type—industrial cyclical and consumer durable stocks of companies whose profits are likely to be influenced by the overall direction of the economy. That is, if the economy is booming, these stocks will do well; if we are in a recession, "their growth stalls and they might even lose money," according to Morningstar.

At the end of December 2010, there were 3,675 Cyclical stocks in Morningstar's database, or 32.4 percent of the total. Examples are Amazon.com (symbol: AMZN), Motorola (symbol: MOT), and Netflix (symbol: NFLX).

Growth

The remaining stocks fall into the "Growth" type, which Morningstar splits into four subtypes, "Speculative Growth," "Aggressive Growth," "Classic Growth," and "Slow Growth." A more conservative investor might be attracted to Classic Growth or Slow Growth, while a more aggressive investor might like Speculative Growth and Aggressive Growth. All stocks in these subtypes are screened based on revenue and earnings growth, and sometimes dividend yield.

Speculative Growth

Speculative Growth stocks exhibit strong revenue growth (greater than four times the rate of gross domestic product [GDP] growth) but slower (or nonexistent) earnings growth (less than three times the rate of GDP growth). The Speculative Growth type also includes companies that had a recent IPO and companies whose annual revenues are less than $5 million.

These are companies that tend to be in the early phase of the growth cycle, where revenues are growing but earnings growth hasn't caught up. At best, profits are spotty, and at worst they are nonexistent, according to Morningstar.

As of the end of December 2010, 542 companies, or 4.8 percent, of the 11,358 in the Morningstar database met these criteria. At the time, Morningstar placed Aetna, Inc. (symbol: AET, yielding 0.1 percent) and Verizon Communications, Inc. (symbol: VZ, yielding 5.4 percent) into Speculative Growth.

Only fifteen paid a dividend, which ranged from 0.1 percent (Aetna Inc, symbol: AET) to 7.4 percent (StoneMar Partners LP, symbol: STON).

Aggressive Growth

Aggressive Growth companies exhibit strong sales and earnings growth, both growing faster than four times the rate of GDP growth. At the end of December 2010, 3.3 percent (378 companies of 11,358) in the Morningstar database were Aggressive Growth. Examples were Avon Products (symbol: AVP, yielding 3 percent) and Coca-Cola (symbol: KO, yielding 2.7 percent).

Of the 358 Aggressive Growth stocks at the end of August 2010, 106 paid a dividend ranging from 0.1 percent (Cooper Companies; symbol: COO) to 5.9 percent (NTELOS Holding Company; symbol: NTLS).

Classic Growth

Classic Growth companies need to exhibit long-term revenue and earnings growth and a "respectable dividend." Morningstar's December 2010 database listed 75 such companies (0.6 percent of the total).

To make the list, the company must have revenue growth of between one and four times GDP growth over the long term (at least three years). Earnings growth must be between one and five times the GDP. Plus, the company must have either good dividend growth over the trailing five years or a dividend yield that is between one-half and two times the average for large cap stocks.

At the end of December 2010, seventy-five stocks passed this screen out of 11,358 in the Morningstar database, but only fifty-one paid a dividend. Those that did pay a dividend yielded between 0.1 percent (Invacare Corporation; symbol: IVC) and 5.8 percent (UIL Holdings Corporation; symbol: UIL).

Other examples are AT&T (symbol: T, yielding 5.8 percent at the time), Procter & Gamble Company (symbol: PG, yielding 2.9 percent), and PepsiCo, Inc. (symbol: PEP, yielding 2.9 percent).

The Class Growth type might be of interest to more conservative retirees who want more stable stocks, especially if they pay dividends.

Slow Growth

Slow Growth companies have slow revenue growth, defined as less than GDP growth, and slow earnings growth, defined as less than two times GDP growth.

At December 2010, 811 stocks (7.2 percent) fell into the Slow Growth type; 225 paid a dividend ranging from 0.1 percent at the end of 2009 (Lincoln National Corp.; symbol: LNR) to 10.2 percent (PHC, Inc.; symbol: PHC). Other examples are Walt Disney Company (symbol: DIS, yielding 1.1 percent), Aflac (symbol: AFL, yielding 2 percent), and Nutrisystem (symbol: NTRI, yielding 3.3 percent).

Different Market Periods

During changing market periods, stocks move from one type to another based on how the company is fairing in that period's economic climate. Let's focus on three periods: (1) a market top and start of the 2000 decade (December 1999), (2) the market bottom of March 2009, and (3) the end of 2010.

Spend a few minutes studying Table 17-1, which shows the percentage representation of each type at these three points in time, as well as Graph 17-1, below, which shows you the data in graphical form.

Table 17-1. Distribution of Morningstar Types at December 1999, March 2009, and December 2010

Morningstar's 8 Types		End of 1999	End of 1999	Market Bottom 3/2009	Market Bottom 3/2009	End of 2010	End of 2010
		Count	% of Total	Count	% of Total	Count	% of Total
1	Distressed	775	10.5%	1,629	21.0%	2,016	24.5%
2	High Yield	1,790	24.1%	288	3.7%	67	0.8%
3	Hard Asset	558	7.5%	669	8.6%	648	7.9%
4	Cyclical	835	11.3%	1,587	20.5%	3,675	44.8%
5	Speculative Growth	1,442	19.4%	1,053	13.6%	542	6.6%
6	Aggressive Growth	618	8.3%	709	9.2%	378	4.6%
7	Classic Growth	600	8.1%	617	8.0%	75	0.9%
8	Slow Growth	797	10.7%	1,191	15.4%	811	9.9%
	Totals	7,415	100.0%	7,743	100.0%	8,212	100.0%

Graph 17-1 shows this data in graph form.

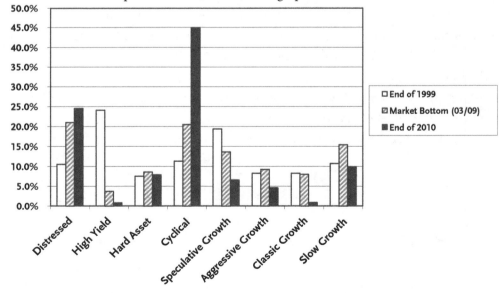

Graph 17-1. Distribution of Morningstar Types at December 1999, March 2009, and December 2010.

Notice that the biggest changes over the three periods occurred with Cyclical stocks, which one would expect. Cyclicals rise and fall with changing economic conditions. And indeed, Cyclicals moved from 11.3 percent (December 1999) to 20.5 percent (March 2009) to 44.8 percent (December 2010).

At the height of the Internet bubble (December 1999), only 10.5 percent of the Morningstar database assigned a type were Distressed. But at the March 2009 market bottom, Distressed stocks represented over 21 percent of the stocks in Morningstar's Principia database, rising slightly to 24.5 percent at December 2010.

High Yield stocks represented the largest percentage of stocks (24.1 percent) at the top of the market and the smallest at the bottom (3.7 percent in March 2009) and even less (0.8 percent) in December 2010.

The number of Classic Growth stocks did not drop from the top in 1999 (600 stocks) to the market bottom of March 2009 (617 stocks), but did drop (to 75) by the end of 2010.

These trends are depicted in Graph 17-2, below.

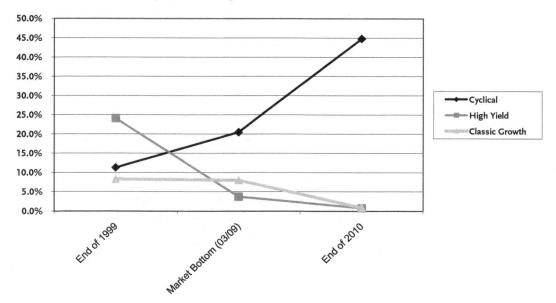

Graph 17-2. Cyclical Trends.

Keep in mind that these changes in types over time are not necessarily reflective of returns.

Aging Process of Types

Using this method of looking at stocks (typing) leads to the question of what an investor can expect as a company matures or ages. Morningstar's senior staff writer Haywood Kelly offered these insights on the topic:

Baby Steps: Speculative Growth

Don't expect consistency from Speculative Growth companies. At best their profits are spotty. At worst they lose money. In fact, many companies never make it beyond Speculative Growth, going instead to bankruptcy court. That's why they're speculative. But current profitability isn't what interests us about Speculative Growth companies. It's future profits. Hopefully, a Speculative Growth company will eventually blossom into a world-class company.

The Awkward Age: Aggressive Growth

Aggressive Growth companies show a bit more maturity than their Speculative Growth counterparts: they post rapid growth in profits, not just in sales—a sign of more staying power. At this point, it's time to make some money.

Prime of Life: Classic Growth

Now we come to firms in their prime—firms with little left to prove. The best classic growers have blossomed into money machines, churning out steady growth, high returns on capital, positive free cash flows, and rising dividends. The catch is, their growth is nowhere near that of the aggressive-growth group.

Senior Citizens: Slow Growth and High Yield

These are the companies whose growth is a fading memory. Having run out of attractive investment opportunities, most of them pay out the bulk of their earnings in dividends—expect high payout ratios—rather than plow the profits back into their business.

Aging Process Conclusion

While there may be an aging process for companies, there's not one for stocks. An investor like Warren Buffet has focused on finding great stocks in and around the Classic Growth category—Peter Lynch was more eclectic, investing in everything from speculative growth to slow growth. . . . Most of us would want a smattering of companies from across the spectrum. By putting each company in context, paying special attention to how it measures up against others in its age bracket, we can do just that. It's one kind of age discrimination that makes eminent sense.

Summary

Morningstar's eight "types" are a way to categorize stocks according to how they might behave. The types include the riskiest stocks (Distressed), those paying high dividends (High Yield), and those that generally perform counter to the economy (Hard Asset) and with the economy (Cyclical). The remaining four types fall into the broad "Growth" category and include riskier subtypes (Speculative and Aggressive) and more conservative stocks (Classic and Slow). Investors looking for capital appreciation need to consider their tolerance for risk when evaluating stocks with growth characteristics.

Key Points

1. When considering how to select stocks, it helps to start with categories, such as Morningstar's types.
2. Some investors with a higher tolerance for risk may be drawn to more aggressive stocks that can be home runs in the right circumstances, or big losses in the wrong circumstances.
3. More conservative investors might be attracted to Classic Growth or Slow Growth stocks.

Steps to Take

1. Review the stock types. Given your investment strategy, pick one or two types that appeal to you for further research.
2. Choose a few stocks of that type for further research.
3. Review your current holdings using Morningstar's type classifications. Are there any surprises?

Selling Rules and Selection Criteria

CHAPTER 18

What's in It for You?

This chapter will introduce you to two types of selling rules, those based on price alone and those based on selection criteria, using Value Line as a resource.

Contents

Background

Irrespective of the type of instrument you are buying to meet your investment objectives, you need to know how to take two types of actions: when to buy and when to sell. It is easier to buy than to sell, and in fact, many people avoid selling because they have not developed their selling skills. In this chapter, let's discuss how you might develop your own selling discipline. There is probably no other aspect of investing that is more affected by the personality and character of the individual. Even professional money managers differ in how they approach selling—there are no universal standards or hard-and-fast rules.

What Is a Selling Rule

A selling rule is a disciplined plan of action that you have in place *before* you buy an investment; the rule defines the circumstances under which you will sell the investment. Having a selling discipline distinguishes the serious investor from the casual investor. It may be the single most important skill to have if you are investing your own money, particularly if you are investing your retirement assets. And, it will prevent you from convincing yourself that you are on the road to making money when you are not—some investments need to be sold because they will not recover.

In this chapter we'll talk about two types of selling rules for stocks: those based on price alone and those based on the original selection criteria.

Price Rules

"Buy low and sell high" is an example of a simple selling rule. The concept underlying the rule is a good one: to make a profit in a stock, you have to sell it at a higher price than you paid for it. Beyond that, the rule has little use and in fact may be harmful if it causes you to think you can make profits only if you buy stocks that are depressed in price. Some stocks decline for a reason: earnings don't support a higher price. Moreover, this selling rule might give you a false sense of security that you actually have a selling discipline.

"Sell your losers and let your profits ride" is an improvement over the first rule. Since you need to sell at a profit to make money, this rule sets an objective without implying that you need to buy undervalued stocks. It adds another element, that of selling losing positions. Here you have a sense of the two essential elements of an effective selling rule: to make money, you must not only take advantage of rising stock prices, but also protect your assets by selling those positions that put you in jeopardy. A further refinement is, "Cut your losses and take your profits."

However, all of these rules fall short of the approach you need to develop for yourself because they don't spell out exactly what you should do after your purchase. Your selling rule needs to help you do two things: (1) protect you from large losses as we've discussed and (2) realize a profit. Let's look at a different type of rule that sets a selling point.

Limiting Losses

One popular selling rule is to limit losses at some percentage point below your purchase price, say 7 to 10 percent. Let's call this type of selling rule a "basis stop" because you calculate the percentage based on your purchase price or cost basis. For example, you buy a stock at $100 a share. If the stock drops 10 percent to $90 a share, you sell.

This type of selling rule helps protect you from serious losses if you apply it religiously to each of your holdings. Theoretically, if executed properly, the basis stop limits your losses to 10 percent of the value of your overall stock portfolio at any point in time.

The basis stop is a big improvement over a fuzzy rule such as "buy low and sell high" since it actually tells you when to get out of a stock. But it does not go far enough because it misses the other side of the coin, profit taking. Remember that the purpose of a selling discipline is not just to protect your downside, but also to take a profit.

Trailing Stop

One way to structure a profit-taking selling rule is to continue to raise the point at which you will sell as the stock rises in price. That's a "trailing stop"—one that floats up with rising stock prices.

Putting the basis stop together with the trailing stop, you might state your selling rule as, "Cut losses with a basis stop, and take profits with a trailing stop." This gives you a basic framework on which to build a selling discipline.

The basis stop is easy. Setting the trailing stop is harder, since you have to keep adjusting it if the stock is actually going up in price. To make things easier for themselves, some people take some of their profits when they make say, 10 percent or 15 percent above their purchase price. The disadvantage of doing that is selling out before a big move in a stock. There is another option, the "conditional order."

Conditional Orders

None of this discussion will be of any value unless you can actually come up with a system that works for you. It takes some thought about what you are trying to achieve, how often you review your holdings, and how much time you have to focus on these issues on a regular basis. Part of the time commitment depends on how you select stocks and how much risk you are taking on.

While these selling rules are not orders, they actually could be placed as such at the time you buy the stock. Some online brokerage firms offer the ability to place conditional orders to accomplish what we've discussed, including a trailing stop.

I caution you to find out the specifics of how those orders execute. Some conditional orders turn into market orders when the price is triggered and some do not. Be vigilant. Read about the trade execution policy of your brokerage firm and be sure to understand under what circumstances the trade will be executed and when it might not. For example, on the May 6, 2010, flash crash, when the markets fell dramatically over a period of minutes, conditional orders that turned to market orders triggered sales at lower prices before the market righted itself minutes later. For that reason, some investors don't enter conditional orders that execute automatically. To start on your research of discount brokers who offer conditional orders, see the Resources section at the end of the book.

Stock Selection and Deselection

Up until now, we've been discussing a selling discipline based on price alone, which is arbitrary in a sense—you pick a percentage above or below the stock price as it moves up and down without regard to fundamental changes in the underlying business represented by the stock.

Let's consider how you could set selling rules based on your selection criteria, which incorporates the concepts we discussed in Parts 3 and 4 of the book in connection with the setting of an investment policy for your portfolio.

Value Line

In this section, I explain how a possible investment policy can be structured using Value Line as a resource. First, let's review how Value Line rankings work.

Value Line's print publication reports on about 100 industries and 1,700 stocks and ranks stocks for purchase criteria, such as timeliness, safety, and technical rankings. The software version reports on 6,000 stocks and includes small and mid-cap stocks as well.

According to Value Line, its highest-ranked stocks have outperformed its lowest ranked stocks for over forty five years, but not every year. These rankings are based on various fundamental and technical conclusions the Value Line proprietary analysis draws about the stocks and are a form of future assessment of how the stocks will do over time. As such, these rankings can be a helpful start to further research. Let me describe the rankings first, and then, let's discuss how you might use them.

Timeliness

"Timeliness" is Value Line's proprietary assessment of the expected price performance of a stock or industry over the next six to twelve months. Value Line determines stock timeliness based on items such as relative earnings and price growth over the prior ten years.

The top 100 stocks are ranked highest (timeliness rank of 1) for expected relative price performance over the next six to twelve months; 300 stocks are ranked 2 (above average); approximately 900 are ranked 3 for average; approximately 300 are ranked 4 for below average; and 100 are ranked 5 for lowest. Stocks ranked 1 and 2 are expected by Value Line to perform better than the rest. Those ranked 4 or 5 have underperformed ranks 1, 2, and 3 in the past, and Value Line expects them to underperform in the future. Ranks are re-evaluated weekly. In addition, Value Line ranks about 100 industry sectors for timeliness by averaging the timeliness ranks of the individual stocks within those industries.

Safety

Value Line also ranks stocks according to safety, with a rank of 1 expected to be the safest, that is, the least volatile and most financially strong, and a rank of 5 being the least safe.

Technical Rank

Then, there is the technical rank. Ranked 1 (highest) to 5 (lowest) based on an analysis of the stock's relative price performance during the prior fifty-two weeks, the technical rank projects the stock's expected price performance relative to the overall market over the next three to six months. The technical rank would be useful to an investor with a short-term horizon and is best used in concert with the timeliness and safety ranks.

Sample Investment Policy

Here is an example of a selection strategy using Value Line rankings. This is not a recommendation, but merely illustrates how you could create an investment policy that includes both selection and deselection criteria using a tool such as Value Line. The investment policy can guide your actions as an investor and take some of the mystery out of when to buy and when to sell.

Sample Investment Policy Statement

Objective: Aggressive growth

Diversification: Ten to twelve stocks in six or more industries

Leverage: None: cash account (no margin)

Industry: Timeliness rank of 1 to 5 (Industry timeliness runs from 1 to 98.)

Stocks: Timeliness rank of 1; safety rank of 1 or 2; technical rank of 1 or 2

Deselection Criteria: Sell when any one or more of the rankings (timeliness, safety, or technical) declines below your initial selection criteria

---

When coming up with your own investment policy, you want to consider when to place an order to buy or sell as well as how often you will look at the portfolio to make your buy and sell determinations, and, if you are using margin, options, or futures, how you will control the extra risk you are assuming.

Key Points

1. If you want to set up selling rules based on price alone, you can set arbitrary limits on the upside and the downside, with a basis stop to protect against severe losses and a trailing stop to protect profits.

2. If you want to use an investment policy approach, you can set rules for deselection that will take you out of a stock when it no longer meets your selection criteria.

3. Or, you can combine the two methods, or develop one of your own based on other criteria, such as technical indicators.

Steps to Take

1. Create your own selling rules based on price.

2. Draft an investment policy statement using the Value Line example as a model.

3. Determine the manner by which and the frequency with which you will monitor your portfolio holdings.

CHAPTER 19

Selecting Stock Mutual Funds

What's in It for You?

This chapter will help you do three things: (1) see how mutual funds can simplify your goal of meeting your investment objectives, (2) improve your ability to make good mutual fund selections based on recognizing red flags and avoiding mistakes, and (3) understand how ETFs and bear funds can be used for hedging.

Contents

Matching Up Investment Objectives

The nice thing about mutual funds is that they are structured to match investors' objectives. There are essentially three types of mutual funds: (1) stock funds, with the objective of growing your capital; (2) bond or fixed-income funds, with the objective of income; and (3) money market funds for stability of principal. (You can also have a hybrid fund that combines stocks and bonds.)

If your objective is growth of capital, the fund you are looking for needs to have the same objective: growth of capital (or a variation of that goal, such as "capital appreciation," or "long-term growth," or "aggressive growth"). Funds with a growth objective invest in stocks.

If your objective is income, you'll be looking for funds that have an "income" objective. Funds with an income objective invest in bonds. Variations include tax-free municipal bond funds, taxable bond funds, international bond funds, high-yield bonds, and so on. They can be sliced and diced by yield, duration, average maturity, credit risk, and other features based on how their portfolios are structured. In addition, you can find funds that invest in both stocks and bonds (called hybrid funds). Hybrid funds can help with both objectives (income and growth).

The investment objective of money market mutual funds is to preserve your capital. (Discussed in Chapter 15.)

In this chapter, we'll focus on selecting stock mutual funds for your growth objective; however, our discussion will also apply to any type of mutual fund.

How Not to Pick a Fund

I'm always amazed when people think that selecting mutual funds is simply a matter of picking top-of-the-chart performers. If you need to convince yourself of why this is not a good idea, all you have to do is look at history.

Take the top-performing "aggressive growth" fund (investment objective) for the beginning of the 2000 decade. If you are a mutual fund junkie, you might remember reading about this small capitalization fund, the Van Wagoner Emerging Growth Fund. It delivered a return of 291 percent in 1999, outperforming the averages by a tremendous margin. In comparison, the benchmark index (the S&P SmallCap 600 Growth Index) clocked in at only 20 percent, according to Morningstar Principia. The broad market, as measured by the S&P 500 Index, returned 21 percent that year.

The fund showed excellent rankings compared to its peers. It ranked in the top 10 percent (#1 decile) for funds in its Morningstar category (Small Blend) for one year, three months, six months, and three years. Morningstar gave the fund its highest rating, five stars. That meant the fund scored in the top 10 percent of all funds in its asset class (Domestic Stock) for returns relative to risk taken ("risk-adjusted returns"). This was clearly a fund that might have attracted your attention if selected based on performance.

However, if you actually bought shares of the fund, you would have been disappointed. You would have lost 21 percent in 2000, 60 percent in 2001, and 65 percent in 2002. Your $10,000 invested in January 2000 would have been worth $1,129 by the end of 2002. In comparison, you would have had $6,239 if you had made a comparable investment in an S&P 500 Index fund. And, if you had made a comparable investment of $10,000 in an S&P SmallCap Growth Index fund, your investment would have been worth $9,248 by the end of 2002.

Could you have spotted potential warning signs before making a purchase? Yes, if you were willing to dig for information.

Performance Was Erratic

This fund's performance was at the bottom of its peer's before gaining momentum in its one big year (1999). Not only was performance erratic before the big run up, but asset declines were not in line with performance, which meant that shareholders fled during bad periods.

The fund performed at the bottom of its peers in 1997, losing 20 percent, but assets declined more sharply, falling more than 50 percent from 1996 ($638 million) to 1997 ($313 million). Assets fell again the following year by about 40 percent (to $189 million), while the fund's returns were disappointing (the fund made 8 percent, far below what the S&P 500 Index delivered that year).

Then came 1999. The fund made 291 percent and leaped in assets (from $189 million to $1.3 billion). This was a fund that seemed to attract investors in good times and lose them in bad times.

Sector Bets

As of June of 1999, the fund was heavily invested in technology (42 percent) and services (21 percent). And, the fund made big bets in individual holdings: almost 17 percent was invested in only two stocks.

Very High Turnover

The fund's turnover ratio was the highest in Morningstar's Small Blend category at a whopping 668 percent. To put things in perspective, the next highest turnover ratio was 45 percent. Turnover is a measure of trading activity, representing the percentage of holdings that changed over the year. Funds with higher turnover have more trading activity and, as a result, have higher trading costs and higher capital gains distributions, which are taxable.

Very High Standard Deviation

The three-year standard deviation for the fund (70.8) was the highest for the category and among the highest in the entire Morningstar database. The next highest standard deviation was 45 for the category. Standard deviation measures how returns vary over time. The higher the standard deviation, the greater the volatility.

Analyst's Cautionary Report

Finally, although Morningstar gave it a thumbs-up with a five-star rating, a closer read of the analyst's report made it clear it was not for everyone: "Clearly, this fund is only appropriate for the most aggressive investors, and then it is best relegated to a niche role in a broader portfolio."

Lessons

There are three lessons investors should take away from this example:

1. Performance rankings are based on what other investors experienced in the past, not what you can expect if you invest after the fact.
2. Ratings are only a starting point. Morningstar cautions that its "rating is only the first step toward a more comprehensive evaluation."
3. Choosing good funds, like choosing good stocks, is not as simple as it may seem.

Your first step is deciding whether you want to shoot for the moon or be satisfied (and comforted) with a well-managed middle-of-the-road performer, which is less volatile and thus more likely to deliver more consistent returns year in and year out. That's my definition of a good fund.

Key Characteristics of Good Funds

In the following section, we'll go through the characteristics you need to look for in a good fund.

Avoid Extremes

When selecting funds, or any investment for that matter, you need to know what you don't want. Weed out funds that have high turnover, high standard deviation, high costs, high sector weightings, large positions in a few individuals stocks, erratic performance (top of the charts one year, bottom of the charts another), and, believe it or not, extraordinary performance. In each instance, you will want to compare the fund's data points against those of other funds in the same category, for example, small cap growth funds.

Select for Good Management

Funds that are managed well exhibit some common characteristics. Long-term investors will want to look for consistent performers that travel in the middle of the pack. Look for low fees (we'll discuss costs later in the chapter). Look for management longevity and experience. Look for a large institution backing up the fund, generally limiting your investments in very small fund complexes. Ultimately, what you want to find is management skill, consistency of performance, and most important, a reasonable expectation that performance will be repeated.

Some research publications rate fund managers. For example, Morningstar grades fund managers for "stewardship." The grade assesses intangibles based on Morningstar's analysts' evaluations of five factors: regulatory history, board quality, manager incentives, fees, and corporate culture. The grades are based on information compiled from public filings and the expertise of Morningstar's fund analysts.

In terms of fees, for example, some managers are paid incentives if they produce short-term performance. They are viewed less favorably under Morningstar's system than those who encourage long-term performance. Having a board led by an independent chairman is viewed positively.

Finding Extraordinary Performers

Aggressive investors might ask, just how do you find a fund that might outperform others? As we discussed, you won't find them in the rearview mirror. You can occasionally stumble on one by sheer luck.

If outperformance is your goal, let me tell you how to go about the research process. You'll have to commit to studying both underachievers and overachievers in different types of markets. Plan to spend quite a bit of time. See if you can identify characteristics such as those we've been discussing (turnover, standard deviation, etc.).

Once you have identified the key components, don't use your own money to test your system—do that with mock trades and be sure to work out a practical way of applying your selling rules (which we discussed in Chapter 18). These funds will be high-momentum, high-relative-strength performers that can drop as quickly as they advance. You can apply the same methodology to stock selection. Software, such as Steele Systems, Value Line and Morningstar, will be helpful.

Next Steps

After you've found some funds that interest you, you'll need to read the prospectus, which is the legally mandated document that describes the manager, what he is trying to achieve with the fund, and what you need to know before becoming a shareholder of the fund.

Tips on How to Read a Prospectus

Having had experience writing mutual fund prospectuses, I can give you some hints on how to tackle the job of reading one. First, don't be intimidated. Follow this very simple rule and you'll find all you need: compare and contrast. That is, don't try to read just one prospectus at a time. Always have two at hand.

Start with the contents. Compare them. You'll notice similarities. For example, every prospectus contains information about the fund's manager and the goal he is setting out to accomplish with the fund (investment objectives), how he gets paid, how an investor can buy shares of the fund, risk, and performance.

Let's focus on just three important items together.

First, you'll want to be sure the fund's objectives line up with yours. As we discussed in the beginning of this chapter, if you are investing for growth, you need to focus on funds that attempt to meet that objective.

Second, you'll want to read about risk, and you'll want to understand how promises are delivered.

Be on the lookout for techniques that are meant to enhance performance, such as leverage, and be sure to understand not only how these techniques work, but also when they can work against you.

For example, FINRA, the body that regulates brokers, issued a special notice called an "Investor Alert" warning investors about tradable leveraged inverse mutual funds (ETFs).

Quoting from the alert:

> Leveraged inverse ETFs (also known as "ultra short" funds) seek to achieve a return that is a multiple of the inverse performance of the underlying index. An inverse ETF that tracks a particular index, for example, seeks to deliver the inverse of the performance of that index, while a 2x (two times) leveraged inverse ETF seeks to deliver double the opposite of that index's performance. To accomplish their objectives, leveraged and inverse ETFs pursue a range of investment strategies through the use of swaps, futures contracts, and other derivative instruments.
>
> Most leveraged and inverse ETFs "reset" daily, meaning that they are designed to achieve their stated objectives on a daily basis. Their performance over longer periods of time—over weeks or months or years—can differ significantly from the performance (or inverse of the performance) of their underlying index or benchmark during the same period of time. This effect can be magnified in volatile markets. . . . [A]n ETF that is set up to deliver twice the performance of a benchmark from the close of trading on Day 1 to the close of trading on Day 2 will not necessarily achieve that goal over weeks, months, or years.

If you don't read the prospectus, which provides this type of information, misunderstandings can arise.

Third, compare costs. Consider (1) the cost to buy fund shares, (2) the cost to hold (or own) them, and (3) the cost to sell ("redeem") shares of the fund.

Some funds, not all, charge a fee to buy and sell shares. All funds have a cost to own—these are the costs of legal expenses, accounting fees, and the costs of printing prospectuses, managing the fund, paying for shareholder services, and the like.

Cost to Buy

The cost to buy shares is the commission ("load"), which can be as low as zero or as high as 8.5 percent of your investment, but only if you invest small amounts. Usually, the load is reduced if you invest higher amounts and eventually goes to zero. The load comes off the top; it reduces the amount of your money that is actually invested in the fund. A "no-load" fund is one whose cost to buy is zero.

Cost to Own

The cost to own the shares is the "total operating expense," which may include a fee ("12b-1 fee") usually paid by the fund to brokers for servicing shareholders. The average total operating expense for all funds in the Morningstar database is over 1.5 percent per year as of March 2011 (including all share classes but excluding money market funds and index funds). You don't see this cost—a daily factor reduces your share price on a daily basis.

Cost to Sell

The cost to redeem, or sell, shares can be a "redemption fee" or a "contingent deferred sales charge" (CDSC). The CDSC can be as high as 6 percent, decreasing to zero over a few years. That is, if you own a fund with a CDSC that starts out at 6 percent, your CDSC may come down to zero if you hold onto the fund long enough (past the deferral period).

Share Classes

If the prospectus mentions share classes, be sure to compare them to each other. They have different costs to buy, own, and redeem. Let me give you an illustration. Amy sold her house for $800,000. She gave the check to her broker, telling him that she wanted to invest in a no-load mutual fund, insisting that she did not want to pay him a commission or load (cost to buy). The broker offered her a Class B mutual fund with no sales charge. Amy received a prospectus, but she did not read it.

Not too long after that, Amy found a new home she wanted to purchase. She called the broker, only to find out that she had to absorb a penalty of 5 percent to get her money out of the Class B fund due to a "contingent deferred sales charge" (CDSC) of $40,000.

Pricing Knowledge

Amy had not paid a load to buy the Class B shares. But, Class B shares came with a CDSC at the time of redemption. In addition, owning them cost about twice as much in total operating expenses (1.6 percent for Class B shares versus 0.7 percent per year for Class A shares), as described in the prospectus.

The Class A shares had a cost to buy of 2 percent. For Amy, 2 percent of $800,000 would have been $16,000. Since brokers are paid between 40 and 90 percent of the commission, Amy's broker would have been paid between $6,400 to $14,400 for the Class A shares, depending on his firm's arrangement with him. In comparison, the broker instead garnered between $16,000 and $36,000 on the Class B share purchase (40 to 90 percent of $40,000, which is 5 percent of $800,000).

Cost Calculator

For more help on understanding share classes and costs, you can use a cost calculator that you can find online at *www.sec.gov*. Look for the "Mutual Fund Cost Calculator."

When to Sell

When you are reviewing your mutual fund holdings to determine if you should hold onto them or sell them, you'll want to compare performance to their peers—funds that have similar investment objectives. You want to compare stock funds with stock funds, bond funds with bond funds, and money market funds with money market funds. In fact, you want to slice even finer. If you own a technology fund, you will *not* want to compare it with a large cap value fund, even though both are stock funds.

Start with performance figures for the most recent period. Compare your fund with other funds that have the same investment objective and category. After you buy a fund, you have to watch it.

Red Flags

While we will discuss monitoring in Chapters 20 and 21, there is something extra that you need to do when reviewing your mutual funds. You'll need to watch two trends: assets and expenses. If your fund's expenses start to trend upward while assets trend downward, that's a huge red flag. If you find yourself in that situation, consider getting out.

ETFs

We can't leave the subject of mutual funds without discussing exchange-traded funds (ETFs). These are mutual funds that trade like stocks throughout the trading day (mutual funds are purchased and redeemed, at "net asset value," not traded). ETFs have become popular vehicles for investors who want low-cost participation in broad market index funds.

The oldest ETF established in 1993 by State Street Global Advisors and the American Stock Exchange is the Standard & Poor's Depository Receipt Trust, or SPDR (ticker: SPY). It actually holds all 500 shares of the S&P 500 Index and mimics the performance of the index. Shares of the fund trade on NYSE Arca just like other stocks.

Recently ETFs have also been set up as managed funds. State Street Global Advisors maintains a robust educational website at *www.spdrs.com*. Start your research there. You can also explore the "Funds Curriculum" at *Morningstar.com*'s Investing Classroom.

Hedging with Funds

You may be interested in using long-short funds, bear funds, or inverse ETFs from time to time or all the time, to add noncorrelated assets to your portfolio—a form of hedging that we discussed in Chapter 7. And indeed this can be a good strategy if you are a very experienced investor, as long as you accept the job of monitoring your holdings closely and frequently. The theory is that adding noncorrelated assets to a portfolio can lessen the volatility and risk of the portfolio, as we discussed in Chapter 5. The higher the correlation between investment options, the more likely the investments will act the same. Choosing lower correlated assets for a portfolio will help dampen volatility and, if used correctly and carefully, potentially improve returns.

Inverse ETFs

An inverse S&P 500 Index fund seeks to deliver the inverse of the S&P 500 Index on a day-to-day basis. For example, Short S&P 500 (ticker: SH) seeks to return 1 percent on a day that SPY loses 1 percent. The correlation does not hold over time, however, because of compounding, as explained in the fund's prospectus. Before buying an inverse ETF, you might want to reread the Investor Alert earlier in the chapter in the section "How to Read a Prospectus." Use inverse ETFs with caution.

Long-Short Funds

Long-short funds buy stocks they think are going up in price and sell short those stocks they think are going down. Short positions are much more risky than long positions, and as a result, these funds are not for neophytes.

You might think that long-short funds can provide profits through good and bad markets. As you can see from Table 19-1 below, you'll notice that's not necessarily the case. If you study the returns for 2008, the year the S&P 500 Index fell by 37 percent, you'll notice that only two funds (#9 and #21 in Table 19-1) had positive returns that year. However, most lost less than the market in 2008. (The bottom row of Table 19-1 compares an S&P 500 Index fund.)

Table 19-1. Morningstar Category: Long-Short Funds 2010

	Fund Name	Ticker	Annual Return 2010 (%)	Annual Return 2009 (%)	Annual Return 2008 (%)	Annual Return 2007 (%)
1	Aberdeen Equity Long-Short C	MLSCX	3.9	6.6	−14.6	14.3
2	Absolute Strategies I	ASFIX	4.2	18.5	−13.5	5.1
3	Autopilot Managed Growth Inv	AUTOX	−4.8	-8.2	−17.9	22.1
4	Bull Path Long Short I	BPFIX	−4.3	9.6	−23.0	12.1
5	Calamos Market Neutral Income A	CVSIX	4.9	13.8	−13.3	5.9
6	Caldwell & Orkin Market Opportunity	COAGX	−1.0	−3.4	−4.7	33.1
7	Diamond Hill Long-Short A	DIAMX	−0.3	17.9	−23.7	3.1
8	Direxion Evolution All-Cap Equity Inv	PEVEX	−0.1	-5.5	−25.3	3.2
9	Driehaus Active Income	LCMAX	5.2	22.1	0.4	1.4
10	Dunham Monthly Distribution A	DAMDX	9.6	9.0	−23.3	1.7
11	Gateway A	GATEX	4.8	6.6	−13.9	7.9

	Fund Name	Ticker	Annual Return 2010 (%)	Annual Return 2009 (%)	Annual Return 2008 (%)	Annual Return 2007 (%)
12	Glenmede Long/ Short	GTAPX	3.6	−0.1	−12.1	−0.8
13	Hatteras Alpha Hedged Strategies	ALPHX	4.5	19.0	−31.6	8.2
14	Hatteras Beta Hedged Strategies	BETAX	5.2	23.3	−37.0	10.4
15	Highland Long/ Short Equity A	HEOAX	4.7	18.1	−10.5	8.4
16	Hussman Strategic Growth	HSGFX	−3.6	4.6	−9.0	4.2
17	ICON Long/ Short I	IOLIX	3.0	14.9	−39.9	9.0
18	Janus Long/ Short C	JCLSX	2.2	3.4	−24.4	15.4
19	Nakoma Absolute Return	NARFX	−5.6	−9.1	−4.3	15.1
20	Old Mutual Analytic Z	ANDEX	6.4	4.8	−33.8	1.7
21	Purisima All-Purpose	PURLX	−1.0	0.8	4.0	6.8
22	Quaker Akros Absolute Strategies A	AARFX	2.1	13.9	−2.9	−0.5
23	Quaker Event Arbitrage A	QEAAX	7.5	27.8	−25.7	0.0
24	Quaker Long-Short Tactical Allc A	QLSAX	−12.0	−14.7	−19.0	15.1
25	RAM Risk-Managed Growth I	RAMIX	1.0	16.1	−18.1	9.9
26	Robeco Long/ Short Eq I	BPLSX	26.4	82.4	−21.2	−4.2
27	Rydex-SGI Alpha Opportunity A	SAOAX	23.5	24.6	−35.1	18.1

	Fund Name	Ticker	Annual Return 2010 (%)	Annual Return 2009 (%)	Annual Return 2008 (%)	Annual Return 2007 (%)
28	Rydex-SGI Multi-Hedge Strategies H	RYMSX	5.3	−2.7	−18.2	4.0
29	Schwab Hedged Equity	SWHEX	6.6	15.9	−20.5	−1.2
30	Sound Mind Investing Managed Volatility	SMIVX	9.3	12.3	−27.4	12.9
31	SSgA Directional Core Equity Instl	SDCQX	3.5	13.7	−22.5	−5.4
32	Virtus AlphaSector Allocation A	PSWAX	12.6	22.4	−26.5	6.7
33	Wasatch-1st Source Long/Short	FMLSX	9.4	30.1	−20.9	5.0
34	Wegener Adaptive Growth	WAGFX	0.7	41.2	−10.8	12.0
	Average		4.0	13.2	−18.8	7.7
	Median		4.0	13.7	−19.8	6.7
	Maximum		26.4	82.4	4.0	33.1
	Minimum		−12.0	−14.7	−39.9	−5.4
	Compare:					
	An S&P 500 Index Fund		14.9	26.5	−37.0	5.4

Long-short funds may be worth further study for even the more cautious investor as a diversifier in the portfolio. They are intended as long-term purchases, unlike inverse ETFs and bear funds, both of which require a conviction that the market is heading south.

Bear Funds

You might think that adding a bear fund to your portfolio might offset bad market periods, and indeed that may be the case if you can anticipate a bear and get out at the right time. In reviewing Table 19-2 below, you should conclude that if you do pursue this strategy, you'll want to be sure to have very tightly established selling rules that get you out when the market rights itself. While the majority of the bear funds had strong performance in 2008, most quickly turned negative in 2009 as the market recaptured positive territory, and ended the year with a positive 26.5 percent return.

Table 19-2. Morningstar Category: Bear Funds 2010

	Fund Name	Ticker	Annual Return 2010 (%)	Annual Return 2009 (%)	Annual Return 2008 (%)	Annual Return 2007 (%)
1	Access Flex Bear High Yield Inv	AFBIX	−20.2	−19.6	0.0	0.6
2	Comstock Capital Value A	DRCVX	−20.6	−31.1	54.3	0.9
3	Direxion High Yield Bear Inv	PHBRX	−12.0	−18.2	7.7	−0.7
4	Direxion Mthly 10 Year Note Bear 2X	DXKSX	−18.0	17.4	−39.2	−12.3
5	Direxion Mthly Dev Mkts Bear 2X	DXDSX	−29.9	−55.0	43.5	−16.6
6	Direxion Mthly Dollar Bear 2X Inv	DXDDX	−5.3	9.1	−15.0	23.5
7	Direxion Mthly Emerg Mkts Bear 2X	DXESX	−39.9	−80.1	−22.7	−52.9
8	Direxion Mthly NASDAQ-100 Bear 2X Inv	DXQSX	−42.3	−74.5	84.5	−36.3
9	Direxion Mthly S&P 500 Bear 2X Inv	DXSSX	−33.7	−59.0	58.7	−8.6
10	Direxion Mthly Small Cap Bear 2X	DXRSX	−50.1	−69.1	11.7	−2.5
11	Federated Prudent Bear A	BEARX	−13.2	−18.5	26.9	13.4

	Fund Name	Ticker	Annual Return 2010 (%)	Annual Return 2009 (%)	Annual Return 2008 (%)	Annual Return 2007 (%)
12	Grizzly Short	GRZZX	−23.2	−47.2	73.7	6.6
13	PIMCO StocksPLUS TR Short Strat Instl	PSTIX	−8.5	−13.9	48.6	6.4
14	ProFunds Bear Inv	BRPIX	−17.4	−28.0	39.8	0.9
15	ProFunds Rising Rates Opp 10 Investor	RTPIX	−10.0	6.6	−17.8	−.2
16	ProFunds Rising Rates Opp Inv	RRPIX	−15.9	32.7	−37.7	−4.9
17	ProFunds Short NASDAQ-100 Inv	SOPIX	−21.4	−40.6	45.4	−11.7
18	ProFunds Short Oil & Gas Inv	SNPIX	−22.8	−25.9	12.1	−23.9
19	ProFunds Short Precious Metals Inv	SPPIX	−33.8	−43.1	−19.9	−22.6
20	ProFunds Short Real Estate Inv	SRPIX	−28.7	−51.8	−5.2	23.7
21	ProFunds Short Small Cap Inv	SHPIX	−28.3	−32.9	23.7	5.1
22	ProFunds UltraBear Inv	URPIX	−33.1	−51.7	65.0	−4.6
23	ProFunds UltraShort Dow 30 Inv	UWPIX	−31.4	−45.6	44.1	−9.0
24	ProFunds UltraShort Emerg Mkt Inv	UVPIX	−35.9	−77.1	13.6	−61.4
25	ProFunds UltraShort Intl Inv	UXPIX	−32.0	−55.6	46.3	−16.0
26	ProFunds UltraShort Japan Inv	UKPIX	−10.8	−41.5	32.8	21.8
27	ProFunds UltraShort Mid-Cap Inv	UIPIX	−46.8	−62.8	47.3	−9.5

	Fund Name	Ticker	Annual Return 2010 (%)	Annual Return 2009 (%)	Annual Return 2008 (%)	Annual Return 2007 (%)
28	ProFunds UltraShort NASDAQ-100 Inv	USPIX	−39.3	−67.0	80.8	−27.7
29	ProFunds UltraShort Small Cap Inv	UCPIX	−51.2	−61.2	23.0	1.9
30	ProShares Short Dow30	DOG	−15.3	−23.7	31.1	−1.3
31	ProShares Short MidCap400	MYY	−25.4	−35.1	34.5	−0.7
32	ProShares Short QQQ	PSQ	−20.6	−40.2	46.6	−11.4
33	ProShares Short S&P500	SH	−16.6	−27.0	39.2	1.4
34	ProShares UltraShort Dow30	DXD	−29.8	−45.0	47.5	−8.7
35	ProShares UltraShort MidCap400	MZZ	−46.2	−62.1	49.5	−7.0
36	ProShares UltraShort QQQ	QID	−38.9	−66.8	77.7	−27.3
37	ProShares UltraShort S&P500	SDS	−32.2	−50.6	61.4	−3.7
38	Rydex Dyn Inverse NASDAQ-100 2X Strat H	RYVNX	−39.3	−66.6	86.9	−27.1
39	Rydex Inverse Dow 2x Strategy H	RYCWX	−30.7	−44.9	53.7	−9.2
40	Rydex Inverse Gov Long Bond Strategy Inv	RYJUX	−13.1	19.5	−29.4	−4.3
41	Rydex Inverse Mid Cap Strategy H	RYMHX	−25.3	−35.5	37.5	−1.5
42	Rydex Inverse NASDAQ-100 Strategy Inv	RYAIX	−20.7	−40.3	48.5	−11.7

	Fund Name	Ticker	Annual Return 2010 (%)	Annual Return 2009 (%)	Annual Return 2008 (%)	Annual Return 2007 (%)
43	Rydex Inverse Russell 2000 2x Strategy H	RYIRX	−49.9	−59.1	25.0	2.0
44	Rydex Inverse Russell 2000 Strategy H	RYSHX	−27.3	−32.3	24.8	5.1
45	Rydex Inverse S&P 500 2x Strategy H	RYTPX	−32.9	−50.6	66.1	−4.0
46	Rydex Inverse S&P 500 Strategy Inv	RYURX	−16.8	−27.3	40.9	1.2
	Average		−27.3	−39.0	31.9	−7.1
	Median		−27.8	−42.3	39.5	−4.2
	Maximum		−5.3	32.7	86.9	23.7
	Minimum		−51.2	−80.1	−39.2	−61.4
	Compare:					
	An S&P 500 Index Fund		14.9	26.5	−37.0	5.4

After reviewing this data, you would conclude that bear funds, as well as inverse ETFs, are short-term strategies for investors who have crystal balls.

Summary

You choose a mutual fund based on what you expect the manager to do for you, which admittedly is much more difficult than just picking a top-performing fund off a list. The best way to become confident in making this judgment is to study managers before buying their funds, something you can do now with the help of software vendors, such as Morningstar and Steele Systems.

Good management is reflected in low fees and consistent, not erratic, performance. Many mutual fund companies that sell directly to investors have excellent websites that can help you review different funds for possible purchase.

I also recommend you read the fund reviews written by the publications mentioned in the reference section of this book, but avoid picking funds off a top-fund ranking list. Sell your funds when they no longer fit your personal investment objectives, when the fund no longer performs as expected, or if the fund exhibits danger signs, especially if assets trend downward while expenses rise.

Key Points

1. Don't pick a fund because it *was* a top performer.
2. If you want to be aggressive, you'll need to create your own system of finding future winners, which you can do by researching data, looking for what works and what does not in different types of markets.
3. Conservative investors will do better if they focus on funds with a history of good management. You want to choose your funds for a particular investment objective.

Steps to Take

1. Review the sections "How Not to Pick a Fund" and "Key Characteristics of Good Funds."
2. Locate the prospectuses of each of the funds you own and compare them to each other. Focus on risk.
3. Review your funds for red flags.

PART 7

The Importance of Monitoring Your Portfolio

Why should you monitor your portfolio? Very simply: to achieve your goals.

In Chapter 20, we'll talk about a few different ways to measure results, what methods might be best to use in your situation, and why it's important to always check to see that you're meeting your investment objectives. We'll also revisit the six elements of quality decision making from Chapter 2 and discuss how they might apply to a portfolio approach to managing your money. Then, in Chapter 21, I'll show you a ten-step system that you can adapt to your own needs.

CHAPTER 20

Why You Need a System

What's in It for You?

How do you know if you are on track to meeting your goals, especially if you have multiple investment accounts with multiple financial institutions? Having a review system will allow you to change direction if you find that you are off course to meeting your objectives. And, here is the key: your review system needs to give you the information you need to make "quality decisions" that are both effective and efficient, as we discussed in Chapter 2.

Contents

Why Bother with a Review System?

In my experience in speaking with investors who contact me because of my practice, column, books, or speeches, I can tell you that it is a rare individual who has a system to review progress even though professionals will tell you that a regularly scheduled portfolio review is the foundation of a constructive and successful investment program. After all, how else can you determine if you are on track? How else can you assess when and how to change direction?

Lack of Oversight

As we discussed in Chapter 3, research concludes that individual investors underperform the market because they enter and exit their investments at the wrong time. Could lack of an effective oversight system explain why individuals might sell at market bottoms and sit on the sidelines as markets rebound? Could improper framing be a culprit? As a reminder, framing is basically asking the right question so that you are reviewing the best information to lead to a good decision. Let's discuss two common methods of review to see if they are properly framed.

What Do Individuals Actually Do?

The individual investors I know who *do* monitor results look at the bottom line on each of their brokerage statements for each of their accounts. Indeed, this is one way to measure if you are ahead or behind the previous month. If that is all you do, however, bad results can follow. Here's why.

First, looking at whether you are ahead or behind measures whether you are making money from month to month. If that is your objective, you might be drawn to scams that promise consistently high returns in all types of markets. Let me remind you that Bernie Madoff, the infamous Ponzi schemer whose game came to an end in 2008, "delivered" steady returns even in down markets (by taking money from others). No stock and bond portfolio can deliver straight-line returns at all times (although inexperienced investors may think so during bubble markets).

Second, looking at whether you are ahead or behind has the advantage of being simple, but it stops short of putting things into decision-making context. If the accounts are down, then what do you do? If the accounts are up, should you do nothing? Looking at your bottom line alone is not enough to enable you to tee up appropriate action steps.

Peaks to Valleys and Valleys to Peaks

Another method individuals use to judge their happiness—or lack thereof—is to measure from valleys (lows) to peaks (highs) and peaks to valleys. This measure is also ineffective.

Say your account is down to $500,000 from its market-high value of $1 million. Now, you want to do whatever it takes to "recover your losses" as quickly as possible.

If you gave that assignment to a portfolio manager you would frame it this way: your investment objective is short-term aggressive growth seeking to profit one hundred percent within three months and if you are successful, there's a bonus in it for you.

Do you see that this objective sets you up to make speculative bets? The person given this mission would have every incentive to do all he can to drive returns as high as possible as quickly as possible. So, he can use performance enhancement techniques, such as leverage, and make bets with abandon. There is nothing stopping him from adopting a "damn the torpedoes" approach.

Your investment objectives need to take into account the fact that you may want to recover your paper "losses"—but *not* at all costs: that is, you don't want to lose more money trying to regain your peak value.

No System?

Without a system—or with an ineffective system such as we've discussed above—it is all too easy to be compelled to action by outside events. In bubble markets, which you will likely see again during your lifetime, many otherwise conservative investors can be drawn into highly speculative trading because they don't want to be left out while others are profiting. During bear markets, normally cautious investors can be spooked into pulling out of the market at the worst time, often without realizing that they are engaging in the risky practice of market timing. It is of utmost importance to remember your own goals and not to bother with anyone else's.

Proper Framing

The system you set up for yourself needs to be easy to implement, aligned with your goals, and lead to effective decision making. The above examples illustrate what happens when you review information without proper framing, the first step toward quality decisions.

Professionals frame-based on (1) risk and reward, as we've discussed in Part 2 of the book, and on (2) whether investment objectives are being met (Parts 3, 4, and 5). Keep this in mind as we review the elements of good decision making, with the goal of setting up a review system for your portfolio that gives you information that you can act upon.

Purpose: Actionable Information

Let's apply the six elements (Chapter 2) that lead to "quality" decision making to Personal Portfolio Management. As you read through them, think about how you would structure your own system of review based on these factors.

1. **AN APPROPRIATE FRAME**—Is my portfolio meeting my investment objectives within acceptable risk parameters?
2. **CREATIVE, DOABLE ALTERNATIVES**—What alternatives have I considered in deciding on my portfolio strategy?
3. **MEANINGFUL, RELIABLE INFORMATION**—What information do I need to assess whether I am on track?
4. **CLEAR VALUES AND TRADE-OFFS**—What risk/reward trade-offs am I making for the portfolio as a whole and for each investment in the portfolio?
5. **LOGICALLY CORRECT REASONING**—Are my desired outcomes, that is, my investment objectives, achievable considering all of the above?
6. **COMMITMENT TO ACTION**—Before making any buy, sell,

or hold decisions, what's the plan of action, how will it be implemented, and how will we know that we are on track?

Summary

The monitoring system that you develop for yourself has to incorporate a realistic view of your desire to participate in the financial marketplace, and it has to give you perspective upon which you can make decisions. In doing so, it also needs to protect you from being influenced to change direction for the wrong reasons. We'll review a system together in the next chapter.

Key Points

1. The way you measure results leads to action. Framing your inquiry properly will help you review information that leads to effective and efficient decision making.
2. If you measure your results based on whether you are ahead or behind from month to month, you will not know if you need to take corrective action. If results are positive, does that mean no action needs to be taken? If results are negative, what next?
3. Your review system needs to provide you with actionable information that supports your goals.

Steps to Take

1. Review your method of monitoring your portfolio.
2. When do you review your accounts? How much time do you spend? What are you looking for in your review?
3. Consider whether your current method delivers the information you need to make quality decisions that lead to good results or whether you need to adapt it as we've discussed in this chapter.

Ten Steps to Measure Progress to Keep You On Track

What's in It for You?

Personal Portfolio Management is about achieving positive outcomes based on personal goals. In this chapter, we'll discuss how to measure progress to make sure that you are on track to achieving financial success. Progress is judged first on risk, then on potential reward. In the next chapter, we'll discuss a ten-step review process that will help you achieve your personal portfolio objectives.

Contents

Measuring Progress

When approaching investing from the broader perspective of portfolio management, you want to measure your progress in the context of the series of trades that you executed over time, focusing first on the risk assumed with each position and the overall portfolio. With an awareness of the risk parameters we discussed in Chapters 5, 6, and 7, you will want to devise a risk strategy for yourself considering the goals you want to achieve. (We'll return to this point at the end of the chapter.)

Looking back over time, you can measure the returns for each holding and the overall portfolio. In the abstract, these measurements tell you little. In context, they can give you information that can help you decide what to do next. What provides context? The process of comparing and contrasting your record for risk and return against meaningful benchmarks and, of course, your personal goals, such as being able to support yourself in retirement.

Attribution Analysis

When you view it from this perspective, you can see that Personal Portfolio Management is more than stock picking, which I define as choosing to buy based on a recommendation from a friend or transaction-oriented stockbroker. What may have worked for a less wealthy youth may not be adequate if you are approaching retirement with significant assets and needs. At that point, graduating to a managed portfolio approach may offer more organization, a set of rules, and the potential for improving results.

You consider each holding in the context of purpose. Is it a contributor or a detractor, again based on risk and reward considerations? That is, is the holding helping or hurting the portfolio achieve intended results? How does each holding relate to others in the portfolio? How much weight does it carry? Is it a correlated or noncorrelated asset? Does it add to safety, diversification, and so on? What role is it playing in the portfolio?

The study of portfolio holdings in this light is called "attribution analysis." Attribution analysis helps to uncover problems for resolution—think of them as action items. It helps you identify holdings that you will want to replace because they are not satisfying your portfolio objectives.

Attribution analysis helps you ascertain whether each investment supports the risk-reward parameters of the overall portfolio, by identifying and eliminating detractors from overall goals and replacing them with better options.

Ten-Step System

Taking these considerations into account, let me give you some general guidelines on how to conduct your own portfolio review.

In the list that follows, you'll see that some steps require no investment knowledge (for example, Step 1) and others call for experience, time, and possibly software (for example, Step 3).

As you read ahead, consider which steps you could realistically adopt. Your comfort level with this process in combination with the complexity and risk level of your portfolio can give you a good indication of whether it is realistic for you to be your own portfolio manager or whether you'd benefit from retaining a professional.

Two people with identical holdings will have different reviews if one uses margin and the other does not. The margined portfolio will take more care and attention, because of leverage. *Be aware that if you engage in strategies that you do not fully understand, you will not be prepared to perform the review on your own.*

Step 1: Situation Analysis

Start with a baseline that encompasses your accounts, your cash flow, and your needs (to save for the future and to spend now), as well as your current advisers, goals, and portfolio manager. If you did any of the action steps presented in earlier chapters (start with Chapter 1), you'll find that you have a lot of this information on hand.

Gather your account statements from the most recent period. Organize them by the owner of the account (you yourself, your spouse, joint, trusts, and so on) and the tax status, whether it is taxable (like a joint account) or tax-deferred (like a traditional IRA or 401[k]). Make a note of any special registrations, such as "transfer on death" registrations or "in trust for" accounts. Make a copy of all beneficiary designations and add the beneficiaries to your log of accounts.

Figure out your current cash flow. How much are you spending? How much are you saving? What do you pay in income taxes? Use these figures to create a simple cash-flow analysis (money coming into and going out of the household for living expenses) to see if you have a current (or retirement) income gap (refer to Chapter 11).

If after doing your cash-flow analysis you find that you need to save for the future, spend some time now to calculate how much you need to save every month to meet your goals. If you need help, refer to chapter 6 of *The AARP Retirement Survival Guide.*

Who are your current advisers? What do they do for you now? Who currently oversees all of your accounts? Who makes strategic portfolio management decisions at present? Who reviews holdings, manages your portfolio? Assess whether there may be room for improvement in how you are currently organized.

Step 2: Revisit Investment Objectives

What are your goals for your portfolio? Do you want to have enough money to live on for the rest of your life after you retire? What do you want your investments to do for you? For example, if you are still working, one investment objective will be to save and invest enough money to be able to retire. Retirement portfolios may have the objective of generating desired cash flow today and tomorrow, plus a long-term goal of capital appreciation for the future as inflation eats away at spending power.

Nothing can be more important in directing investment decisions than setting appropriate investment objectives: these are the goals that define where you are heading.

Step 3: Review Your Risk Expectations for Your Portfolio as a Whole

Managing risk is a key determinant of success. You can raise and lower the risk level of your portfolio as we discussed in Chapter 7 and, by doing so, raise and lower your potential returns (and exposure to losses).

How will you deal with volatility of your portfolio? Will you use hedging techniques to dampen the effect of down markets? Will you use leverage to increase potential returns? Will you invest in illiquid investments? Will you set up a diversified portfolio with noncorrelated assets, or will you concentrate in a few sectors or stocks, and if you do the latter, how will you determine which sectors or stocks to choose and when to get out?

How will you measure risk? One method is to measure standard deviation as discussed in Chapter 7. You can use a spreadsheet or purchase a portfolio management program to do so. (American Association of

Individual Investors, *www.aaii.com,* reviews software and online resources periodically.) A high standard deviation implies higher risk. Without a risk measure, you can't put returns into context.

Warning: Be alert to changes in your risk profile. In good markets, people tend to accept more risk than they do in bad markets. After experiencing declines, people might find themselves taking on more risk if they set out to "recover losses." That's not a good strategy.

Step 4: Review Your Portfolio Strategy

Strategy sets the stage for results. For example, if you need to create income for retirement you may choose to follow a total-return strategy or a demand-based strategy, both of which we discussed in Chapter 10. If your portfolio is constructed to produce income, it takes more time and effort to monitor results and a greater understanding of the bond markets, interest rates, and inflation than a growth portfolio. For example, if your goal is to produce $72,000 of income per year from your investment portfolio and you are producing interest and dividends of only $50,000, this will tell you more work is in order. Is the $72,000 goal realistic in the current market? Are you actually withdrawing $72,000 and only producing $50,000? If so, it's coming out of principal—are you addressing your future income needs if you are withdrawing principal?

Another strategic consideration is the current economy. Professional investors might develop a thesis based on how they view the economy and their expectations for the future.

For example, during the disturbing market of 2007 and 2008, especially in September 2008 when Lehman Brothers filed bankruptcy, one strategy was to get out of the way, to protect assets as much as possible. The operative thesis was the market was in a state of severe uncertainty, therefore, run for cover.

Then, as markets started to stabilize, some theorized that our government would step in to protect the banking system; one strategy was to buy severely depressed bank stocks. The former was a defensive strategy; the latter offensive, opportunistic, and quite risky. Both were based on an operative thesis that was yet unproven at the time.

Step 5: Review the Tactics That You Will Use to Implement Your Strategy

Each tactic should have a logical basis (a thesis from which it is derived, such as described above) and an entry and exit strategy. For example, you believe the market is declining. You may choose to (1) stay the course, (2) increase your cash position (by selling holdings), or (3) hedge some of your holdings by buying put options or inverse ETFs (exchange-traded funds) for protection. (Buying puts and inverse ETFs are both down-market tactics.) You monitor these holdings closely and close out the positions according to plan.

Step 6: Review Your Selling Rules

You will want to lessen the likelihood of losses in order to preserve your capital. As we discussed in Chapter 18, for example, you can sell an investment if it drops a certain percentage from your purchase price. You will also want to sell to take profits.

Step 7: Review Each Holding

What types of investment vehicles do you hold? Structured products, options, futures, and stocks call for more frequent monitoring, whereas mutual funds, bonds, and broadly diversified vehicles may take less time and effort to monitor.

What do you look for? Professionals want to know how each holding has contributed to the overall risk-adjusted results of the portfolio through an attribution analysis, as discussed earlier in this chapter.

Attribution can be benchmarked against asset class (growth, income, cash), sector (using the ten Standard & Poor's sectors), and even more finely, by industry and subindustry.

You can do such an analysis on your own using a spreadsheet. Look at the holding, and see if it added to or detracted from your overall results based on the risk assumed. Following attribution closely helps you make buy and sell decisions and determine whether a particular holding is in line with your goals.

Also consider the role the investment is playing in the portfolio. Is it generating income (interest and dividends)? Is it contributing to profits (capital appreciation)? Is it tax efficient (some investments will trigger higher taxes than others)?

Warning: Before we leave this topic, let me caution that this exercise should not lead you to replace a lower-yielding investment with a higher-yielding one without assessing the risk assumed with such a change. Some investments have a place in your portfolio even if the yield is negligible, for example; T-bills and money market funds stabilize the portfolio and serve as a parking place for cash, but they do not outpace inflation.

Step 8: Review the Overall Portfolio

Consider whether you are achieving the results that you would expect in light of how much risk you have taken on and how you are invested. The most often used benchmark for a stock portfolio is the S&P 500 Index. Assuming the beta of the S&P 500 is 1, what are the betas of each holding? What is the beta of your portfolio? If greater than 1, your portfolio is more risky than the market.

What about the standard deviation of each holding and the portfolio? A more volatile portfolio, as measured by standard deviation, may represent both a bigger downside and a bigger potential upside.

In a rapidly deteriorating market such as 2008, neither measure (beta nor standard deviation) alone would have prevented lost ground. However, you could you have identified positions that were dropping faster than the market and taken action to curtail losses.

You also have to have an absolute measure, but that cannot be your only measure, as we discussed in Chapter 20: are my investments holding up or losing money? How do they compare to what is going on in the market?

Step 9: Reassess Your Holdings in Light of Step 8

Assess your goals and needs (both short and long term). Then, you will be able to determine whether your current investments are in line with your goals. Very simply, each holding should have a reason for being, either the potential for producing income, developing capital appreciation, or providing stability to the portfolio.

Step 10: Retool Your Portfolio

After performing this review, you'll find areas that you'll want to improve. Reconsider your holdings based on your investment objectives, strategy, and desired results.

How Often Should You Do a Review?

Once you design your review system, you'll want to be sure that it's something you can live with and use. Some people review their portfolios yearly, some quarterly, some monthly. There is no optimal answer. Pick a frequency that you can stick with.

Summary

Once you know where you are going by setting appropriate investment objectives, your portfolio review will help you reach your destination. How? By identifying problems and mistakes that you can correct midcourse. The individual investor's job is to stay on target so that he or she can reach his or her destination in a safe and timely manner. Risk is always a consideration for your overall portfolio and for each and every holding. Every investment must be assessed from the point of view of liquidity (can I get my money out?), potential for success (will this achieve my goals?), and potential for failure (how much can I lose?).

Key Points

1. Attribution analysis allows you to see whether each holding is supporting or detracting from your goals.
2. The ten steps to a portfolio review help you take a holistic overview of your portfolio so that you can see if you are on track to meeting your goals.
3. You'll want to adapt the review process to something that works for your particular situation, considering the

complexity of your portfolio, the goals you are trying to achieve, your experience, and your desire to commit to research.

Steps to Take

1. Refer to the binder that you put together after reading Chapter 1.
2. Review your goals for each account. Make a note of your goals for your overall portfolio so that you have a unified theme to apply to all of your accounts.
3. Consider how you might adapt the ten-step review that we discussed in this chapter to one that you can follow on a regular basis. Keep in mind that the goal is to identify action points—problems that need to be dealt with, and opportunities that need to be pursued.

Part 8

Who Should Manage Your Portfolio?

Up to now, we have assumed that you will serve as your own portfolio manager. But, what if you don't want to take on that task? In Chapter 22, let's explore functions a Personal Portfolio Manager would perform. Then, let's identify the type of financial service provider who might be able to perform those functions for you. In Chapter 23, we'll discuss how to find potential candidates you might want to interview. In Chapter 24, I'd like to offer some parting thoughts and insights as you develop your own Personal Portfolio Management style.

CHAPTER 22

Who Manages Customized Portfolios?

What's in It for You

This chapter will help you understand the functions involved in Personal Portfolio Management and to discern who provides such services.

Contents

Functions of a Personal Portfolio Manager

First, let's agree to use the descriptive term "Personal Portfolio Manager" to describe the person you might retain for the job of managing your portfolio for you, and the term "financial adviser" as a catchall for anyone who sells financial services or products.

Your Personal Portfolio Manager will need to perform the following six functions.

1. **ARTICULATE A PORTFOLIO STRATEGY FOR YOU** based on a situation analysis (see Chapter 21), considering your particular circumstances and needs for the present and with a view to the future, taking into account your investment horizon, your need for income, and how "uncertainties" will be addressed.

2. **ORGANIZE A PORTFOLIO CUSTOMIZED TO MEET YOUR OBJECTIVES,** with due attention to appropriate asset allocation, correlation, diversification, tax efficiency, and, for those who need live off of their portfolios throughout retirement, the demands that will be placed on the portfolio due to lifelong withdrawals that will increase over time to offset inflation.

3. **SUPERVISE THE INVESTMENT PROGRAM,** review individual holdings regularly in light of their contribution to the whole, and replace them as necessary.

4. **MONITOR YOUR OVERALL PORTFOLIO** to make sure your objectives are being met at the proper level of reward for the assumed level of risk.

5. **REVIEW PROGRESS** with you periodically so that activity can be adapted to changing needs and circumstances, and limitations, flaws, or constraints can be addressed.

6. **PARTNER WITH YOU** in the provision of these services in such a way that mutual interests are aligned, and potential conflicts are disclosed and addressed openly and in writing. (We'll discuss examples in this chapter.)

These six functions describe a close, ongoing relationship that puts you at the center of the equation. As you can see, it goes beyond investment recommendations, product offerings, and asset allocation suggestions.

Who provides these services? Let's go through the possibilities. First we have to address the fact that financial advisors appear to provide the same services but they don't.

Regulators Are Aware of Customer Confusion

Regulators are aware that investors are confused about financial service providers. As SEC Chairman Mary Schapiro said: "As it stands now, investors who turn to a financial professional often *do not realize* there's a difference between a *broker* and an *adviser* [emphasis added]—and that *the investor can be treated differently* [emphasis added] based on who they're getting their investment advice from."

While titles and services may appear to be similar, "brokers" are regulated under the Securities and Exchange Act of 1934 (the 1934 Act) and "advisers" (registered investment advisers) are regulated under the Investment Advisers Act of 1940 (the Advisers Act). Regulation exacts accountability, and indeed different standards apply.

A broker is transaction oriented. Regulation is focused on the point of sale, calling for the broker to make recommendations that are suitable, but for which there is no duty to disclose conflicts of interest, such as incentives to sell you a product or service that may be more lucrative to the broker.

In contrast, a registered investment adviser is required by law to provide you with a written document that lays out any compensation received directly or indirectly and other potential conflicts, along with an explanation of how the adviser addresses those conflicts. The disclosure document is called a "Brochure," also known as a Form ADV-Part 2A. In addition, the person working for the adviser who actually gives investment advice to the client must provide a Form ADV-Part 2B which provides his or her background and disciplinary history. Unless they are also registered as investment advisers, brokers are not required to provide the same disclosure, placing the burden on their clients to initiate a dialogue about fees, services and conflicts.

Brokers

Historically, brokers ("registered representatives") were once referred to as "customer's men" and simply took orders to buy or sell stocks and bonds for their customers.

Things have changed dramatically. Today's broker can sell you an array of stocks, bonds, mutual funds, and other traditional investments, as well as limited partnerships, REITS, structured products, private placements (Reg D offerings), options, mortgages, lines of credit, and just about any financial device you can think of, including serving as the intermediary who refers his customers to an in-house or outside investment adviser through a "managed account." If the broker is also licensed to sell life insurance, he can offer variable annuities, immediate annuities, indexed annuities, life insurance, long-term care, and other insurance.

The broker's compensation for these services can be tucked away inside a product so that your payment is not visible to you (for example, a financial product sale may earn the broker a 4-percent one-time commission plus a 0.25-percent annual "trail"). Or, it may be included as part of a fee that you do see (for example, if a managed account charges customers 1.5 percent per year, the broker may receive the lion's share of 1 percent with 0.5 percent going to the adviser who manages the portfolio).

To add to the mystery, brokers are no longer called stockbrokers or registered representatives or RRs. Now they are called wealth managers, financial consultants, financial advisers, financial planners, vice presidents of investments, and other titles that might leave the impression that their services go beyond relationship management and the sale of financial products and services.

However, regulation of brokers remains focused on the point of sale, as I mentioned before, as it has since the regulatory scheme was put in place decades ago with the passage of the 1934 Act. The standard of care is called "suitability." Namely, at the time of the sale of the product or service to you, the recommendation must have been appropriate for you considering the circumstances. There is no ongoing management responsibility.

Because some brokers offer services that appear to be advisory in nature (managed accounts, for example), for a time regulators actually did require brokerage firms to make written disclosures—somewhat like a notice on a cigarette package.

While this particular SEC disclosure (see the quote below) is no longer required, I suggest reading it carefully, since it is still an accurate statement of the need for you, the customer, to initiate a dialogue with your broker to ask for a disclosure of self-interest, since none is required under the laws that regulate brokers.

> Your account is a brokerage account and not an advisory account. Our interests may not always be the same as yours. Please ask us questions to make sure you understand your rights and our obligations to you, including the extent of our obligations to disclose conflicts of interest and to act in your best interest. We are paid both by you and, sometimes, by people who compensate us based on what you buy. Therefore, our profits, and our salespersons' compensation, may vary by product and over time.

This quote is the official language that the SEC used to require brokers to prominently display on advertising for services that appeared to be investment advisory in nature.

The nuance that may not be apparent to the casual reader is this: by contrasting a brokerage account to "an advisory account," regulators are referring to SEC Chairman Schapiro's distinction between a "broker" and an "adviser," the latter term referring to a registered investment adviser under the Advisers Act who is held to the higher standard of a "fiduciary" by law. A fiduciary must disclose potential conflicts and resolve them in your favor.

Investment Counsel

Who manages portfolios for individuals? A certain type of registered investment adviser called "investment counsel" regularly provides Personal Portfolio Management services as we are using that term. The service is provided under a contract that spells out the specific duties the adviser will be taking on for the client.

In order to be called "investment counsel," a substantial part of the business must consist of supervisory services, which are defined by the Advisers Act as continuous advice about the investment of funds according to the individual needs of each client.

Unlike other titles that were created by marketers, such as "wealth manager" or "financial consultant" or even "financial adviser," the term "investment counsel" is statutory, making it unlawful for anyone to use that title unless he or she falls within the Adviser's Act framework I've described.

The Intelligent Investor

To get a flavor of what investment counsel do, let me quote from Benjamin Graham's *The Intelligent Investor.* Legendary investor Warren Buffet was one of Graham's students.

> The leading investment counsel firms make no claims to being brilliant; they do pride themselves on being careful, conservative, and competent. Their primary aim is to conserve the principal value over the years and produce a conservatively acceptable rate of income. Any accomplishment beyond that—and they do strive to better the goal—they regard in the nature of extra service rendered. Perhaps their chief value to their clients lies in shielding them from costly mistakes. They offer as much as the defensive investor has the right to expect from any counselor serving the general public.

This description of investment counsel still holds true today.

Minimum Requirements

Investment counsel typically have minimum account requirements, which they disclose in their Brochures or Forms ADV-Part 2A. For example, the minimum might be $250,000 or in the tens of millions of dollars. You'll want to address minimums when you interview potential candidates as we'll discuss in the next chapter.

Other Options

Keep in mind that some registered investment advisers provide Personal Portfolio Management services on a limited basis. Although they may not call themselves investment counsel, they may be good candidates. You may also want to approach a larger financial adviser, such as The Vanguard Group or Fidelity Investments, to explore their investment advisory services. Or, you may wish to manage your portfolio yourself while continuing to use your broker for *recommendations,* but keeping in mind that it will be your job to *manage* your portfolio.

When You Should *Not* Manage Your Portfolio Yourself

You will probably be better off retaining a Personal Portfolio Manager than taking on the job yourself in these situations.

1. You are not experienced in making investment decisions.
2. You need your portfolio to support you in retirement.
3. Your spouse has no interest in finances.

Your Experience

If you have no experience setting strategy for an investment program and making investment decisions in the context of particular objectives, you may find that it will not be to your advantage to manage your own portfolio.

You Need Income

People whose living expenses are not covered by pensions and Social Security will need to turn their savings into an income stream that will not only last a lifetime but also outpace inflation and possibly leave a legacy for children. This is a big-picture advisory activity that needs to be conceptualized, coordinated, and managed over time. If your strengths don't match up with these demands, you may not want to manage your own portfolio.

Your Spouse Is Not Interested

I am a firm believer that retirement investing needs to be a joint venture between spouses. If your spouse has no interest in things financial and you are the financial decision maker in the family, your spouse will be at a disadvantage if you become incapacitated or predecease him or her. If that is the case, there are advantages to be gained from establishing a relationship with a Personal Portfolio Manager when both of you can benefit.

Summary

Either you or a Personal Portfolio Manager you select needs to make portfolio management decisions for your portfolio, especially if you need your savings to provide for your income needs in retirement.

Experienced do-it-yourself investors who are comfortable doing research and making their own investment decisions will likely want to manage their own portfolios. Investors with less interest, experience, or time will need to think about retaining a Personal Portfolio Manager to do it all.

Advisers who specialize in Personal Portfolio Management—investment counsel—can have high minimums. Larger financial institutions that sell mutual funds directly to the public, such as Vanguard and Fidelity, offer advisory services at lower minimum account thresholds. They may be worth exploring.

Another option is to manage the portfolio yourself, working on your own or with a broker who offers investment recommendations, with the understanding that it's not the broker's job to offer management services—the exception is a broker who is also registered as an investment adviser offering portfolio management services under a written contract.

Key Points

1. There is no doubt that the investing public is confused by the differences between financial service providers, which

can lead to misunderstandings of service offerings and standards of care.

2. Regulation of brokers is different from regulation of registered investment advisers, most importantly in terms of disclosure of potential conflicts of interest and the nature of the services offered. Another complication: now many brokerage firms are dually registered (brokers and investment advisers), making it even more important for you to clarify the role your financial adviser is playing.

3. "Investment counsel," while not a well-known term, is the type of adviser who typically performs the six key functions that go into Personal Portfolio Management. The services he or she will perform for you are described in an investment advisory contract that you sign before the engagement. They are also described in a Brochure (Form ADV-Part 2A), which is a legally mandated disclosure document that sets out services, fees, and conflicts of interest.

Steps to Take

1. Make a list of the benefits and drawbacks of managing your own portfolio.

2. Make a list of the benefits and drawbacks of retaining investment counsel.

3. If you are currently working with a financial adviser who is not investment counsel or an investment adviser, make a list of benefits and drawbacks of continuing the relationship.

CHAPTER 23

How to Find a Personal Portfolio Manager

What's in It for You?

The chapter describes how to find and select a Personal Portfolio Manager.

Contents

What's It Worth?

The value of a good Personal Portfolio Manager is the organization and discipline he or she brings to the enterprise, and this is in essence the professional service you pay for. As in every professional relationship, you expect a certain level of knowledge and skill to be brought to bear on your behalf. You also want a relationship in which there are no conflicting agendas. Ideally, you want someone whose interests align with yours.

Assuming you find the required level of skill, knowledge, and honesty, the ability to understand each other and agree on philosophical grounds becomes extremely important. Personalities need to complement each other. There has to be mutual respect and an understanding of common goals. Responsibilities and expectations have to be understood and agreed upon. These are the "soft" characteristics of a working relationship that cannot be defined up front. They can only be discovered after getting to know the person with whom you will be working.

The other characteristics are based on how the individual sees his or her role, the strategies used to deliver on promises, how risk is defined and dealt with, the system used to review holdings and monitor portfolios, how progress is followed and reported on, and the manner and frequency of client interaction.

How to Locate a Personal Portfolio Manager

Since registered investment advisers such as investment counsel don't typically hang up shingles or advertise in the yellow pages, it is unlikely that you know any off the top of your head. Part of the reason is that the group is quite small in relation to the hundreds of thousands of other financial advisers. There are over 600,000 brokers, according to the Financial Industry Regulatory Authority (FINRA). In contrast, there are only about 10,000 advisory firms registered with the SEC, and most (over 80 percent) have ten or fewer employees performing advisory functions.

When I am looking for expertise, I search through professional publications and organizations, particularly committees focused on the areas of expertise that I want to find. For example, if I'm looking for a trust and estates lawyer, I would start with the trust and estates committee of the local bar association.

I cannot use the same process to find a Personal Portfolio Manager, because investment counsel do not tend to participate in organizations comparable to bar associations. One nonprofit organization, of which my firm is a member, the Investment Adviser Association (*InvestmentAdviser.org*), might be helpful as a starting point.

The IAA, founded in 1937, is a membership organization of registered investment advisers that prescribes principles of conduct for its members. Financial planning organizations do exist, as do accountant organizations that have financial planning committees, but I am distinguishing investment counsel from financial planners and accountants.

Get a list of prospects together based on the criteria you are looking for. You might research prospective candidates through friends or colleagues. You might turn to financial literature. If you ask your lawyer or accountant for advice, be sure to find out if there are any referral fees or other incentives or relationships that may influence the referral.

Some accounting firms and law firms are setting up related advisory arms that provide investment advice. This arrangement may increase the likelihood for a potential conflict of interest. I like to see accounting services provided by accountants, legal advice given by lawyers, and investment advice given by investment advisers.

Don't rush. If you feel pressure to make a quick decision, you may make a bad move. Take your time to explore possibilities. Choosing the right Personal Portfolio Manager for important assets is like getting married. It is a long-term relationship. You want to be sure you are compatible before you tie the knot.

Questions to Ask at the Interview

When you meet with potential candidates, try to assess skill as well as ability to understand your mission and meet your goals.

Anticipating that you will be interviewing people who may use any number of titles, this list of questions focuses on the services they provide, rather than what they call themselves. That way, your search will not exclude any particular type of purveyor of financial advice, including the person you use now, whom you might want to interview for the job of managing your portfolio. If you choose to include your current financial adviser in the interview process, keep in mind that he or she may be performing a different function for you now.

1. How Will You Handle My Portfolio?

With this question, you are looking for clues on whether the candidate does indeed shoulder the burden of managing customized portfolios for clients, the standard of care to which he or she is held under the law (fiduciary or suitability), and how he or she sees *your* role in the relationship.

To give you a good answer, the people you interview have to

understand your goals. Beware if they offer you a financial product or managed account solution too early, which would indicate that they may see themselves as "asset gatherers" (translation: salespersons) who act as intermediaries between you and the firm that manages your money.

Listen for clues about expertise, skill, and approach. Do they spend time assessing your holdings and goals? What about doing a cash-flow analysis? And, importantly, what do they do about monitoring your portfolio regularly? How do they explain their selling discipline? How do they address risk?

Listen and observe. Candidates will have different strengths and weaknesses. Some consider themselves expert stock pickers. Some are fixed-income experts. Some stick to insurance products. Some manage aggressive-growth portfolios. Get a feel for whether there is a proper fit with your particular needs.

2. Tell Me About How You Handle Other Clients Who Have Goals Similar to Mine.

First, you want to know that the candidate regularly handles situations like yours. Listen to how they monitor performance and their rule set for buying and selling positions. Based on the description, you can judge the candidate's familiarity with your type of situation. This should also give you an idea of the types of investment vehicles they would use in your portfolio.

The clients who are similarly situated to you are the people you will want to call for a reference, assuming you think the candidate may be a good choice for you. The candidate should be happy to give you names and phone numbers of one or two clients. When you call the clients, ask open-ended questions about the candidate's services. Asking specific questions about the client's personal finances would be off limits, of course. As a courtesy, let the candidate know how the call went. Also let the candidate know if for some reason you did not connect with his or her clients.

3. Tell Me About Your Background.

The purpose of this question is to understand how the candidate developed his or her skill set. People in the financial services industry come from all kinds of backgrounds. You may be talking to an engineer who decided to become a financial planner. You may be talking to a successful luxury automobile salesperson recruited as a broker.

An unrelated background doesn't necessarily mean you won't get good service. But it gives you something to explore further and evaluate in light of the backgrounds and services of other candidates you will be interviewing.

When probing about background, it's fair to ask about customer complaints. Investment counsel and other candidates who are regulated as investment advisers are required by law to provide you with written disclosure of disciplinary history in their Brochure Supplements (ADV-Part 2B). Others financial advisers have no such disclosure obligation.

4. Please Describe the Services That You Will Be Providing Me.

You want to listen carefully to see if the candidate includes all or only some of the six functions of a Personal Portfolio Manager that we discussed in the last chapter. Some financial advisers don't perform any of these functions. If he or she sells investments or insurance products, perhaps the candidate can be helpful to you by offering investment recommendations, research, and possibly assistance with some asset allocation planning. In that case, you will need to jump in to take care of the other functions, essentially serving as your own Personal Portfolio Manager.

5. How Do You Get Paid?

Notice the question is not "How much do you charge?" While investment counsel and other registered investment advisers are required to disclose their fees to you in writing, that is not the case with other financial advisers.

Investment counsel typically charge a percentage of assets managed (for example, 1 percent per year for the first $2 million, and a lower percentage for higher asset amounts). These fees may be tax deductible, depending on your tax situation.

If a registered investment adviser is paid indirectly through product sales, which can be hidden from view, this conflict of interest must be addressed in writing in his Form ADV-Part 2A. Other financial advisers are not required to make comparable disclosures. Compensation can affect advice. Taking an extreme example, you may be talking to a candidate who only gets paid if he or she sells you a certain type of product. You pay nothing extra when you buy that product. But the candidate gets paid a commission for selling it to you. You would want to know that up front.

If a candidate is uneasy about talking about the subject of how he or she gets paid, that would be enough for me to go elsewhere. Full disclosure of (a) fees you pay directly to the candidate and (b) compensation the candidate receives indirectly helps maintain an arm's-length relationship, which is an absolute must. It helps you understand if there are any reasons a particular product or service is being recommended over any other.

6. Tell Me About Conflicts of Interest That You Have in Working with Clients.

Here, you'll want to hear about indirect compensation, sales of product from inventory, referral arrangements, payments to finders, limitations on products or services, incentives to sell products or services, bonus arrangements, and any other factors that can influence the candidate to act against your interests. Again, these types of conflicts are disclosed in writing by registered investment advisers in their ADV-Part 2A's.

Summary

At some point in your life, you will want to graduate from casual investing to Personal Portfolio Management. If you don't want to handle that function yourself, you'll want to interview potential candidates for the job. If you enjoy working with your current broker, you may want to interview him or her for the role. Be sure to review the contract under which he or she would be providing Personal Money Management services to you, so that you understand how you will be dividing your duties. If you decide to include him or her in your search, don't stop there. Speak with a few other candidates before making a decision.

Key Points

1. Finding an appropriate Personal Portfolio Manager to work with will require interviewing potential candidates. Since there are so many different ways to deliver financial services, it's important to understand precisely what the financial adviser is offering.
2. The purpose of the interview is to find someone who understands what you are trying to achieve and can deliver results.
3. It's best to ask open-ended questions that focus on the actual functions the candidate will be providing, so that you are not tripped up by the candidate's title.

Steps to Take

1. Expand your list of benefits and drawbacks of working with investment counsel versus a broker that you completed in Chapter 22.
2. Decide on whom you would like to work with and do some research to determine whom you would like to interview for the job.
3. Arrange a few interviews to review the types of services that are being offered. Review the terms of the arrangement to see if the services you are looking for are provided by the adviser you are interviewing.

CHAPTER 24

Where to Go from Here

What's in It for You?

In this chapter, I'll help you assess how to implement your own management process so that it is doable considering the time and attention you want to devote. I'll also offer some additional insights that can help improve your results.

Contents

Time, Effort, and Devotion

Goal: Improving Results

Additional Thoughts and Considerations

And Some Personal Advice

Time, Effort, and Devotion

Some of the concepts that we discussed together in this book are very straightforward and simple to understand, for example, how to use assets to achieve different purposes (Chapter 8). Others, such as the capital asset pricing model (Chapter 6), may be appreciated by more experienced investors. Whether you have many years of experience or none, my hope is that this book helped you gain a few insights that you can apply to your situation. In this final chapter, I'd like to talk with you about how to go to the next step toward managing your portfolio on your own or through an adviser.

Goal: Improving Results

When you step back and consider all we've discussed, you'll realize that there are some key concepts that can help you get organized and potentially improve your results by applying Personal Portfolio Management principles to your investing: recognizing that the investment environment is always uncertain, understanding that investment decisions need to be scrutinized, setting investment objectives so they drive results, putting risk management in its proper place (ahead of everything else), and setting up a system to watch developments so that alternative decisions can be made when necessary—all based on understanding your own personal needs and goals.

To set up that system, you need to think about: (1) organizing yourself, (2) doing some research of the type we've discussed, (3) setting objectives, and (4) monitoring results. Let's take these one at a time.

Organizing Yourself

We've already discussed in other chapters how to get your holdings organized. Now is the time to pull together all the information that you will need to make reasoned judgments about yourself and your finances. Let's plan how much time and effort you'll want to set aside.

First, decide on how much time you'd like to devote to portfolio management functions and when you will tackle them. Calendar a day and time to start. Plan on a weekly review to begin with; you'll be able to cut back to quarterly reviews later as your portfolio starts to show results.

Second, decide on who will help you. If you are married, I highly recommend that both spouses get involved—as I said before, I see retirement as a joint venture between spouses. It would be beneficial to the couple if both spouses worked together on organizing and setting objectives. If one spouse has more interest in research, that person might take the leading role on that function, as well as perhaps the monitoring function. Consider dividing duties based on each spouse's strengths and interests.

If you are widowed or divorced, consider involving one or more children, at least for help in research if not in the total review process. You'll have to decide if that works for you, based on your relationship and your communication style. Before you go this route, be aware that once you open the door to children participating in portfolio management, it cannot be closed easily.

Research

It goes without saying that sound investing requires a commitment to doing research of the kind that we explored together in this book and much more. How much research you will want to do will depend on your interests. There are many valuable research tools available to investors, including real-time databases that help you assess the current markets.

You'll want to pick a few tools that you'll use. Libraries carry various databases and research services, such as Standard & Poor's, Morningstar, and Value Line. Explore those resources and the many other research tools that you can find online, including AAII resources at *aaii.com*. Think about whether you need any training to use these resources.

Objectives

As we have discussed, objectives will guide your actions, as they do for professional money managers. Set those objectives. They will give you something solid to measure when you assess your progress.

Monitoring

As we discussed in Chapters 20 and 21, doing your own review periodically will help you understand whether you are on course to meeting your goals, or whether you need to change your strategy or tactics. The objective of such a review is to catch mistakes and to correct course on a timely basis, with the ultimate view to improving your results. And indeed, this practice of monitoring is probably the single most important distinction between casual investing and Personal Portfolio Management.

The level of complexity of your overall financial picture will determine the information you will need to consider in your review. For example, you may have multiple goals without realizing it, a shorter-term more conservative goal (college tuition for your kids) and a longer-term more aggressive goal (retirement). Or, if you don't have a sufficient pension, you will need to produce income from your portfolio that lasts a lifetime.

The Role of Your Adviser

If you are currently working with a financial adviser, now is the time to define roles. As you adapt portfolio management principles and functions, what will you want your adviser to do for you? What will you want to do yourself?

If you are working directly with investment counsel (Chapter 22), your role will likely be more strategic. You'll be involved in setting investment objectives and you'll receive performance reviews on a regular basis to make sure the portfolio is on track to meeting your needs as they may change over time.

If instead you are working with a transaction-based broker, you will need to play the role of manager, from establishing portfolio objectives to setting up a review system to make sure that the investments work together to meet your income objectives, and long-term goals, all within acceptable risk parameters.

Before we leave the subject of reviews, let me share a few more observations.

Additional Thoughts and Considerations

Diversification and Correlation

Until the market meltdown of 2008, those who believed in modern portfolio theory assumed that asset allocation and diversification among asset classes (such as stocks, bonds, money markets, and real estate) would protect you from a major decline of your portfolio. As long as investments were not correlated, returns would not suffer greatly. This logic has merit, but as we saw in 2008, unusual events caused assets to decline at the same time, as they might in a financial catastrophe.

Individual investors might want to consider adding to their portfolios alternative investments that were previously available only to the wealthy through hedge funds, futures, or other alternative investments. Mutual funds in alternative classes are available to the individual investor, including currency funds, long-short funds, precious metals funds, and bear-market funds. In addition, there are dozens of ETFs that give you the diversification of commodities, including grains and livestock. I'm not suggesting that the average investor partake in alternatives, only that if you do seek diversification in this manner, that you make certain to include a framework for monitoring your results.

Asset Allocation

If you have a total-return strategy (discussed in Chapter 10), you will want to be aware of asset allocation—how much should be set aside in growth investments versus income-producing bonds, and so on. If you use a demand-based portfolio strategy, allocations are driven by desired income production.

Rebalancing

Individuals who set up total-return portfolios using asset allocation methodology may rebalance on a regular basis, perhaps once a year, perhaps more frequently. The effect of rebalancing is to readjust asset classes to an agreed-upon percentage allocation. For example, if you want 60 percent stocks and you have 70 percent, you would sell enough to bring the porfolio back down to 60 percent. The effect of the reallocation is to lower the portion of the portfolio that has grown, while increasing the portion that has declined. Before embarking on such a program, be sure to understand the benefits and drawbacks of such a program, including the tax and other consequences of buys and sells.

Leverage

If you borrow to invest and you make correct decisions, you can boost your returns. If your decisions are wrong, you can wipe out your savings. Leverage in the form of margin borrowing (your broker lends you money) or imbedded in a product (such as a leveraged ETF or a leveraged closed-end fund) must be understood and monitored.

Benchmarks

When studying how an individual holding (or your overall portfolio) is performing, you always need to compare to an appropriate benchmark. The S&P 500 Index is a widely accepted benchmark for the overall stock market; the Barclays Aggregate Bond Index is the benchmark for the bond market. These are helpful benchmarks when reviewing the portfolio as a whole. When it comes to monitoring results of individual holdings, you'll want to compare your results more finely to the sectors and industries those holdings represent.

Income Taxes

Your personal income tax situation will determine whether you need to add tax expertise to your review. You may need to consider various tax-advantaged strategies, including harvesting losses, buying tax-free municipal bonds, and considering tax-deferred vehicles, such as IRAs, and tax-free Roth IRAs.

If you are over 70.5 years old, are you taking required minimum distributions from your tax-deferred accounts? Keep in mind that inherited IRAs are subject to required minimum distributions for beneficiaries of any age.

Planning Issues

Consider other financial, legal, and tax considerations that impact your retirement investing. Are you maximizing your company retirement plans? If you are self-employed or earning directors' fees or consulting income, are you taking advantage of deductible retirement plans, such as solo 401(k)s?

If you are married, should your assets be held in joint name? Should they be held in individual name? Have you considered what happens to your spouse if you predecease him or her? What assets will pass directly? What assets will pass through the probate process? Have you reviewed your life insurance policies recently, including whether proceeds will pass outside of probate? Have you reviewed beneficiary designations recently? Have you reread your will recently?

And Some Personal Advice

Personal Portfolio Management goes beyond simply making good buy and sell decisions. It goes beyond the steps that most people take when they invest on their own or through a broker. And, it takes time and effort and dedication.

I know from my experiences meeting with many individual investors over the years that people need to establish a sense of security about their financial futures. I know from my experience as investment counsel that organization and disciplined monitoring determines success. And, I know from my experience as a mere mortal that implementing a regularly scheduled review of the type we've discussed might fall by the wayside when "life" intervenes.

Consequently, I recommend that you approach the exercise of Personal Portfolio Management as a process to be implemented over time. Do the high-pay off tasks first. For example, you do need to know how much you will need to live on in retirement and whether you have a gap that will need to be covered from your investments. That piece of information will help you plan for the future.

Next, tackle assignments that match your interests and strengths. If you are a people person, interview some potential advisers. If you are a researcher, start with a review of your holdings. If you are a planner, chart a course that you will cover over the next year.

Then, come back to this book after a while and let's talk again.

This is an iterative process. As you learn about your own needs and your own interests, you will build on your knowledge and move closer to a system that you can live with and, in fact, enjoy.

Keep in mind that your job is to set a goal, start on a path, and watch for missteps so that you can correct midcourse.

When monitoring your portfolio, you need to know where you are starting, where you are headed, and whether you are on track. Just as the wind can take an airplane off course, so do the workings of the Federal Reserve, the markets, earnings reports, wars, accidents, extreme weather conditions, and a multitude of other factors that you may not even consider. Like a pilot, you need to check progress and correct course when necessary, check and correct, check and correct, over and over as time goes on. If you do this, your investing has a greater chance of achieving desired results.

What Financial Statements Reveal About a Firm

This material provided in Appendices A through D was prepared by the American Association of Individual Investors (AAII) and is reprinted by permission. Every purchaser of this book is entitled to a complimentary one-year membership in AAII. For details, see page 306.

Contents

Step 1: Why Should I Study a Company's Financial Statements?

Successful investing has no secret formula. A good strategy and a basic understanding of the rules of the game are required to do well in the long run. Since financial statements are basic tools of fundamental analysis, it is important to be able to read and analyze them.

Financial statements provide the means to measure the performance of the company and its management. These statements allow investors to compare one company's performance to that of other companies and industry norms. Items reported in the financial statements, such as sales, earnings, and cash flow, help value and growth investors gauge the worth of the stock price.

The amount of emphasis you place on various parts of financial statement analysis depends upon your viewpoint. A credit analyst extending a short-term, unsecured loan to a company might emphasize the firm's cash flow and liquidity. An investor with a growth strategy looking at stock may look closely at items that impact a firm's ability to produce future earnings. A value investor examining a distressed company may also concern himself with the financial structure of a firm to identify whether it has the resources to work its way through a difficult period. When working with financial statements, you must keep in mind that they are historical records and public information. Spending a great deal of time scrutinizing financial statements with the hope of finding hidden assets is generally not a productive use of spare time.

There are three primary financial statements—the balance sheet, the income statement, and the cash-flow statement. The balance sheet indicates the current financial position of the firm. The income statement summarizes the sales and profit performance over a period of time, while the cash-flow statement details the use and generation of cash over a period of time.

Annual and quarterly reports remain the best, most readily available sources of financial statements. Companies produce formal reports for two main groups—shareholders and the Securities and Exchange Commission (SEC). Although the reports sent to shareholders are similar to those filed with the SEC—the annual report is similar to the Form 10-K filed with the SEC, and the quarterly shareholder report is similar to Form 10-Q—there are some differences.

Under the Securities Exchange Act of 1934, public companies are required to file with the SEC a number of very informative reports, including 10-Qs and 10-Ks. The SEC specifies the contents of each report and the frequency with which each report must be filed. In contrast to the slick reports produced for shareholders, the SEC reports may seem very drab. However, the financial statements presented for both the shareholder reports and SEC reports will be the same. For example, the annual report must include audited financial statements (balance sheets for the two most recent fiscal years, and income and cash-flow statements for the three most recent years), selected quarterly data for the two most recent years, and a summary of selected financial data for the five most recent years. Most professionals choose to read the SEC-filed reports, because they are typically more detailed in describing the company's line of business and competitive environment, and they present data in an order mandated by the SEC.

You can request copies of a firm's 10-K and 10-Q filings directly from the company, but now that companies are required to file the forms electronically, they can also be retrieved from the SEC website at *www.sec.gov*. Companies must file their quarterly 10-Q reports within 45 days of completing a quarter and within 90 days after their fiscal year end. A firm's fiscal year may or may not correspond to the calendar year. Companies also typically release their quarterly performance figures to the public prior to filing their statements with the SEC. Normally these announcements come about a month after completing a quarter, and publications such as the *Wall Street Journal* provide an Earnings Digest section to summarize these announcements.

Step 2: What's the Purpose of the Balance Sheet?

The balance sheet of a firm represents the financial history of a firm at one point in time—normally the end of a company's fiscal quarter or year. The income and cash flow that occur during the period into and out of the accounts represented on the balance sheet are not reported, but the end-of-period account balances reflect a summary of all transactions. It is best to think of the balance sheet as a single snapshot at the end of the quarter or year, while looking at the income and cash-flow statements as photo albums that capture events over a period of time.

While the balance sheet is also called the "statement of financial position" or "statement of financial condition," the term balance sheet indicates an important characteristic—the balance sheet must balance.

Asset values must equal the sum of liabilities and owner's interest (or equity).

Assets = Liabilities + Equity

The assets consist of the items owned by the firm and used to conduct business. The liabilities and equity represent the claims against the value of the assets. Liabilities are what the company owes to others, while the owner's interest or equity essentially is what is left over. Equity is the value of all your assets less all your debts, similar to your personal net worth.

A typical, if simplified, balance sheet is presented in Figure 1. The complexity and detail of the balance sheet presentation varies from company to company and industry to industry. Figure 2 on page 246 shows a company's presentation of the same information. Companies also publish notes to accompany the financial statement, which help to explain the construction of the various accounts listed in the balance sheet as well as some of the assumptions made by management when presenting the figures. While we will not cover these notes, they are an important element that should be examined during the analysis process.

The balance sheet format is relatively standardized, although due to the unique nature of some industries, such as banks, the format does differ. Standardization makes it easier to become familiar with the statements, allowing investors to identify key elements and compare company performance.

Within the balance sheet, various accounts are placed in standard classes and presented in order of liquidity. More liquid short-term assets and current liabilities are placed first. A brief examination of each account should help bring the balance sheet into focus.

Figure 1. The Balance Sheet: An Example

Cash	320
Accounts receivable	1,070
Less: allowance for doubtful accounts	90
Net accounts receivable	980
Inventory	1,400
Prepaid expenses	100
Total Current Assets	**2,800**
Investments	350
Property, Plant, and Equipment	
Land, buildings machines, equipment, and furniture	930
Less: accumulated depreciation	230
Net property, plant & equipment	700
Other assets	
Goodwill	300
TOTAL ASSETS	**4,150**
Accounts payable	540
Accrued expenses	230
Income tax payable	60
Notes payable	170
Current portion of long-term debt	100
Total Current Liabilities	**1,100**
Deferred income tax	150
Long-term debt	1,000
Total Liabilities	**2,250**
Common stock	800
Paid in capital	800
Retained earnings	300
Total Stockholder's Equity	**1,900**
TOTAL LIABILITIES AND STOCKHOLDER'S EQUITY	**4,150**

(All figures in millions of dollars)

Step 3: What Are the Crucial Figures in the Assets Column?

Current Assets

CASH is the most liquid of the assets and is watched carefully by equity and credit analysts. Keep in mind that when we are referring to cash, we are also including marketable securities and other cash-equivalent interest-bearing accounts. Too little cash may make it difficult for a firm to meet its cash obligations, such as the interest payment on a bond. However, too much cash reduces the potential earnings of the firm. Attractive companies should be able to earn more in their normal business lines than the prevailing short-term interest rate.

ACCOUNTS RECEIVABLE is the credit extended to customers to purchase goods. The accounts receivable balance is the total money owed to the company by customers at the end of the reporting period. A low accounts receivable balance may indicate that the firm is efficient in its collections or that credit standards are too restrictive and depressing sales. A large balance may indicate that the company is having difficulty collecting the money it is owed and its credit standards are too lax. Once a company recognizes that an accounts receivable will not be collected, it must reduce the value of the account and write the uncollectable accounts off. The recognition of this charge will ultimately impact the company. Companies maintain a reserve against potentially uncollectable accounts receivables, titled an allowance for doubtful accounts. It represents management's estimate of how much customers will default on their bills. The allowance reduces (is charged against) the accounts receivable account. The higher the *allowance for doubtful accounts*, the more conservative the company is in its estimates. Acceptable levels vary by industry, so it is important to compare a company against similar firms.

INVENTORY levels are also crucial. A low level of inventory may make it difficult for the firm to meet demand, thereby losing sales opportunities; an inventory level that is too high reduces the return on assets and may also imply that the inventory may not be easily converted to sales. Acceptable inventory levels vary by industry and are tied to the useful life, cost, and replacement pattern of the goods. For example, personal computer manufacturers must balance the risk of not being able to finish goods because of the shortage of a critical component, such as a processor, against the possibility of being stuck with out-of-date or devalued inventory due to product enhancements or price declines. Inventory is generally a wasting asset that must be written off once it becomes obsolete. Inventory levels should be checked against sales. The two items should grow at roughly the same rate. Deviations merit further examination.

The overall level of total current assets also becomes important in comparison to the level of current liabilities (explained in "Putting the Numbers to Work: The Magic of Ratios" in Appendix B).

Property, Plant, and Equipment

PROPERTY, PLANT, AND EQUIPMENT consists of fixed assets used to generate sales over a period of years. Depending upon the business, it may include buildings, computers, office equipment, machinery, etc. With the exception of land, a portion of the original cost of these items is written off as an expense each year over the estimated life of the asset. These expense write-offs are totaled in the accumulated depreciation account. The cost of property, plant, and equipment less accumulated depreciation equals *net property, plant, and equipment*.

The importance of the property, plant, and equipment account will vary from industry to industry. For a manufacturing enterprise, it should be watched carefully. For a company selling services, or even software enterprises, it takes on less importance.

Goodwill

Other assets can include securities held by the company as long-term investments (important for financial firms) and intangible assets such as goodwill and patents. "Goodwill" is created when one company acquires another and pays a price above the book or accounting value of the firm. It is termed an "intangible asset" because it cannot be linked directly to the cost or value of a real, tangible item. Companies are required to test goodwill at least annually for possible impairment: they must estimate the fair value of all components that goodwill is attributed to and compare that value with the carrying amount currently being reported. If the carrying amount exceeds the estimated value, the difference must be realized as an impairment loss. This creates a noncash charge that lowers reported earnings but not cash flow. Some analysts like to subtract the intangibles account from the owner's equity account to calculate a more conservative tangible net worth value. The need to adjust for intangibles varies from company to company. The potential intangible value of a brand name such as Coke, Disney, or McDonald's is high and can justify a rich premium above the book value. For other firms, a purchase premium may not be justifiable.

Intangibles

What are intangibles?

Most of us are familiar with physical assets such as property, plant, and equipment. These tangible assets can be counted or measured with a high level of certainty. Tangibles, however, make up only half of the picture of a company's assets. The other half, which is intangible in nature, is an entirely different beast. Intangible assets have no physical presence, nor do they carry with them any certainty of future benefits. In addition, they are non-separable from a company, have indefinite benefit periods, and are valued based on competitive circumstances. Because of these characteristics, intangible assets are also more difficult to value.

The common types of intangible assets are patents and copyrights, franchises and licenses, brand names and trademarks, computer software, and goodwill. Excluding goodwill, these types of intangible assets are sometimes referred to as "identifiable intangibles." Identifiable intangibles can be developed internally or acquired, and they are linked with specific rights or privileges with limited benefit periods. On an accounting basis, identifiable intangibles are recorded at cost and are then amortized over their benefit period.

How Is the Amount for "Goodwill" Determined?

Those intangible assets that cannot be specifically identified and have indefinite benefit periods are often called "unidentifiable intangibles." The most common unidentifiable intangible asset is goodwill. Goodwill is the excess of the price paid for a company or business unit over the sum of the fair market value of the net assets of the company or business unit. In simpler terms, it is the residual between the acquisition cost and the sum of the fair market values of all identifiable assets and liabilities. Goodwill is recorded only upon the purchase of another business entity. Goodwill is an attempt to balance the allocation of the cost of an acquisition against the fair market value of the assets being acquired.

Why Do Companies Try to Avoid Creating Goodwill?

A key issue surrounding intangibles is the need to ultimately amortize, impair, or write them off over their expected benefit period, not to exceed 40 years. The length of the period is dependent upon factors such as the type of intangible, the competitive environment, contractual agreements, and legal or regulatory limitations. Goodwill, unlike other intangibles, cannot be amortized. Firms are required to test for impairment at least annually. This means companies must estimate the fair value of all components that goodwill is attributed to and compare that value with the carrying amount currently being reported. If the carrying amount exceeds the estimated value, the difference must be realized as an impairment loss, creating a noncash charge that lowers reported earnings.

The other issue to remember is that impairment of goodwill and amortization of other intangibles are not tax-deductible and therefore create no economic benefit. Management has latitude in amortizing intangibles, and since reducing amortization expenses improves reported earnings, pressure exists to extend the amortization period as much as possible to keep the annual amortization expense low. Some companies will also try to write off a large chunk through a reassessment of economic value and one-time extraordinary charge of income, often called a "big

Figure 2. The Balance Sheet: Presentation

Assets*		
Current Assets		
Cash		320
Accounts receivable	1070	
Less: allowance for doubtful accounts	90	
Net accounts receivable		980
Inventory		1,400
Prepaid expenses		100
Total Current Assets		2,800
Investments		
Property, Plant, and Equipment		
Land, buildings machines, equipment and furniture	930	
Less: accumulated depreciation	230	
Net property, plant & equipment		700
Other assets		
Goodwill		300
TOTAL ASSETS		4,150
Liabilities and Stockholder's Equity*		
Current Liabilities		
Accounts payable		540
Accrued expenses		230
Income tax payable		60
Notes payable		170
Current portion of long-term debt		100
Total Current Liabilities		1,100
Long-Term Liabilities		
Deferred income tax		150
Long-term debt		1,000
Total Liabilities		2,250
Stockholder's Equity		
Common stock		800
Paid in capital		800
Retained earnings		300
Total Stockholder's Equity		1,900
TOTAL LIABILITIES AND STOCKHOLDER'S EQUITY		4,150
*All figures in millions of dollars		

bath." This provides a one-time hit to earnings but eliminates the slow burn of amortization. The SEC carries out a broad-based investigation of potential abuses to these types of write-downs.

Step 4: Why Does the Balance Sheet Show Different Types of Liabilities?

Current Liabilities

CURRENT LIABILITIES, generally, are all debts that have a maturity of less than one year. Most of the current liabilities for the average company are tied to trade credit extended by suppliers (*accounts payable*). These liabilities will be paid as the inventories are sold and converted to cash. *Accrued expenses* represent costs that have been incurred but not yet paid. This account may include items such as rent, interest, or salaries.

INCOME TAXES PAYABLE are simply that, and *notes payable* reflect promissory notes, signed when borrowing short-term funds from financial institutions. The *current portion of long-term debt* reflects the amount of long-term debt that comes due and must be paid within the next year. The company must have the financial resources to make good on this debt or be in a strong enough position to issue new debt.

Long-Term Liabilities

LONG-TERM LIABILITIES are loans and obligations payable in more than one year out. There can include accounts such as bonds, deferred income taxes, and pension obligations. Long-term bonds are the most common long-term liability and represent debt that has a maturity date and usually requires periodic interest payments.

Step 5: What Is Stockholder's Equity?

This is the ownership interest in the company and is composed of a *common stock* account and a retained earnings account. A common stock account will appear on the balance sheet when common stock with a stated par value (such as one dollar), meaningless from an investor's viewpoint, is sold. The account will reflect the par value of the shares sold. The *paid-in-capital* account records the amount initially paid by the shareholders above the par value of the common stock. *Retained earnings* are the accumulation of earnings, after all expenses and dividend payments. In effect, retained earnings represent the reinvestment of earnings into the firm.

STOCKHOLDER'S EQUITY is often referred to as the "net worth" of the firm. This represents the residual value after liabilities are subtracted from assets. "Book value" is another label attached to stockholder's equity. The usefulness of book value is limited because the balance sheet represents an accounting value that may be dramatically different from the market value. The market value of some of the unfinished goods in inventory may be below the accounting book value, while the market value of some of the property owned by the firm may be well above the stated book value. Service firms may have a substantial level of hidden intangible assets that will never be valued on the balance sheet. It is often said that the assets of a service company walk out the door every evening. While some investors select stocks for their hidden asset values, the majority of investors are concerned with the future earnings and cash-flow generation potential of the assets held by the firm.

More on Stockholder's Equity

Common stock represents ownership in a company and bears the ultimate rewards and risks for the owner. Common stock has no preference over other claims to the assets of a firm. It does, however, reap the residual profits and assume net losses. For some companies, especially those with more complex capital structures, there may be different classes of stock. Typically, these classes are distinguishable by their dividends and their voting rights.

Common stock may carry a "par" value, which usually has little analytical significance. The par value of a stock is more a matter of legal and historical significance.

The contributed or paid-in capital of a company is the amount received from shareholders in return for shares of common stock. This item is typically divided into two parts:

The first part is assigned to the stated or par value of the shares; the remainder is reported as additional paid-in capital (also called paid-in capital in excess of par, paid-in capital, etc.).

When you look at the shareholder's equity section of the balance sheet, you may well run across some additional accounts. These may include:

Treasury stock, which represents shares of company stock that have been reacquired by the issuing company after having been previously issued. It is important to realize that treasury stock is not an asset. It is a contra equity account that reduces both assets and shareholder's equity.

Retained earnings, which is the accounting of undistributed earnings or losses of a company since inception. The contribution to retained earnings for any given year is the residual amount of net income (or loss) after dividends, if any, have been paid.

Prior period adjustments, which are corrections for errors in prior periods' financial statements. These adjustments are made directly to the beginning balance of retained earnings in order to exclude them from the income statement.

Appropriations of retained earnings, which are reclassifications of retained earnings for specific purposes. These appropriations recognize the fact that a company does not plan to distribute these amounts as dividends. Instead, the company reserves them for future expenditures such as expansion.

Restrictions (or covenants) on retained earnings, which are constraints placed on a certain amount of retained earnings. A common example is the limitation a company has in paying dividends. These restrictions typically arise from bond indentures or through loan agreements.

Putting the Numbers to Work: The Magic of Ratios

Contents

Step 1: Is There an Easy Way to Use a Firm's Numbers to Judge Its Prospects?

Financial ratio analysis relies on financial statements to study the past and develop a feel for a company's attractiveness measured through factors such as its competitive position, financial strength, and profitability.

Knowledge of financial ratios should give investors a feel for how a company might react to shifts in industrial, financial, and economic environments.

In Table 1, we have selected some widely used ratios of interest to investors. The financial data used to illustrate the ratios are taken from a sample balance sheet and income statement

As with all ratios, a comparison with other firms in similar industries is useful, and a comparison of these ratios for the same firm from period to period is important in pinpointing trends and changes. It is also important to keep in mind that these ratios are interrelated and should be examined together rather than independently.

Table 1. Financial Ratios

Operating Performance Asset Management			
Total asset turnover =	$\dfrac{\text{Net sales revenue}}{\text{Total assets}}$ =	$\dfrac{\$8,500}{\$4,150}$ =	2.0x
Inventory turnover =	$\dfrac{\text{Cost of goods sold}}{\text{Inventory}}$ =	$\dfrac{\$5,600}{\$1,400}$ =	4.0x
Receivables turnover =	$\dfrac{\text{Net sales revenue}}{\text{Net account receivables}}$ =	$\dfrac{\$8,500}{\$980}$ =	8.7x
Average collection period =	$\dfrac{\text{365 days}}{\text{Receivables turnover}}$ =	$\dfrac{365}{8.7}$ =	42.0 days
Profitability			
Gross profit margin =	$\dfrac{\text{Gross income}}{\text{Sales revenue}}$ =	$\dfrac{\$2,900}{\$8,500}$ =	34.10%
Operating profit margin =	$\dfrac{\text{Operating income (EBIT)}}{\text{Sales revenue}}$ =	$\dfrac{\$750}{\$8,500}$ =	8.80%
Profit margin =	$\dfrac{\text{Net income}}{\text{Sales revenue}}$ =	$\dfrac{\$380}{\$8,500}$ =	4.50%
Return on assets =	$\dfrac{\text{Net income}}{\text{Total assets}}$ =	$\dfrac{\$380}{\$4,150}$ =	9.20%
Return on stockholder's equity =	$\dfrac{\text{Net income} - \text{preferred dividends}}{\text{Common equity*}}$ =	$\dfrac{\$380 - \$10}{\$1,700}$ =	21.80%

* Total stockholder's equity less preferred stock

Table 1. Financial Ratios, continued

Liquidity and Financial Risk				
Liquidity				
Current ratio	=	$\dfrac{\text{Current assets}}{\text{Current liabilities}}$	$= \dfrac{\$2,800}{\$1,100}$	= 2.5x
Quick ratio	=	$\dfrac{\text{Current assets } -\text{inventory}}{\text{Current liabilities}}$	$= \dfrac{\$2,800 - \$1,400}{\$1,100}$	= 1.3x
Financial Risk				
Times interest earned	=	$\dfrac{\text{Operating income (EBIT)}}{\text{Interest expense}}$	$= \dfrac{\$750}{\$120}$	= 6.3x
Debt to total assets	=	$\dfrac{\text{Total liabilities}}{\text{Total assets}}$	$= \dfrac{\$2,250}{\$4,150}$	= 0.5x
Debt to capital	=	$\dfrac{\text{Long-term debt}}{\text{Total capital**}}$	$= \dfrac{\$1,000}{\$2,900}$	= 0.3x

** Long-term debt plus stockholder's equity

Step 2: How Do I Check on Whether a Company Is Using Its Assets Effectively?

Operating performance ratios are usually grouped into asset management (efficiency) ratios and profitability ratios. Asset management ratios examine how well the firm's assets are being used and managed, while profitability ratios summarize earnings performance relative to sales or investment. Both of these categories attempt to measure management's abilities and the company's accomplishments.

TOTAL ASSET TURNOVER measures how well the company's assets have generated sales. Industries differ dramatically in asset turnover, so comparison to firms in similar industries is crucial. Too high a ratio relative to other firms may indicate insufficient assets for future growth and sales generation, while too low an asset turnover figure points to redundant or low productivity assets.

Whenever the level of a given asset group changes significantly during the analysis, it may help the analysis to compute the average level over the period. This can be calculated by adding the asset level at the beginning of the period to the level at the end of the period and dividing by two, or in the case of an annual figure, averaging the quarter-end periods.

INVENTORY TURNOVER is similar in concept and interpretation to total asset turnover, but examines inventory. We have used cost of goods sold rather than revenues because cost of goods sold and inventory are both recorded at cost. If using published industry ratios for company comparisons, make sure that the figures are computed using the same method. Some services may use sales instead of cost of goods sold. Inventory turnover approximates the number of times inventory is used up and replenished during the year. A higher ratio indicates that inventory does not languish in warehouses or on the shelves. Like total asset turnover, inventory turnover is very industry specific. For example, supermarket chains will have a higher turnover ratio than jewelry store chains.

RECEIVABLES TURNOVER measures the effectiveness of the firm's credit policies and helps to indicate the level of investment in receivables needed to maintain the firm's level of sales. The receivables turnover tells us how many times each period the company collects (turns into cash) its accounts receivable. The higher the turnover, the shorter the time between the typical sale and cash collection. A decreasing figure over time is a red flag.

Seasonality may affect the ratio if the period ends at a time of year when accounts receivable are normally high. Experts advocate using an average of the month-ending figures to better gauge the level over the course of the year and produce a figure more comparable to other firms. When averaging receivables, most investors will have to rely on quarter-ending figures to calculate average accounts receivable.

AVERAGE COLLECTION PERIOD converts the receivables turnover ratio into a more intuitive unit—days. The ratio indicates the average number of days accounts receivable are outstanding before they are collected. Note that a very high number is not good and a very low number may point to a credit policy that is too restrictive, leading to lost sales opportunities.

Meaningful industry comparisons and an understanding of credit sales policy of the firm are critical when examining these figures.

Step 3: Which Ratios Put a Firm's Profits in Perspective for Me?

Long-term investors buy shares of a company with the expectation that the company will produce a growing future stream of cash or earnings even when investing in emerging industries such as the Internet sector. Profits point to the company's long-term growth and staying power. There are a number of interrelated ratios that help to measure the profitability of a firm.

GROSS PROFIT MARGIN reflects the firm's basic pricing decisions and its material costs. The greater the margin and the more stable the margin over time, the greater the company's expected profitability. Trends should be closely followed because they generally signal changes in market competition.

OPERATING PROFIT MARGIN examines the relationship between sales and management-controllable costs before interest, taxes, and non-operational expenses. As with the gross profit margin, one is looking for a high, stable margin.

PROFIT MARGIN is the "bottom line" margin frequently quoted for companies. It indicates how well management has been able to turn revenues into earnings available for shareholders. For our example, about 4 ½ cents out of every dollar in sales flows into profits for the shareholder.

Industry comparisons are critical for all of the profitability ratios. Margins vary from industry to industry. A high margin relative to an industry norm may point to a company with a competitive advantage over its competitors. The advantage may range from patent protection to a highly efficient operation operating near capacity.

RETURN ON TOTAL ASSETS examines the return generated by the assets of the firm. A high return implies the assets are productive and well managed.

RETURN ON STOCKHOLDER'S EQUITY (ROE) takes this examination one step further and examines the financial structure of the firm and its impact on earnings. Return on stockholder's equity indicates how much the stockholders earned for their investment in the company. The level of debt (financial leverage) on the balance sheet has a large impact on this ratio. Debt magnifies the impact of earnings on ROE during both good and bad years. When large differences between return on total assets and ROE exist, an investor should closely examine the liquidity and financial risk ratios.

Step 4: How Can I Tell if a Firm Is at Risk for Financial Trouble?

Liquidity ratios examine how easily the firm could meet its short-term obligations.

THE CURRENT RATIO compares the level of the most liquid assets (current assets) against that of the shortest maturity liabilities (current liabilities). A high current ratio indicates high level of liquidity and less risk of financial trouble. Too high a ratio may point to unnecessary investment in current assets, failure to collect receivables, or a bloated inventory, all negatively affecting earnings. Too low a ratio implies illiquidity and the potential for being unable to meet current liabilities and random shocks like strikes that may temporarily reduce the inflow of cash.

THE QUICK RATIO, or acid test, is similar to the current ratio, but it is a more conservative measure. It subtracts inventory from the current assets side of the comparisons because inventory may not always be quickly converted into cash or may have to be greatly marked down in price before it can be converted into cash.

Step 5: What Measures Show whether a Firm Might Default on Its Debts?

Financial risk ratios examine a company's ability to meet all liability obligations and the impact of these liabilities on the balance sheet structure.

TIMES INTEREST EARNED, or interest coverage ratio, is the traditional measure of a company's ability to meet its interest payments. Times interest earned indicates how well a company is able to generate earnings to pay interest. The larger and more stable the ratio, the less risk of default. Interest on debt obligations must be paid, regardless of company cash flow. Failure to do so results in default if the lender will not restructure the debt obligations.

THE DEBT-TO-TOTAL-ASSETS RATIO measures the percentage of assets financed by all forms of debt. The higher the percentage and the greater the potential variability of earnings translate into a greater potential for default. Yet, prudent use of debt can boost return on equity.

THE DEBT-TO-TOTAL-CAPITAL RATIO is a popular measure of financial leverage, but its name may cause confusion. Debt for this ratio consists only of long-term debt, not total debt. Capital refers to all sources of long-term financing—long-term debt and stockholder's equity. This ratio is interpreted in the same way as the debt-to-total-assets ratio; a high ratio indicates high risk. However, a low level may not be an indication of low risk if current liabilities are high.

Mapping Earnings: Finding the Bottom Line of Profits

Contents

Step 1: What Can I Determine About a Company from the Income Sheet?

THE INCOME STATEMENT reports on one of the most critical company figures—its earnings per share. Over the long run, a stock's value is dependent upon its earnings potential. Investors closely monitor earnings announcements. Stock price can nosedive when earnings expectations are missed by even a few pennies. Therefore, it is important to be able to read and understand an income statement and identify trends of key items that impact earnings.

The goal of the income statement is to determine revenue for the period that it covers and then match the corresponding expenses to the revenue. The income statement, sometimes referred to as the "statement of earnings" or "statement of operations," presents a picture of a company's profitability over the entire period of time covered. This is in contrast to the balance sheet, which presents a snapshot of a company's financial 257 condition at a specific point in time.

The income statement cumulates revenues and expenses and presents the results in a statement that is designed to be read from top to bottom. Like the balance sheet, the income statement reflects management's decisions, estimates, and accounting choices. Just looking at the bottom-line profits may mislead investors. A careful, step-by-step review of the income statement is useful in order to judge the quality and content of the bottom-line earnings figure.

The income statement outline presented in Table 1 has five income steps: (1) gross income, (2) operating income, (3) income before taxes, (4) income after taxes, and (5) net income. There is wide latitude for the format of the income statement used by firms, but the five-step format is useful in explaining the information provided by the statement.

Accrual Accounting

Before the income statement can be analyzed correctly, it is important to understand that most companies report their financials using the accrual principle of accounting. Sales revenues and expenses are recorded when they are earned and incurred whether or not cash has been received or paid. Sales should only be recorded once the exchange of goods or services has been completed and the sale has been completed. Expenses are recorded when the goods and services that generate expenses are used.

Accrual accounting includes credit sales in the sales line and records them as accounts receivable on the asset side of the balance sheet. Likewise, unpaid (accrued) expenses are presented as expenses on the income statement, but recorded as liabilities on the balance sheet.

Table 1. Income Statement Structure

Net sales revenue*	8500
Less cost of goods sold	5600
Gross income	2900

Operating Expenses

Selling, administrative, and general	1,600
Research and development	450
Depreciation	80
Impairment of goodwill	20
Total operating expenses	2,150
Operating income	750

Other Income (Expense)

Interest income (expense)	−120
Nonoperating income (expense)	50
Gain (loss) on sale of assets	−10
Total other income (expense)	−80
Income before taxes	670
Income taxes	240
Income after taxes	430
Extraordinary gain (loss)	15
Gain (loss) on discontinued operations	−60
Cumulative effect of change in accounting	−5
Net income	380
Less preferred dividends	10
Net earnings available for common	370
Common dividends	100
Earnings per share—basic	—
Earnings per share—diluted	3.66
Dividends per share	1

Consolidated Statement of Retained Earnings

Balance, beginning of year	30
Net income	370
Cash dividend declared on common	−100
Retained earnings balance, end of year	300

All figures in millions of dollars

Step 2: How Are Sales Logged by a Company?

SALES REVENUE is the total of sales for the period. Sales should not be booked unless there is a high probability that the goods will not be returned and the customer will pay for them. Risk and benefit of ownership of the goods should have been transferred to the buyer in order to be considered a finished sale.

For example, it is common for publishers to sell books to bookstores under the provision that the bookstore may return unsold books. Under this circumstance it would not be proper to record all of the revenue from this type of sale. Companies are required to estimate an allowance for future returns on sales made during the reporting period. Most companies report net sales within the income statement, which is sales less this allowance and other sales discounts. The notes to the financial statements would typically have to be studied to see the estimated annual allowance.

Accounts receivable, a balance sheet item, should roughly move in tandem with sales. Accounts receivable is the credit extended to customers to purchase goods. Accounts receivable increasing at a faster rate than sales may point to more lenient change in a firm's credit policy toward customers or a firm pushing unwanted products out to customers to boost short-term sales. The quarter-end period is a noteworthy time for companies to push this sales recognition frontier. Some firms have gone so far as to send unfinished, returned, and defective goods just to meet a sales growth objective. While outright fraud is difficult for an outsider to detect, a sudden increase in accounts receivable relative to sales is a warning flag that merits further investigation.

Not all cash received in connection with a sale can be booked as sales for a given reporting period. Firms must match up the sales revenue to the period in which the good or service is delivered. A magazine publisher that receives cash for a multiyear subscription should count only that portion of the subscription delivered during the current reporting period as sales, and establish a balance sheet liability titled "unearned revenue" for the remainder of the subscription. In subsequent periods, the appropriate portion of unearned revenue account can be converted into sales.

Trends in sales are extremely important in judging the current health and prospects of the firm.

Step 3: What Makes Up a Firm's Gross Profit?

THE COST OF GOODS SOLD item indicates the cost to produce the goods sold and includes the raw materials and labor costs to create the finished product. The cost of goods sold is often a substantial line item for traditional manufacturers, wholesalers, and retailers, so the method used to determine this expense can have a dramatic effect on the company's bottom line. Switching from a LIFO (last-in, first-out) to a FIFO (first-in, first-out) inventory valuation system in an inflationary period can boost earnings temporarily as inventory tagged with older, lower prices is matched up with sales. Companies have some discretion on the accounting method used to determine the cost of inventory sold, and any changes to the methods must be disclosed in the notes accompanying the financial statements.

Subtracting the cost of goods sold from the net sales revenue produces *gross income* (or gross profit). This is the first income step and indicates the profitability before operating, financial, and tax expenses are considered. The nature and efficiency of the product's manufacturing cycle will greatly affect the gross income.

Step 4: Why Do Other Revenue and Expenses Need to Be Factored into the Gross Profit?

Operating Expenses

OPERATING EXPENSES are diverse and may include advertising, selling, and administrative expenses, depreciation, research and development, maintenance and repairs, and even lease payments.

Items such as *research and development* are required to be listed as separate line items only if they represent a significant and material value. Only about a third of listed companies disclose their research and development expenses; the vast majority of these firms operate in the technology and health care sectors.

DEPRECIATION expense is the allocation to this year's revenue of a portion of the cost of long-lived assets such as buildings, machinery, trucks, and autos. Depreciation charges reflect the useful lives of the assets, their original cost, and estimated salvage value. Depreciation expense is a noncash expense. The cash for the asset depreciating in value was spent when the asset was purchased. Depreciation attempts to capture the use and depletion of the asset over the course of the reporting periods. It reduces reported taxable income, although it does not actually represent the use of cash. By lowering the pretax income and thereby the firm's tax liability, it may actually help to decrease cash outflow from the company. Various depreciation methods are available to the firm, such as straight-line and accelerated. The choice of depreciation methods will affect earnings over the depreciation schedule of the asset. For example, an accelerated depreciation schedule will reduce the value of an asset at a faster pace early in the asset's life, but more slowly at the end of the asset's life. Under an accelerated depreciation schedule, depreciation will be higher early in the asset's life accompanied with a higher operating expense, lower pretax income, lower tax liability, and lower reported earnings. The firm must also estimate the useful life of the asset. A longer life will result in a lower annual expense at the cost of stretching out the expenses over a longer period. While guidance is provided for common assets such as cars (5 years) and buildings (31.5 years), companies still have some discretion. For example, two airlines may estimate different useful lives for the same type of airplane.

Subtracting operating expenses from gross income provides the next income step—operating income. *Operating income* or earnings before interest and taxes (EBIT) represents income generated for the period after all costs except interest, taxes, nonoperating costs, and extraordinary charges. Operating income reflects the organizational and productive efficiency of the firm before considering how the firm was financed or the contribution (or drag) of nonbusiness activities.

Nonoperating Expenses

INTEREST EXPENSE includes interest paid by the firm on all outstanding debt and may also include loan fees and other related financing costs. The special nature of interest leads to separate reporting. Interest is a financial cost, not an operating cost. Interest cost is dependent upon the financial policies of the firm without regard to nature or efficiency of the firm's operation.

If the company had additional nonoperating expenses or profits, they would also be listed after the operating expenses, but before the tax liabilities. Common elements include interest income from investments and gain or loss from the sale of assets. These are items not related to the sales revenue activity of the firm and need to be tracked separately to measure their impact on bottom-line income.

Subtracting nonoperating expense from operating income leaves *income or earnings before taxes* (EBT). This is the third income step and a step that cumulates all revenue and expenses with the exception of a potential tax liability.

Step 5: How Do Taxes Affect Income?

THE INCOME TAX expense lists the federal and state tax liability incurred by the firm. Other types of taxes, such as property and Social Security, appear under operating expenses.

Note that companies usually maintain separate accounting books for tax reporting purposes. Taxes are paid on income, so companies try to keep profits as low as possible to minimize their tax liability when reporting to the IRS. While generally accepted accounting principles must be followed for both sets of books, differences can arise in the calculation of tax liabilities between the accounting statements prepared for the IRS and those presented to investors. For example, a firm may use an accelerated depreciation schedule when reporting income to the IRS, but a straight-line method for reporting income to investors. Since more depreciation and lower income would be recorded in the early years of the asset for tax purposes, the tax liability would be smaller for the IRS-prepared statements. The difference would be considered deferred income taxes and would show up as a liability on the balance sheet. This temporary difference would reverse itself in the later years of the asset life when the annual straight-line depreciation amounts exceed the annual accelerated depreciation expense.

Adjustments to Income

Subtracting income tax expense from income before taxes produces *after-tax income*. For most firms this figure will also be the net income; however, there are three notable items that may be listed after taxes—extraordinary items, discontinued operations, and cumulative effect of change in accounting.

EXTRAORDINARY ITEMS are distinguished by their unusual nature and by the infrequency of their occurrence. An uninsured loss from an earthquake would qualify as an extraordinary item. The event should not be related to the firm's normal course of business.

THE DISCONTINUED OPERATIONS line can detail the gain or loss from disposing a segment of a firm's business or closing down a line of business.

As companies adapt new accounting policies or make corrections to past financial statements, there may be the need take a special one-time, noncash charge. This charge would be reflected in the line item *cumulative effect of change in accounting* and described in the footnotes.

Investors need to be aware of management's propensity to determine these types of adjustments. Management has control over factors such as the timing of selling a business or closing down a line. Some firms have shown a tendency to bunch up adjustments to clear the slate for future profits. When earnings are expected to be weak during a particular period, there may be a push to take a "big bath." When new management takes over a company, there is also a strong temptation to writeoff old projects and assets to show strong improvements during future periods.

Step 6: What Is the Bottom Line for Earnings?

Net income or earnings is the bottom-line figure that attracts the most attention. Usually, however, it is reported in a different format, as earnings per share. The *earnings per share figure* (*basic earnings per share*) is simply the net income of the firm, less any preferred dividend payments, divided by the average number of common shares outstanding during the period. If a company had convertible bonds or stocks, stock options, and warrants, it must also calculate *diluted earnings per share*, which measures the impact on earnings per share created by the conversion and exercising of all of these securities into common stock. Both the basic and fully diluted earnings per share must be reported in the income statement. The same line item may be labeled "basic" and "diluted" if the company has no convertible securities. The notes to financial statements should include a table describing the calculation of basic and diluted earnings per share.

The Statement of Retained Earnings section details how the *retained earnings* figure on the balance sheet is affected by the current period earnings and dividend decisions. The retained earnings are not necessarily available cash, but instead may be invested in other current and long-term assets of the firm.

More on Diluted Earnings

I'm having trouble understanding exactly what is meant by the term "diluted EPS." Would you clarify it for me?

Companies have been required to report basic and diluted earnings per share (EPS) since December 15, 1997. Basic EPS is computed by dividing income available to common stockholders by the weighted-average number of common shares outstanding during the reporting period. Diluted EPS tries to capture the impact the holders of securities convertible into stock might have on the basic EPS figure. Some companies issue securities, such as preferred stock and bonds, that can be converted into a number of common stock shares at a given price. With a larger number of outstanding shares, a given level of income would reduce or dilute earnings for a given share. Diluted EPS reflects the potential dilution that could occur if securities with rights to issue common stock were exercised or converted into common stock. If there are no convertible securities, basic EPS and diluted EPS will be the same. However, if a company has convertibles, the diluted EPS will be less than the basic EPS.

More on Earnings and Earnings Estimates

Some companies are reporting "cash" earnings or "pro forma" income. What are cash earnings, and why are companies reporting them?

Traditional valuation measures rely on the value and growth potential of variables such as earnings, cash flow, and dividends. However, it is difficult to value many technology and Internet companies because of their lack of bottom-line profitability—net income. These companies have been pushing for analysts to judge them higher up the income statement on a figure they are calling *cash earnings* or *pro forma income*—operating income before depreciation and amortization. Cash earnings consider sales and expenses such as cost of goods and selling, administrative, and general expenses, but ignore items such as amortization, depreciation, nonoperating expenses, interest, taxes, and extraordinary expenses.

Summary

The income statement provides insights on how well management can translate sales revenues into earnings. There are many management judgments, estimates, and choices of accounting methods that affect the bottom line, so it is important to be aware and alert to these issues when judging the quality of the firm's earnings.

No single year will capture the dynamics of the firm. A careful comparison of changes and an identification of trends can aid in judging the attractiveness of the stock. The income statement provides valuable guidance on the sales and earnings trend of a firm, but it does not identify whether the company is producing cash flow.

Show Me the Money: Tracing a Firm's Cash Flow

Contents

Step 1: Can I See How a Company Raises Money and What It Is Used For?

Earnings, dividends, and asset values are important factors, but it is ultimately a company's ability to generate cash that fuels the growth in these factors. Strong cash flow allows a company to increase dividends, develop new products, enter new markets, pay off liabilities, buy back shares, and even become an acquisition target. It is important to understand the statement of cash flows and the elements that impact upon cash-flow trends.

Earnings and earnings multiples dominate standard measures of company performance and stock price valuation. However, slight accounting differences can make it difficult to track earnings over time or between firms. Net income reports on a company's performance under principles of accrual accounting, which attempts to match expenses to revenues when the revenues are recognized.

267

Accrual accounting introduces many interpretations and estimates by management into the financial statements. Decisions regarding the capitalization of expenses, the recognition of revenue, the creation of reserves against losses, and the writing off of assets are examples of just a few of the factors that may vary from firm to firm. Many of these issues are factors that relate to the "quality" of a firm's earnings.

For example, cash used to build up inventory will not be reflected as an expense on the income statement until the inventory is sold. But even the recognition of this inventory cost may vary from firm to firm if one company uses a last-in, first-out (LIFO) method to measure the cost of inventory sold while another firm uses a first-in, first-out (FIFO) method. Higher sales may not translate into higher cash flow if accounts receivable is allowed to grow. Prepaid expenses such as income taxes and software development costs may not flow through the income statement when the payments are actually made. On the other hand, much like a personal checkbook, cash accounting tracks cash inflows and outflows directly when they actually occur.

Fortunately, companies have been required to provide a statement of cash flows since 1987. The purpose of the statement is to disclose information about the events that affected cash during an accounting period. The statement looks at the changes in the levels of cash directly.

A sample cash-flow statement is presented in Table 1. The statement divides company uses and sources of cash into three mutually exclusive segments—operating activities, investing activities, and financing activities.

Table 1. Statement of Cash Flows

Cash Flows from Operations (Indirect Method)*

Net income	380

Adjustments to Reconcile Net Income to Net Cash Provided by Cash Activities

Depreciation	80
Impairment of goodwill	20
Income from unconsolidated entities	−5
Increase (decrease) in deferred taxes	15
Loss (gain) on sale of equipment	50

Changes in Current Assets and Liabilities

Decrease (increase) in accounts receivable	(105)
Decrease (increase) in inventory	(125)
Increase (decrease) in accounts payable	50
Net cash provided by operating activities	360

Cash Flows from Investing Activities*

Acquisitions, net of cash acquired	(400)
(Payments) for property, plant, and equipment	(30)
Proceeds from the sale of assets	50
Distributions from unconsolidated entities	5
Proceeds from notes receivable	300
Net cash provided by operating activities	(75)

Cash Flows from Financing Activities*

Increase (decrease) in notes payable	10
Long-term debt issued (retired)	100
Increase (decrease) in common stock	(200)
Dividends paid	(100)
Net cash provided by financing activities	(190)
Effect of exchange rate changes on cash	(5)
Net increase (decrease) in cash	90

Cash at the Beginning of Year	**230**
Cash at the End of Year	**320**

Bracketed items ( ) represent use of cash
All figures in millions of dollars

Step 2: How Can I Tell if a Firm Is Making Enough Money to Cover Its Day-to-Day Operation?

The operating cash-flow segment is designed to measure a company's ability to generate cash from day-to-day operations as it provides goods and services to its customers. It considers factors such as cash from the collection of accounts receivable, cash incurred to produce any goods or services, payments made to suppliers, labor costs, taxes, and interest payments. A positive cash flow from operations implies that a firm was able to generate enough cash from continuing operations without the need for additional funds. A negative cash flow from operations indicates that additional cash inflows were required for day-to-day operations of the firm.

Companies can determine the cash from operations using either the direct or indirect method. However, the vast majority of companies report operating cash flow using the indirect method, which is presented in Table 1.

Under the indirect method, net income is the starting point for cash flow from operations. Adjustments for noncash expenses, nonoperating income and expenses, as well as changes on the balance sheet attributed to operating activities are presented to reflect the sources and uses of cash beyond profit. Table 1 provides samples and explanations of types of adjustments found on a typical statement of cash flows prepared under the indirect method.

In contrast, under the direct method, the actual operating cash flows are reported for each primary operating segment such as collections received from customers, payments made to employees, payments to suppliers of goods and services such as goods used in inventory and advertising, interest expenses, and taxes. If the cash flow from operations begins with the net income, the company is using the indirect method. However, if the cash flow from operations begins with collections received from customers, the statement is prepared under the direct method.

Step 3: How Are Company Purchases and Sales Recorded?

The investing segment of the cash-flow statement captures changes in a company's investment in the firm. Financial and tangible assets allow the company to produce future profits. Factors such as purchases of property, plant, and equipment; investment or sale of marketable securities; and investments or divestitures in subsidiaries can be recorded in this segment.

The elements displayed in this area will vary depending upon the nature of the industry. Financial firms will use cash to make loans, while industrial firms will have higher cash flows used for property, plant, and equipment.

Purchases and investments are uses of cash, so they are recorded as a negative, while the receipts from the sale of assets represent a source of cash and are reported as a positive figure. Accounting rules dictate that only investments with maturities of three months or less qualify under the definition of cash equivalent. Therefore even the purchase of short-term, near cash instruments can show up as an investment and corresponding use of cash.

Negative cash flow from investing activities indicates that the company made additional long-term investments in the company's assets or outside investments. A positive cash flow from investing activities indicates a divestiture or sale of the long-term assets of the firm.

Step 4: Do the Stocks and Bonds a Firm Issues Count as Cash?

The financial segment of the cash-flow statement examines how the company finances its endeavors and how it rewards its shareholders through dividend payments. Factors such as cash received from the issuance of new shares of stock or debt, payment of dividends to stockholders, and the cash used to repurchase stocks or to retire debt are summarized by this segment. Note that interest payments are considered part of normal operational expenses and are factored into the operations segment, not the financing segment, of the cash-flow statement. Interest income will not appear as a separate line item on the cash flows from operations segment if the indirect method is used, because it is already factored into the calculation of net income. Cash dividends paid to shareholders are considered a return of capital, so they are reported within the financing section.

When it comes to sources and uses of cash, cash inflows include proceeds from issuing stock, notes, bonds, mortgages, and other short-term or long-term borrowing. Cash outflows for financing activities include payments of dividends to owners, repayments of money borrowed, and repurchase of stock.

The cash-flow statement also includes a separate section that details the impact of foreign currency translation on the company's cash flow. This line item will not appear for companies in which the effect was negligible. However, the line item can be substantial for multinational companies.

Step 5: How Does a Firm's Cash Flow Relate to Its Income?

The net cash flow or net increase (decrease) in cash for a company is the sum of operating, investing, and financing activities plus any foreign exchange effects. It indicates whether the company generated or used cash during the reporting period. Normally, the net change in cash is added to the beginning level of cash and cash equivalents to calculate the cash at the end of the period. This cash line will match the cash and cash equivalents reported on the period-ending balance sheet.

Investors look closely at the operating cash flow because it relates most closely to the income statement and earnings. Both statements should be considered together because each has its own limitations. The cash-oriented accounting of the operating cash flow ignores sales from which money can reasonably be expected in the near term as well as expenses that are owed and must be paid in the future. The accrual-based income statement includes noncash elements and is affected by management's estimates and discretion of account treatments. The income statement does not show the timing of cash flows and the effect of operations on liquidity and solvency.

For established companies, both cash flows from operations and net income should follow similar trends. The comparison of the operating cash-flow segment to the net income statement is less applicable to younger, rapidly growing companies that must use significant levels of cash to fund their growth through increases in items such as accounts receivable and inventory.

Step 6: Why Should a Company Have Excess Cash Flow?

Ideally, a company should not only cover the costs of producing its goods and services, but also actually produce excess cash flow for its shareholders. Cash flow from operations represents a good starting point for this type of analysis. However, beyond current production, a growing company must reinvest its cash to maintain its operations and expand. While management may neglect capital expenditures in the short term, there are fundamental negative long-term growth implications to such neglect. Free cash flow refines the cash-flow-from-operations measure by subtracting capital expenditures and dividend payments from operating cash flow. While you can argue that dividend payments are not required, they are expected by shareholders and they are paid in cash, so they must be subtracted from cash flow to calculate a free cash-flow figure.

This free cash-flow figure is considered to be excess cash flow that the company can use as it deems most beneficial. With strong free cash flow, debt can be retired, new products can be developed, stock can be repurchased, and dividend payments can be increased. Excess cash flow also makes a company a more attractive takeover target.

You may need to make adjustments to the free cash-flow figure depending upon the company's industry. Financials do not typically have large expenditures in brick and mortar property, plant, and equipment expenditures. However, they make significant investments in marketable securities, which are not considered in the standard free cash-flow calculation. When looking at the cash flow of a financial firm, it would be best to examine total cash-flow figures from the statement of cash flows.

Cyclical firms and companies with long development and construction cycles may have periods of slow sales, inventory buildup, and strong capital expenditures that occur over the normal course of business. A firm such as Boeing, which has a long development cycle for new planes, a long ramp-up period when starting production, and an extended and expensive product-construction cycle, may show negative free cash flow until it starts to deliver its planes in quantity.

Summary

A firm's cash flows are driven by its sales growth and management's ability to manage expenses, capital investment, and financing in response to that growth. The cash-flow statement can give valuable insight into how well a company is managing its growth. Sales, inventory control, production and employee costs, accounts receivable management, interest payment levels, product development, and capital expenditures are some of the elements that impact the cash-flow statement. It is critical to understand industry norms to gain a complete understanding of the numbers. Ultimately, firms have to produce cash to do well in the long run.

Notes

Introduction

xii "Millions of these everyday Americans have substantial assets . . ." Almost 25 million households have investable assets of $250,000 to $1 million, according to the September 2010 Phoenix AMS Market Sizing Report. Investable assets exclude 401(k)s and real estate. Another 5.5 million households have investable assets of $1 million or more. Almost 12 million affluent households are headed by Baby Boomers, people born between 1946 and 1964, according to Phoenix, based on December 2010 data. "Affluent" means having investable assets of $250,000 or more or $150,000 or more in annual income. There were 117,538,000 households in the U.S. at the end of 2010 according to the U.S. Census Bureau.

Chapter 1

4 "Survey data tell us that people with substantial assets . . ." Walter Zultowski, *Tenth Annual Phoenix Wealth Survey for 2009*, The Phoenix Companies, Inc.

4 "Research tells us that affluent baby boomers . . ." Spectrem Group, *Affluent Market Insight 2009*.

4 "A good portfolio is more than . . ." Harry M. Markowitz, *Portfolio Selection: Efficient Diversification of Investments*, Cambridge: John Wiley and Sons, Inc. (1959).

5 "For help with cash-flow management . . ." Julie Jason's book *The AARP Retirement Survival Guide: How to Make Smart Financial Decisions in Good Times and Bad* (Sterling 2009) was recognized as a Top Ten Business Book by Booklist (the American Library Association) for 2010, the EIFLE Award (Excellence in Financial Literacy Education 2010), The International Book Award (2010), the National Best Books Award (2010), and the Axiom Business Book Award (2011).

Chapter 2

11 "And indeed, in such situations . . ." Professor Ron Howard of Stanford University, Carl Spetzler, CEO, Strategic Decisions Group (SDG), a decision consulting firm, et al. "Why Decisions Go Bad," Stanford University, Stanford Center for Professional Development, March 17–28, 2008.

14 "It is better to be vaguely right . . ." Carveth Read, *Logic: Deductive and*

Inductive. (London: Simpkin, Marshall, Hamilton, Kent & Co., Ltd., 1898, rewritten 1920) 351.

Chapter 3

21   "Historically, a diversified portfolio of . . ." *Ibbotson SBBI Classic Yearbook* (Chicago: Morningstar Inc., 2010). © 2011.

Chapter 4

24   "As such, investor return is probably . . ." See Fact Sheet: Morningstar Investor Return. As Morningstar explains, investor returns measure the return earned collectively by all the investors in the fund.

24   "Ten-year investor returns are more reliable . . ." Fact Sheet: Morningstar Investor Return.

26   "'When investor return is greater than total return . . .'" Ibid.

27   "Some conclude that how well an investor does is actually . . ." *Quantitative Analysis of Investor Behavior: Investor Behavior in the New Paradigm*, DALBAR, Inc. Research and Communications Division March 2010, and *Quantitative Analysis of Investor Behavior: Helping Investors Change Behavior to Capture Alpha*, DALBAR, Inc. Research and Communications Division, March 2011.

32   "To answer that question, I used . . ." Morningstar, Inc., headquartered in Chicago, is a provider of independent investment research in North America, Europe, Australia, and Asia. The company offers an extensive line of Internet, software, and print-based products and services for individuals, financial advisers, and institutions. Morningstar provides data on approximately 370,000 investment offerings, including stocks, mutual funds, and similar vehicles, along with real-time global market data on more than 4 million equities, indexes, futures, options, commodities, and precious metals, in addition to foreign exchange and Treasury markets. (Website: Morningstar.com)

33   "Of the 5,295 stocks . . ." Morningstar.com

Chapter 5

50   "Nobel Prize–winning economist, Harry Markowitz . . ." Harry Markowitz, *Portfolio Selection: Efficient Diversification of Investments* (Cambridge: John Wiley and Sons, Inc., 1959).

50   "Many are Chartered Financial Analyst designees . . ." The CFA credential, which is earned through a self-study, graduate-level program offered by

the CFA Institute (www.cfainstitute.org), is recognized globally as the gold standard investment credential.

50 "According to Markowitz: . . ." Ibid., 5.

52 "In Markowitz's words: . . ." Ibid., 6.

52 "A salient . . ." Ibid., 6.

52 "If a portfolio holds assets . . ." Ibid., 6.

53 "The efficient market theory essentially . . ." Eugene Fama, "Efficient Capital Markets: A Review of Theory and Empirical Work," *The Journal of Finance*, 25, no2:383–417.

54 "Whether or not you believe in all . . ."William F. Sharpe, "Practical Aspects of Portfolio Optimization" (Stanford University: Graduate School of Business, 1984).

54 "Sharpe introduced the . . ." William F. Sharpe, "The Sharpe Ratio," *Journal of Portfolio Management,* Fall 1994.

55 "As Nassim Nicholas Taleb . . ." Nassim Nicholas Taleb, *The Black Swan: The Impact of the Highly Improbable* (New York: Random House, 2007), 348.

55 "Buffett prefers to concentrate . . ." *1996 Berkshire Hathaway Annual Report*, 1997.

Chapter 6

58 "This is based on three elements . . ." Time value of money assumes that money invested today will be worth more in the future due to earnings.

58 "You'll have to compare and contrast . . ." An example of an online tool for determining a target price is the Online Stock Selection Guide offered at betterinvesting.org, which is available through BetterInvesting (formerly the National Association of Investors Corporation or NAIC), a nonprofit organization providing investment information to its members (betterinvesting.org).

Chapter 7

72 "The book, *The Black Swan* . . ." Nassim Nicholas Taleb, *The Black Swan: The Impact of the Highly Improbable* (New York: Random House, 2007).

Chapter 13

117 "Benjamin Graham, coauthor of . . ." Benjamin Graham, *Security Analysis: Principles and Technique* (New York: McGraw-Hill Books, 1934).

117 "and author of . . ." Benjamin Graham, *The Intelligent Investor* (New York: Harper & Brothers, 1949, Revised edition published in 1973).

117 "Graham separates investors into two . . ." Ibid., 6.

120 "As Buffett says, . . ." *Berkshire Hathaway Annual Report,* 2008.

124 "From Graph 13-1, you can see . . ." "How to Read a Financial Statement," American Institute for Economic Research, August 2008, XLVIII, no. 8: 90.

Chapter 14

131 "If the income streams of new bonds . . ." If you would like to price a bond, try a bond calculator, such as the one at www.investopedia.com/calculator/BondPrice.aspx.

134 "As former bond analyst Annette Thau . . ." Annette Thau, *The Bond Book* (New York: McGraw Hill, 2011) 34.

136 "A good resource for additional information . . ." "About the Financial Industry Regulatory Authority," FINRA.org, n.d., Internet accessed January 5, 2010. http://apps.finra.org/investor_information/smart/bonds/000100.asp

Chapter 15

142 "Although money market mutual funds . . ." These two funds were the Reserve Fund's Primary Fund, which "broke" net asset value on September 16, 2008, and the Community Bankers Mutual Fund, which broke net asset value in 1994.

Chapter 16

152 "The problem however, challenges Benjamin Graham, . . ." Benjamin Graham, *The Intelligent Investor* (New York: Harper Collins, 1949, 2006 Revised Edition), 6.

152 "Graham concludes that . . ." Ibid., 7.

152 "Even experts have no . . ." Ibid., 7.

154 "You can find a more current list . . ." "S&P Dividend Aristocrats Index," Standard & Poor's, Internet accessed April 2011, www.standardandpoors.com

Chapter 17

166 "Aging process . . ." Haywood Kelly, "Aging Process of Types," *Morningstar Report: Stock Data Definitions*, Morningstar, Inc.

Chapter 19

183 "Most leveraged and inverse ETFs 'reset' daily . . ." FINRA Investor Alert "Leveraged and Inverse ETFs: Specialized Products with Extra Risks for Buy-and-Hold Investors," August, 8, 2009. http://www.finra.org/Investors/ ProtectYourself/InvestorAlerts/MutualFunds/P119778

186 "The oldest ETF established in 1993 . . ." NYSE Arca is an electronic exchange for the trading of U.S. stocks and options.

187 "The correlation does not hold over time . . ." You can use the Correlation Tracker at www.spdr.com to check current correlations and to compare and contrast different ETFs. Go to www.spdrs.com and search for Correlation Tracker.

Chapter 22

216 "As SEC Chairman Mary Schapiro said . . ." Mary Schapiro, Remarks: "Moving Forward: The Next Phase in Financial Regulatory Reform, July 27, 2010. "

218 "Your account is a brokerage account. . . ." Rule 202(a)(11) under the Investment Advisers Act of 1940.

218 "This quote is the official language that the . . ." The quoted language is set out in Rule 202(a)(11)-1 under the Advisers Act, which was adopted on April 15, 2005, in Release IA-2376 (April 19, 2005), "Certain Broker-Dealers Deemed Not to Be Investment Advisers" (http://www.investorscoalition. com/brokerdealersfinalruleapril05.pdf). While this disclosure is no longer required, the statement is still an accurate statement. Unfortunately, the District of Columbia Circuit Court of Appeals overturned the rule when the Financial Planning Association challenged the SEC's authority to issue the rule. For a copy of the court's decision, go to http://pacer.cadc.uscourts.gov/ docs/common/opinions/200703/04-1242a.pdf.

218 "The nuance that may not be apparent . . ." You might ask why the Advisers Act and the higher fiduciary standard that applies to advisers doesn't extend to brokers who provide investment advice. If they (1) are providing advice that is "solely incidental" to their primary business and (2) are not receiving "special compensation" (historically defined as anything other than commissions), they are excused from the registration requirements of the Advisers Act (Section 202(A)). That gives an "out" to just about every broker. However, a broker to whom you have given written authority to make buy and sell decisions on your behalf without getting your approval is a fiduciary under the law, even though he is not regulated under the Advisers Act as an investment advisor. A broker can also be held to a fiduciary standard if he works as a representative of a registered investment adviser.

218 "The service is provided under a contract . . ." As defined in the Advisers Act, "'Investment adviser' means any person who, for compensation, engages in the business of advising others, either directly or through publications or writings, as to be value of securities or as to the advisability of investing."

216 "Historically, brokers . . ." U.S. Supreme Court Justice William O. Douglas (then commissioner of the Securities and Exchange Commission [SEC]), spoke about the differences between stockbrokers and investment counsel in his remarks to the New York Stock Exchange Institute on November 12, 1936.

219 "Unlike other titles that were created by marketers . . ." Section 80b-8(c) of the Advisers Act provides: "It shall be unlawful for any person registered under section 80b–3 of this title to represent that he is an investment counselor to use the name 'investment counsel' as descriptive of his business unless (1) his or its principal business consists of acting as investment adviser, and (2) a substantial part of his or its business consists of rendering investment supervisory services." As defined in the Advisers Act, "'Investment adviser' means any person who, for compensation, engages in the business of advising others, either directly or through publications or writings, as to the value of securities or as to the advisability of investing in, purchasing, or selling securities, or who, for compensation and as part of a regular business, issues or promulgates analyses or reports concerning securities . . ." As defined in the Advisers Act, "'Investment supervisory services' means the giving of continuous advice as to the investment of funds on the basis of the individual needs of each client."

219 "This description of investment counsel . . ." Benjamin Graham is the father of "value investing." A value investor believes that it is best to buy stocks when they cost less than they are really worth—when price is less than "intrinsic value."

219 "The leading investment counsel . . ." Benjamin Graham, *The Intelligent Investor* (New York: Harper Collins, 1949, 2006 Revised Edition), 259. Graham taught at Columbia University and coauthored *Security Analysis* with David Dodd in 1934.

211 "There is no doubt that the investing public . . ." Part of the confusion comes about because of the confusing array of titles: brokers refer to themselves as "investment executives," "account executives," "financial consultants," "financial advisers," and more recently, "wealth managers," and give themselves titles with apparent (but nonexistent) corporate authority, such as "vice-president of investments."

Internally, however, managers still, even today, refer to stockbrokers as "the retail sales force," and measure their performance based on commissions and fees generated for the firm. How their clients' accounts perform is not measured, and portfolio management services are not provided.

Some stockbrokers work in teams or groups. They might offer investment advice or professional portfolio management through a "managed account" program offered by their firms or external money managers. The best salesmen focus on "gathering assets," which means they are good at bringing new clients into the brokerage firm.

Chapter 23

224 "In contrast, there are only about . . ." SEC, SEC Release No. IA-2711 (Amendment to Form ADV) adopted March 3, 2008, 79. Final rule adopted July 21, 2010.

Resources

Bond Research

www.bondinfo.com—website featuring transaction reports captured by the Trade Reporting and Compliance Engine (TRACE), from all NASD registered firms on more than 30,000 corporate bonds.

www.finra.org/Investors/InvestmentChoices/Bonds/—investor education about bonds from the Financial Industry Regulatory Authority (FINRA).

www.investinginbonds.com—website run by the Securities Industry and Financial Markets Association (SIFMA).

www.morningstar.com/Cover/Bonds.aspx—Morningstar's website has news and commentary on bonds, bond funds, corporate credit ratings, bond data, and calculators. Their "Investing Classroom" has a series of topics relating to bonds.

Bond Ratings

(Free access to ratings after registering as a user.)
- Standard & Poor's (S&P)—www.standardandpoors.com/ratings/en/us
- Moody's Investor Service—www.moodys.com
- Fitch's—www.fitchratings.com

Municipal Bond Research

www.emma.msrb.org—website operated by the Municipal Securities Rulemaking Board.

www.sec.gov/info/municipal/nrmsir.htm—the Securities and Exchange Commission's updates, disclosures, and information on municipal bonds.

Discount Brokers

- Charles Schwab—www.schwab.com
- E-Trade—www.etrade.com

- Fidelity—www.fidelity.com
- Firstrade—www.firstrade.com
- Just2Trade—www.just2trade.com
- Scottrade—www.scottrade.com
- TD Ameritrade—www.tdameritrade.com
- TradeKing—www.tradeking.com
- Vanguard—www.vanguard.com

Educational Organizations

www.aaii.com—website of the American Association of Individual Investors featuring a wide array of educational tools, research, screens, model portfolios, financial planning, and investing tools.

- Free one year membership for readers of this book—see page 306 for details or visit www.juliejason.com and click on Julie's Special Offers.

www.betterinvesting.org—Website of the National Association of Investors Corporation, a non-profit, volunteer-based organization for individual investors. Founded in 1951, BetterInvesting provides members with investing classes and webinars, web-based mutual fund and stock tools, "First cut" stock studies, in-person learning events sponsored through local chapters, the digital edition of BetterInvesting magazine, an active online community of individual investors and member-only investing content. For a free trial, go to their "Open House" link under the "Education" tab on their home page.

www.cfainstitute.org—website of the CFA Institute has educational resources for investors including articles on investing basics and insights, evaluating investments and investment advice, and financial planning for various circumstances.

www.cfainstitute.org/ABOUT/INVESTOR/Pages/index.aspx

The CFA Institute offers a self-study program for individuals who want to earn the Chartered Financial Analyst (CFA) charter. The books for this program are divided into three levels, cover all aspects of investing and are appropriate as a resource for more experienced investors. To purchase, visit www.cfainstitute.org/learning/products/publications/Pages/cfa_program_curriculum.aspx

The site also offers "learning topics" based on the Global Body of Investment Knowledge (GBIK), which are the 10 topics studied in the CFA program. www.cfainstitute.org/learning/topics/Pages/index.aspx

ETFs (Exchange Traded Funds) Resource

www.spdrs.com—State Street Global Advisors' website featuring investor education, tools, and information about ETFs.

Investment Adviser Resource

www.investmentadviser.org—website of the Investment Adviser Association. Includes an investor information section with guidelines for choosing a financial adviser.

Quotes, Tools, and Graphs

www.morningstar.com—website with research, ratings, rankings, commentary, tools, etc. covering stocks, bonds, mutual funds, ETFs, options, and hedge funds. Free membership or premium membership (free trial, then fee).

www.mutualfundexpert.com—highly rated software by Steele Systems for screening and selecting mutual funds. Free trial, then fee.

www.standardandpoors.com—website featuring "benchmarks, research, data, and analytics."

www.valueline.com—website with research, rankings, reports, and commentary covering stocks, mutual funds, ETFs, options, and convertibles.
- Free offer for readers of this book—see page 306 for details or visit juliejason.com and click on Julie's Special Offers.

www.worden.com—TC2000® stock charting and analysis software offers a handful of tools to make managing thousands of charts a breeze. EasyScan® instantly returns lists of charts that meet a common set of criteria. Custom Date Sort allows you to create sorts such as which industries and stocks outperformed the S&P 500 during specific time periods. Access a library of 70+ technical indicators including Worden's own MoneyStream®, Time Segmented Volume® (TSV) and Balance of Power® (BOP).
- Free 30 day trial for readers of this book—see page 306 for details or visit juliejason.com and click on Julie's Special Offers.

Regulatory Authorities

www.finra.org—website of the Financial Industry Regulatory Authority featuring investor education, market data, investor alerts, and a variety of calculators and tools.

www.sec.gov—website of the Securities and Exchange Commission which has information on corporate filings and regulatory actions as well as investor information, including tools such as the mutual fund cost calculator.

Risk Calculators

www.palisade.com/risk—Palisade's@Risk Monte Carlo simulator (free trial, then fee).

www.solver.com/risksolver—Frontline System's Risk Solver Monte Carlo simulator (free trial, then fee).

Stock Research

finance.yahoo.com—free website with real-time stock quotes, news, calculators, and ability to create and monitor personal portfolios.

www.bigcharts.com—free website providing research tools such as "interactive charts, quotes, industry analysis, and intraday stock screeners, as well as market news and commentary." Big Charts is operated by MarketWatch, a service of Dow Jones & Co.

www.google.com/finance—free website with real-time stock quotes and charts, stock screens, news, and the ability to create and monitor personal portfolios.

www.investors.com—website of Investor's Business Daily. Stock research tools including charts and screens, with resources for options and ETFs as well. News and commentary and online version of Investor's Business Daily—eIBD.

- Free offer for readers of this book—see page 306 for details or visit www.juliejason.com and click on Julie's Special Offers.

www.marketsmith.com—Online equity research tools created by Investor's Business Daily. Geared toward the experienced investor, this subscription-based product provides an "institutional-quality database," along with charts, screens, and exclusive ratings and rankings (free trial, then fee).

www.standardandpoors.com/products-services/outlook/en/us—*Standard & Poor's Outlook*—a subscription-based weekly newsletter available in print or online editions. Includes analytical research on sectors and industries, investment strategies and proprietary S&P Portfolio information, S&P's STARS stock reports, analysts' rankings, screens, charts, etc. Online version available with limited access (free) or premium access (fee).

www.stocktrak.com—Portfolio simulations website featuring virtual trading platforms and access to websites which help "individuals learn about the markets and practice their trading skills."

U.S. Treasury Information

http://www.treasurydirect.gov—website with information about U.S. Treasury bills, notes, bonds, and Treasury Inflation-Protected Securities (TIPS). Investors can buy these securities online through this site.

Reading List

Altucher, James. *Trade Like a Hedge Fund: 20 Successful Uncorrelated Strategies & Techniques to Winning Profits.* Hoboken, NJ: Wiley, 2004.

Buffett, Mary, and David Clark. *Buffettology: The Previously Unexplained Techniques That Have Made Warren Buffett the World's Most Famous Investor.* New York: Fireside (Simon & Schuster), 1999.

CFA Program Curriculum: Corporate Finance. New York, CFA Institute, 2011.

Dorsey, Pat. *The Little Book That Builds Wealth: The Knockout Formula for Finding Great Investments.* Hoboken, NJ: Wiley, 2008.

Elmiger, Gregory, and Steve S. Kim. *RiskGrade Your Investments: Measure Your Risk and Create Wealth.* Hoboken, NJ: Wiley, 2003.

Gitman, Lawrence J., et al. *Fundamentals of Investing.* 11th ed. Boston: Prentice Hall, 2011.

Graham, Benjamin. *The Intelligent Investor: A Book of Practical Counsel.* Updated with new commentary by Jason Zweig. New York: HarperCollins, 2006.

Graham, Benjamin, and David L. Dodd. *Security Analysis: Principles and Techniques.* 6th ed. New York: McGraw-Hill, 2009.

Greenwald, Bruce C. N., et al. *Value Investing: From Graham to Buffett and Beyond.* Hoboken, NJ: Wiley, 2001.

Hackel, Kenneth S. *Security Valuation and Risk Analysis: Assessing Value in Investment Decision Making.* New York: McGraw-Hill, 2011.

Hirt, Geoffrey A., and Stanley B. Block. *Fundamentals of Investment Management.* 7th ed. Boston: McGraw-Hill, 2003.

"How to Read a Financial Statement." *Economic Education Bulletin.* XLVIII 8 (Aug 2008). Published by the American Institute for Economic Research.

Ibbotson Stocks, Bonds, Bills, and Inflation (SBBI) Classic Yearbook. Chicago: Morningstar, 2010.

Jason, Julie. *The AARP Retirement Survival Guide: How to Make Smart Financial Decisions in Good Times and Bad.* New York: Sterling, 2009.

Kelly, Jason. *The Neatest Little Guide to Stock Market Investing.* New York: Penguin, 2008.

Leder, Michelle. *Financial Fine Print: Uncovering a Company's True Value.* Hoboken, NJ: Wiley, 2003.

Maginn, John L., et al. *Managing Investment Portfolios: A Dynamic Process.* Hoboken, NJ: Wiley, 2007.

Malkiel, Burton G. *A Random Walk Down Wall Street: The Time-Tested Strategy for Successful Investing.* New York: W. W. Norton, 2011.

Markowitz, Harry M. *Portfolio Selection: Efficient Diversification of Investments.* 2nd ed. Malden, MA: Blackwell, 1991.

Mergent's Handbook of Dividend Achievers. Summer 2010. (Published quarterly by Mergent).

Morningstar Investing Workbook Series: Stocks Book 1: How Get Started in Stocks. Hoboken, NJ: Wiley, 2005.

Morningstar Investing Workbook Series: Stocks Book 2: How to Select Winning Stocks. Hoboken, NJ: Wiley, 2005.

Morningstar Investing Workbook Series: Stocks Book 3: How to Refine Your Stock Strategy. Hoboken, NJ: Wiley, 2005.

O'Neil, William J. *How to Make Money in Stocks: A Winning System in Good Times or Bad.* 4th ed. New York: McGraw-Hill, 2009.

Pinto, Jerald E., et al. *Equity Asset Valuation.* 2nd ed. Hoboken, NJ: Wiley, 2010. (CFA Inst.)

Pompian, Michael M. *Behavioral Finance and Wealth Management: How to Build Optimal Portfolios That Account for Investor Biases.* Hoboken, NJ: Wiley, 2006.

Shilling, A. Gary. *The Age of Deleveraging: Investment Strategies for a Decade of Slow Growth and Deflation.* Hoboken, NJ: Wiley, 2011.

Siegel, Jeremy J. *Stocks for the Long Run: The Definitive Guide to Financial Market Returns and Long-Term Investment Strategies.* 4th ed. New York: McGraw-Hill, 2008.

Sipley, Richard. *Market Indicators: The Best-Kept Secret to More Effective Trading and Investing.* New York: Bloomberg Press, 2009.

Solin, Daniel R. *The Smartest Investment Book You'll Ever Read.* New York, Penguin, 2006.

Thau, Annette. *The Bond Book: Everything Investors Need to Know about Treasuries, Municipals, GNMAs, Corporates, Zeros, Bond Funds, Money Market Funds, and More.* 3rd ed. New York: McGraw-Hill, 2011.

Tortoriello, Richard. *Quantitative Strategies for Achieving Alpha.* New York: McGraw-Hill, 2009.

Acknowledgments

This book has been in the making for the last two years (truth be told, the last twenty years) and I am grateful to all who had a hand in it, from my agent, Marilyn Allen of Allen and O'Shea, whom I embarrass with the moniker "best agent on earth" (she is), to Michael Fragnito, Editorial Director of Sterling Publishing Co., Inc., whose wisdom and professionalism I admire, to Kate Zimmermann, my efficient and supportive editor (I love to work with you Kate), and to the many others who took the time to contribute to this project.

Thanks to the friends and colleagues who gave me their reactions to the manuscript as it developed: Tony Aiken, Manny Bernardo, Ronnie Braun, Peter De Nicola, Wendy Reilly Harris, Frank Henderson, John and Aileen Lowe, Bill Lyons, Rick Ryder, Robert Sadofsky, Peter Spielman, Celine Stahl, Jay Terzis, Irene and Chris Theriot, Charles Zatzkin, and Carl Zimmerman. You challenged me to keep the reader in the center of the equation.

A number of subject matter experts were kind enough to offer critiques, insights, and data. Thank you Ron Howard, Professor/Director, Decisions and Ethics Center at Stanford University, and Carl Spetzler, CEO of Strategic Decisions Group; David G. Tittsworth, Executive Director, Investment Adviser Association; Stephanie Ptak of DALBAR; David Thompson, Managing Director, Phoenix Marketing International; Alexa Auerbach, Allison R. Pagni (Ibbotson), Fani D. Koutsovitis, Margaret Kirch Cohen, Andrew Webb, and Shawn Malayter, Morningstar; Marc Eiger, Howard Silverblatt, Justin Hom, Bill Griffis, Susan Cheng and Susan Fagg, Standard & Poor's; Lena Kempe, Associate General Counsel, and Jeanne McLaughlin, Value Line; Michael W. Thompson and Patrick Argo at Worden Brothers, Inc.; Jonathan Hahn and Matt Galgani at Investor's Business Daily; and Adam Ritt at BetterInvesting. I am grateful for your interest and your help.

I appreciate the generosity of the experts who liked the book enough to write forewords and endorsements, namely, Gregg Brewer, Executive Director of Research, Value Line Publishing LLC; Jonathan Dahl, Editor in Chief of SmartMoney Magazine; Peter Hathaway, retired, former portfolio manager, GE Asset Management's US Equity Large Cap Value Strategy; and Charles Rotblut, CFA, Vice President, American Association of Individual Investors (AAII); as well as Richard Berkowitz, Esq., Senior Partner, Berkowitz, Trager & Trager, LLC of Westport, CT; Pam Krueger, Executive Producer and Co-host of the award winning PBS series, MoneyTrack; Don Phillips, Managing Director, Morningstar; John Wasik, Reuters columnist; Tom Robinson, Ph.D., CFA, CAIA, CFP®, Managing Director, Education Division, CFA Institute; and Ben Stein.

An important aspect of Personal Portfolio Management is research. A special thank you goes to Morningstar for making available 11 years of Principia software, which I used for the stock and mutual fund analyses that you see throughout the book. Because I wanted readers of this book to be able to try out different resources, I am very happy to arrange special offers for readers from the AAII, Investor's Business Daily, Morningstar, Value Line, and Worden Brothers, Inc. Thank you all.

Many thanks to my editorial assistants, Alison Zomb and Emily Smalter, who shouldered the burden of fact checking and managing countless re-writes, as well as other colleagues at Jackson, Grant who provided research and feedback on the manuscript, particularly Patty Debias, Ilona Kucharczyk, and Janella Joyner.

Last but certainly not least, I thank my far-from-retirement children, Ilona and Onur, and Leila and Mark, for their feedback and understanding throughout the writing process. And, I thank Howard, whose support has been constant and unwavering through a journey of six books.

Thank you all for the very important part that each and every one of you played in making this book vastly better than I could have made it on my own.

Index

About the Author

JULIE JASON directs the Personal Porfolio Management practice of Jackson, Grant Investment Advisers, Inc. of Stamford, CT (www.jacksongrant.us). She started her Wall Street career as a lawyer after earning an advanced law degree from Columbia University. Also the author of *The AARP Retirement Survival Guide: How to Make Smart Financial Decisions in Good Times and Bad* (Sterling 2009), she writes an award-winning investor-education column in which she tackles readers' investment, tax, and retirement-finance questions.

Jason's award-winning *Retirement Survival Guide* was recognized as a Top Ten Business Book by Booklist (the American Library Association) for 2010, and received:

- The International Book Award (2010)

- The National Best Books Award (2010)

- The EIFLE Award (2010)

- The Axiom Business Book Award (2011)

Write to her at readers@juliejason.com.

This book, *Managing Retirement Wealth*, received the following awards in 2012: the Axiom Business Book Award; the USA Best Books Award; the International Book Award; and the EIFLE (Excellence in Financial Literacy Education) Award.

Special Offers for Readers of
Managing Retirement Wealth

American Association of Individual Investors
The Stock Analysis process described in the Appendices of this book is from the Classroom area of www.aaii.com, an investment education website developed by the American Association of Individual Investors (AAII). I have arranged for you to receive a free 12 month trial membership with the AAII, which starts the day you register. You'll receive monthly online issues of the AAII Journal, access to online investor classrooms, and much more. Simply visit www.aaii.com/emembership and enter in "juliejason" as your group login name and "AAII" as your group password.

Morningstar
In chapter 17 (and throughout this book), I relied on Morningstar for stock insights and information. To start, you can access Morningstar's free content online at www.Morningstar.com. For more comprehensive resources, you'll want to try Morningstar Premium, the members-only content on Morningstar.com, which includes Morningstar's analyst reports and screeners to uncover stocks, funds, and ETFs that you might want to explore further, as well as tools like Portfolio X-Ray, that can help uncover investment strengths and weaknesses. If you would like a $20 discount from the $199 annual membership fee, call 1-866-486-9750 and mention Save20.

Value Line
Value Line, which is the subject of Chapter 18, is another excellent resource for target price and a variety of proprietary ratings. Comprehensive stock reports and independent analysis in an easy-to-use format provide a wealth of information to help you make investment decisions when planning for a secure retirement. As a special offer for my readers, Value Line is offering a free 14 day trial to their signature service "Value Line Investment Survey." Visit www.valueline.com/JJ to start your trial.

Worden Brothers, Inc.
As mentioned in Chapter 16, TC2000® stock charting and analysis software will help you compare stocks and manage thousands of charts with ease. EasyScan® instantly returns lists of charts that meet a common set of criteria. Custom Date Sort allows you to create sorts such as which industries and stock outperformed the S&P 500 during specific time periods. Access a library of 70+ technical indicators including Worden's own MoneyStream®, Time Segmented Volume® (TSV) and Balance of Power® (BOP). As a Managing Retirement Wealth reader, you will receive a $25 discount to Worden's TC2000. Visit www.TC2000.com/bonus/juliejason to sign up.